W9-ADZ-834

SOVIET
& EAST
EUROPEAN
FOREIGN
POLICY

SOVIET & EAST EUROPEAN FOREIGN POLICY

A Bibliography of English- & Russian-Language Publications 1967-1971

ROGER E. KANET

Santa Barbara, California
Oxford, England

Library of Congress Catalog Card Number 73–76444
ISBN Clothbound Edition 87436–137–0

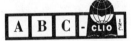

American Bibliographical Center—Clio Press, Inc.
2040 Alameda Padre Serra
Santa Barbara, California

European Bibliographical Center—Clio Press
30 Cornmarket Street
Oxford OX1 3EY, England

Designed by Barbara Monahan
Composed by Datagraphics
Printed and bound by Publishers Press
in the United States of America

CONTENTS

PREFACE

One of the major problems faced by students of Soviet and East European affairs, as well as most scholars in other areas of the social sciences, is the difficulty of keeping abreast of the materials published in that field. During the past two decades publications on Soviet foreign policy and the foreign policies of other Eastern European countries have proliferated, and the bibliographical control over this growing collection of books and articles has not improved significantly.[1] The only major bibliography on Soviet foreign policy published to date was edited by Thomas T. Hammond, *Soviet Foreign Relations and World Communism: A Selected, Annotated Bibliography of 7,000 Books in 30 Languages.*[2] Hammond's work is an excellent tool for the study of Soviet foreign policy prior to 1964, but it is almost ten years old and suffers from the failure to include periodical literature. Besides Hammond's volume the only sources of bibliographic assistance available for the study of Soviet and East European foreign policy have been lists of published books prepared by various East European countries, occasional listings in general bibliographies,[3] sporadic listings of books and articles in *Canadian* (now *Canadian-American*) *Slavic Studies, Bibliography,* current lists of books and

[1] Two discussions of the present state of bibliography in the Slavic field are included in Eric H. Boehm, "Bibliography: Current State and Prospects," in Lyman H. Legters, ed., *Russia. Essays in History and Literature.* Leyden: Brill, 1972, pp. 152–164 and Roger E. Kanet, "Some Problems with Current Methods of Bibliography Management in Slavic and East European Studies," *Slavic Bibliographic and Documentation Center Newsletter,* no. 5 (1971), pp. 2–3.

[2] Princeton: Princeton University Press, 1965.

[3] Among the more useful English-language bibliographies of periodical literature are *Humanities and Social Science Index, Public Affairs Information Service,* and *Reader's Guide to Periodical Literature.*

articles in such journals as *Foreign Affairs, ORBIS,* and *Osteuropa,* and a few similar bibliographical aids. The only consistently useful listing of articles on Soviet and East European foreign policy available during the past twenty years has appeared in *Historical Abstracts,* published quarterly since 1955.

This volume is an attempt to remedy, at least partially, the problem noted above by making an indexed listing of books and articles published in English and Russian during the period 1967–1971 available to scholars in the field. The entries are not annotated, and no attempt has been made to note the relative significance of the items listed. In spite of these limitations, it will hopefully fill part of the almost total gap in bibliographical aids for the study of Soviet and East European foreign policy. The work lists all of the items published in English and Russian uncovered during the past several years. Unfortunately, time limitations and language difficulties have prevented the inclusion of East European publications.

This bibliography grew during the several years that Soviet books and articles on international relations were compiled for listing in *Canadian Slavic Studies, Bibliography.* Those quarterly lists were compiled by culling Soviet publications, in Russian and in English, and lists of published Soviet books. During a stint as a contributing editor on Soviet and East European foreign policies to *The American Bibliography of Russian and East European Studies* from 1967 to 1971,[4] The editor regularly surveyed more than one hundred English-language journals, and catalogues of published books and monographs. The journals, in English and Russian, which included entries on Soviet and/or East European foreign policy are listed in this bibliography, and those periodicals which were found to have no items on the subject are also listed.

The selection of items for this bibliography is as inclusive as possible and all non-Soviet items published in English noted by the editor are included. All of the Russian-language and Soviet-published English materials that concern Soviet or East European foreign policy directly have been included. In addition, there is a selection of Soviet books and articles which deal primarily with such general topics as developing countries and imperialism and also concern Soviet or East European foreign policy. Items published in other East European countries, whether they are published in English or in the native language are not included. Finally, articles from English-language translation journals have not been included. The student of Soviet and East European

---

[4] *The American Bibliography* has suffered from rather serious problems during the past few years. In fact, it is at present (early 1973) seriously behind schedule. However, with the financial assistance of The Ohio State University and grants from the Ford Foundation and the National Endowment for the Humanities the problems of producing the bibliography are being solved and it should soon begin to appear once again on a regular basis. The issues for 1967 through 1972 are under preparation at The Ohio State University and should be published during 1973 and 1974 under the editorship of Kenneth Naylor (1967–1969 issues) and James Scanlan (1970–1972 issues). Beginning with the 1973 issue the bibliography will be prepared at the Library of Congress under the sponsorship of The American Association for the Advancement of Slavic Studies and will be edited by David Kraus.

foreign policy should be aware of certain valuable sources of information not included in this bibliography. The most important are:

Absees: Soviet and East European Abstracts Series. This quarterly, published by the University of Glasgow, includes excerpts and brief summaries of articles from the press of the Soviet Union and other East European countries.

Current Digest of the Soviet Press. Published weekly, this journal includes translations from Soviet newspapers, journals, and magazines. In addition, each issue includes a weekly index to *Pravda and Izvestiia.*

Translation journals of the International Arts and Sciences Press (IASP). Among the most important for Soviet and East European foreign relations are: *Eastern European Economics, Problems of Economics, Soviet and Eastern European Foreign Trade, Soviet Law and Government, Soviet Review.*

Joint Publications Research Service (JPRS Reports). This publication includes translations from the press of all communist countries (as well as that of other countries) on all subjects. All reports are listed in the *Monthly Catalog of U.S. Government Publications.*

Radio Free Europe Research Reports. There are three major series that provide analysis of developments in the USSR and Eastern Europe, as well as translations of articles from the press and radio of the area: *Background Papers* on each of the countries; *Situations Reports* on the individual countries; and *Press Surveys* for Bulgaria, Czechoslovakia, Hungary, Poland, and Rumania. Each series has a quarterly or monthly index.

Radio Liberty publishes two series which are useful for the study of foreign policy: *Radio Liberty Dispatch,* which includes information and brief analyses of current developments in the USSR, and *Radio Liberty Research Papers,* which provide more extended analyses.

U.S. Foreign Broadcast Information. Daily Report and *Daily Report Supplement.* These two publications include monitored broadcasts translated into English from all countries of the world, including the USSR and Eastern Europe.

Finally, a useful listing of English-language journals on all communist countries and aspects of communism, including East European and Soviet English-language publications is included in Harry G. Shaffer, *English-Language Periodic Publications on Communism: An Annotated Index.* New York: Research Institute on Communist Affairs, Columbia University, 1971.

The entries in the following bibliography are arranged in alphabetical order according to author (or title, if no author's name is given). Each item is numbered and the numbers after entries in the index refer to the corresponding book or article in the main body of the bibliography. Most of the items are indexed under several categories.

Several of my former students were involved in the collection of items for this bibliography or in the bibliographical efforts on which it is based. I am especially grateful for the assistance of Barry Bede, Hans Brisch, J. Russell Mills, Jr., and Faria Vahdat. In addition, I am also indebted to the Research Institute on Communist Affairs and the Russian Institute of Columbia University, which provided the time to complete this project, and to the Graduate School of The University of Kansas which provided financial assistance for the collection and typing of the materials. I am especially pleased to commend the editorial staff of ABC-CLIO for its technical assistance in preparing my work for publication—James Crane and Barbara Monahan were particularly helpful. Finally, I wish to thank my wife Joan and my daughter Suzanne for their help during the tedious task of checking all of the reference numbers in the index.

ROGER E. KANET

New York
February 1973

LIST OF JOURNAL
ABBREVIATIONS

A,AAPSS	*Annals, American Academy of Political and Social Science*
AAS	*Aziia i Afrika segodnia* [Asia and Africa Today]
ACQ	*Atlantic Community Quarterly*
AER	*American Economic Review*
AfA	*African Affairs*
AfR	*Africa Report*
Ag	*Agenor*
AJIL	*American Journal of International Law*
AJPH	*Australian Journal of Politics and History*
AO	*Asian Outlook*
AP	*Adelphi Papers*
APS,P	*Academy of Political Science, Proceedings*
APSR	*American Political Science Review*
AQ	*Australian Quarterly*
AR	*Antioch Review*
ArQ	*Army Quarterly*
AsQ	*Asia Quarterly*
AsS	*Asian Survey*
ASt	*Asian Studies*
AuO	*Australian Outlook*
AUR	*Air University Review*
BAS	*Bulletin of the Atomic Scientists*
BH	*Behind the Headlines*
B,ISUSSR	*Bulletin, Institute for the Study of the USSR*
BR	*Baltic Review*

BSJA	Bulletin on Soviet Jewish Affairs
CA	Communist Affairs
CaC	Cooperation and Conflict
CAR	Central
car	Central Asian Review
CEF	Central European Federationist
CEJ	Central Europe Journal
CH	Current History
CJTL	Columbia Journal of Transnational Law
CLR	Columbia Law Review
Co	Coexistence
Comm	Commentary
CM	Center Magazine
CP	Comparative Politics
CQ	China Quarterly
CR	Contemporary Review
CSlP	Canadian Slavonic Papers
CSlSt	Canadian Slavic Studies
CSlSt,BS	Canadian Slavic Studies, Bibliography Supplement
CSSH	Comparative Studies in Society and History
DAI	Dissertation Abstracts International
EBB	Economics and Business Bulletin
EBE	Economic Bulletin for Europe
EE	East Europe
EEM	East European Monographs
EEQ	East European Quarterly
Enc	Encounter
ERR	Editorial Research Reports
ESE-E	Études Slaves et Est-Européennes
FA	Foreign Affairs
FEER	Far Eastern Economic Review
FP	Foreign Policy
GM	Gewerkschaftliche Monatshefte [Labor Monthly]
GO	Government and Opposition
HILJ	Harvard International Law Journal
HJ	Historical Journal
IA(L)	International Affairs (London)
IA(M)	International Affairs (Moscow)
IC	International Conciliation
IJ	International Journal
IJPS	International Journal of Political Science
ILM	International Legal Materials
IlP	Il Politico
InP	Internasjonal Politikk

Int	*Interplay*
Inte	*Intereconomics*
IO	*International Organization*
IP	*International Problems*
IPUB	*International Peasant Union Bulletin*
IQ	*India Quarterly*
IR	*International Relations*
IS	*International Studies*
ISp	*Internationale Spectator* [International Spectator]
ISSJ	*International Social Science Journal*
IStQ	*International Studies Quarterly*
JASt	*Journal of Asian Studies*
JCH	*Journal of Contemporary History*
JCMSt	*Journal of Common Market Studies*
JCR	*Journal of Conflict Resolution*
JCRV	*Journal of Contemporary Revolutions*
JIA	*Journal of International Affairs*
JI-ASt	*Journal of Inter-American Studies*
JICSt	*Journal of International and Comparative Studies*
JISt	*Journal of International Studies*
JMAS	*Journal of Modern African Studies*
JMH	*Journal of Modern History*
JP	*Journal of Politics*
JPL	*Journal of Public Law*
JSEASt	*Journal of Southeast Asia Studies*
Komm	*Kommunist* [Communist]
Kyk	*Kyklos*
LA	*Latinskaia Amerika* [Latin America]
LARR	*Latin American Research Review*
MA	*Masters Abstracts*
ME	*Middle East*
MEJ	*Middle East Journal*
MEMO	*Mirovaia ekonomika i mezhdunarodnye otnosheniia* [World Economics and International Relations]
MESt	*Middle East Studies*
Mid	*Midstream*
Min	*Minerva*
Miz	*Mizan: U.S.S.R., China, Asia, Africa*
MJPS	*Midwest Journal of Political Science*
ModA	*Modern Age*
ModR	*Modern Review*
MR	*Military Review*
NAA	*Narody Azii i Afriki* [Peoples of Asia and Africa]
NLR	*New Left Review*

NME	New Middle East
NNI	Novaia i noveishaia istoriia [Modern and Contemporary History]
NP	New Politics
NT	New Times
NWCR	Naval War College Review
NYUJIL	New York University Journal of International Law and Politics
Oe-R	Osteuropa-Recht [East Europe Law]
Orb	Orbis
PA	Pacific Affairs
PC	Pacific Community
PG	Poland and Germany
PH	Pakistan Horizon
PHR	Pacific Historical Review
PoC	Problems of Communism
Pol	Politics
PolS	Politics and Society
POQ	Public Opinion Quarterly
PP	Past and Present
P,PRS	Papers of the Peace Research Society
PQ	Political Quarterly
Prog	Progressive
PS	Politicheskoe samoobrazovanie [Political Self-Education]
PSQ	Political Science Quarterly
PSR	Political Science Review
QQ	Queen's Quarterly
RCIIS	Report of California Institute of International Studies
RMSSJ	Rocky Mountain Social Science Journal
RP	Review of Politics
RPu	Res Publica
RR	Russian Review
SAIS	SAIS Review
SAQ	South Atlantic Quarterly
SDT	Sovety deputatov trudiashchikhsia [Soviets of the Workers' Deputies]
SGP	Sovetskoe gosudarstvo i pravo [Soviet Government and Law]
SJISt	Stanford Journal of International Studies
SlEER	Slavic and East European Review
SlR	Slavic Review
SoR	Social Research
SShA	SShA [USA]
SSQ	Social Science Quarterly
SSt	Soviet Studies

StCC	*Studies in Comparative Communism*
StNCE	*Studies for a New Central Europe*
StST	*Studies in Soviet Thought*
StSU	*Studies on the Soviet Union*
Sur	*Survey*
Surv	*Survival*
T-A	*Trans-Action*
TSJIA	*Towson State Journal of International Affairs*
UA	*United Asia*
UPLR	*University of Pennsylvania Law Review*
UQ	*Ukranian Quarterly*
USNI,P	*U.S. Naval Institute, Proceedings*
VE	*Voprosy ekonomiki* [Problems of Economics]
VF	*Voprosy filosofii* [Problems of Philosophy]
VI	*Voprosy istorii* [Problems of History]
VQR	*Virginia Quarterly Review*
VT	*Vneshniaia torgovlia* [Foreign Trade]
WA	*Weltwirtschaftliches Archiv* [World Economic Archive]
WAf	*World Affairs*
WMR	*World Marxist Review*
WP	*World Politics*
WPQ	*Western Political Quarterly*
W/PR	*War/Peace Report*
WT	*The World Today*
YLJ	*The Yale Law Journal*
YR	*Yale Review*

LIST OF OTHER JOURNALS CONSULTED

African Studies
Asian Forum
Canadian Journal of Political Science
Comparative Political Studies
Daedalus
Dissent
Hudson Review
International Journal of Middle East Studies
Journal of Common Market Studies
Journal of Latin American Studies
Journal of Peace Research
Law and Contemporary Problems
Modern Asian Studies
Osteuropa
Partisan Review
Peace Research Reviews
Political Science
Political Studies
Polity
Rumanian Studies
St. Anthony's Papers

SOVIET
& EAST
EUROPEAN
FOREIGN
POLICY

BIBLIOGRAPHY

[1] ABDULLAH, FUAD A. "Soviet Economic Aid in the Middle East: An Economic Evaluation." *EBB* 1967 19(3): 3-19.

[2] ABOLTIN, V. IA. *Gonka iadernykh vooruzhenii ugroza miru* [The nuclear arms race—threat to peace]. Moscow: Znanie, 1968.

[3] _____.*Politika gosudarstv i razoruzhenie* [The politics of governments and disarmament]. Moscow: Nauka, 1967.

[4] _____.*Sovremennye problemy razoruzheniia* [Contemporary problems of disarmament]. Moscow: Mysl', 1970.

[5] ABRAMOWITZ, MORTON. "Moving the Glacier: The Two Koreas and the Powers." *AP* 1971 80: 1-26.

[6] ABRAVANEL, MARTIN. "Affect, Belief and International Affairs: Soviet-American Competition and the National Images of Mass Publics." *DAI* 1971 32: 2148-A.

[7] ABROSIMOV, I. "Ekonomicheskoe sotrudnichestvo SSSR s Alzhirom" [Economic cooperation of the USSR with Algeria]. *VT* 1969 10: 14-16.

[8] ABU-JABER, FAIZ S. "The Origins of the Soviet-Arab Co-operation." *Miz* 1969 11: 211-233.

[9] ABUTALIPOV, CH. *Razvitie mezhdunarodynkh sviazei Uzbekskoi SSR —torzhestvo Leninskikh idei internatsionalizma* [The development of international ties of the Uzbek SSR—the victory of Leninist ideas of internationalism]. Tashkent: Uzbekistan, 1970.

3

[10] ACHIMINOW, HERMAN F. "Crisis in Mao's Realm and Moscow's China Policy." *Orb* 1968 11: 1179-1192.

[11] ACZEL, TAMAS, ED. *Ten Years After: The Hungarian Revolution in the Perspective of History.* New York: Holt, Rinehart and Winston, 1967.

[12] ADLER, LESLIE KIRBY. "The Red Image: American Attitudes Toward Communism in the Cold War Era." *DAI* 1971 31: 5309-A.

[13] ADLER-KARLSON, GUNNAR. *Western Economic Warfare 1947-1967: A Case in Foreign Economic Policy.* Stockholm: Almqvist and Wicksell, 1968.

[14] *Afrika v Sovetskikh issledovaniiakh* [Africa in Soviet research]. Moscow: Nauka, 1968.

[15] *L'Afrique dans les études soviétiques. Annuaire* [Africa in Soviet studies. Annual]. Moscow: Nauka, published annually.

[16] *Against Modern Anti-Communism (Proceedings of a Conference Held in Moscow, January 19-23, 1970).* Prague: Peace and Socialism Publishers, 1970.

[17] AHSEN CHAUDHRI, MOHAMMED. *Pakistan and the Great Powers.* Karachi: Council for Pakistan Studies, 1970.

[18] AINSZTEIN, R. "Soviet Policy on the Trail of the Golden Horde: Soviet Policy in Perspective [In the Middle East]." *NME* August 1970 (2): 31-35.

[19] AIR FORCE ACADEMY ASSEMBLY. *The United States and Eastern Europe.* Colorado Springs, Colorado: United States Air Force Academy, 1968.

[20] AIZIN, B. A. *Lenin v bor'be za revoliutsionnyi internatsional* [Lenin in the struggle for a revolutionary international]. Moscow: Nauka, 1970.

[21] AKERS, ALBERT B. "The Cuban Missile Crisis: A Study in Multilateral Diplomacy." *MA* 1967 5(2): 15.

[22] AKHARI, SHABROUGH. "The Egyptian Image of the Soviet Union, 1954-1968: A Study in Press Communications." *DAI* 1970 31: 2449-A.

[23] AKHMEDOV, B., AND M. NISHAKOV. *Kto ugrozhaet Evropeiskoi bezopasnosti?* [Who threatens European security?]. Tashkent: Izd. TsK. KP Uzbekistana, 1970.

[24] AKHRAMOVICH, R. "Leninskaia diplomatiia i Afganistan" [Leninist diplomacy and Afghanistan]. *AAS* 1969 (9): 5-7.

[25] AKHTAMZIAN, A. A. "Lenin's Foreign Policy Activity (April-August 1920)." *IA(M)* 1969 (8): 82-86.

[26] ———. "Lenin's Foreign Policy Activity (April-October 1921)." *IA(M)* 1969 (11): 50-53.

[27] ———. "Osnovnye etapy Sovetskoi vneshnei politiki (1917-1967)" [Basic stages of Soviet foreign policy (1917-1967)]. *VI* 1967 (10): 113-134.

[28] AKIMOV, E. "Problems of CMEA Countries' Economic Integration." *IA(M)* 1969 (12): 7-11.

[29] ALAMPIEV, P. M. "Lenin i sotrudnichestvo sotsialisticheskikh natsii" [V. I. Lenin and the cooperation of the socialist nations]. *MEMO* 1970 (1): 3-12.

[30] ———. "Socialist Internationalism and National Interests." *NT* 1970 (8): 22-23.

[31] ———.*Problemy mezhdunarodnogo sotsialisticheskogo razdeleniia truda* [Problems of international socialist division of labor]. Leningrad: Nauka, 1967.

[32] ALBERT, E. H. "Bonn's Moscow Treaty and Its Implications." *IA(L)* 1971 47: 316-326.

[33] ———. "The Brandt Doctrine of Two States in Germany." *IA(L)* 1970 46: 293-303.

[34] ALBINSKI, HENRY. "Chinese and Soviet Policies in the Vietnam Crisis." *AQ* March 1968 15: 65-74.

[35] ALDOSHIN V. "Outer Space Must Be a Peace Zone." *IA(M)* 1968 (12): 38-41.

[36] ALEKSANDROV, I. "The Poverty of Anti-Communism." *WMR* 1971 (1): 23-28.

[37] ALEKSANDROV, V. V. *O taktike i strategii mezhdunarodnogo Kommunisticheskogo dvizheniia* [On the tactics and strategy of the international Communist movement]. Moscow: Politizdat, 1968.

[38] ALEKSEEV, A. "Important Initiative for Disarmament." *IA(M)* 1968 (9): 7-11.

[39] ———. "Non-Proliferation Talks." *IA(M)* 1968 (5): 19-23.

[40] ———. "Non-Proliferation Treaty and Security." *IA(M)* 1969 (1): 10-14.

[41] ———. "Non-Proliferation Treaty and the Non-Nuclear States." *IA(M)* 1969 (3): 9-13.

[42] _____. "Prohibiting Military Use of the Sea-Bed." *IA(M)* 1971 (2): 60-62.

[43] _____, AND IU. SAVENKO. "Problemy sotsialisticheskoi integratsii" [Problems of socialist integration]. *MEMO* 1970 (12): 3-14.

[44] _____, AND A. VASIL'EV. "Bulgarian-Soviet Fraternity." *IA(M)* 1967 (7): 34-39.

[45] ALEKSEEVA, E., AND R. VASIL'EVA. "An Important Stage in the Development of Soviet-Hungarian Friendship." *IA(M)* 1970 (8): 100-101.

[46] ALEXANDER, ROBERT J. "Marx, Lenin and Developing Countries." *NP* 1971 9(2): 87-95.

[47] ALEXANDROV, L., AND V. SHESTOV. "Important Initiative of Socialist Countries" (Elimination of Bacteriological Weapons). *IA(M)* 1971 (7): 88-91.

[48] ALIMOV, E., AND V. POLIANSKII. "The Struggle Against Imperialism and Anti-Imperialist Unity." *IA(M)* 1969 (4): 16-24.

[49] ALKHIMOV, V. "Mezhdunarodnye platezhnye otnosheniia SSSR" [International payments relations of the USSR]. *VT* 1967 (7): 3-9.

[50] _____. "Novyi znachitel'nyi shag v razvitii vneshnei torgovli SSSR" [A new important step in the development of the foreign trade of the USSR]. *VT* 1971 (5): 6-7.

[51] _____. "Soviet Foreign Trade Today and Tomorrow." *NT* 1971 (14): 10-11.

[52] ALLARD, SVEN. *Russia and the Austrian State Treaty: A Case Study of Soviet Policy in Europe.* University Park: Pennsylvania State University Press, 1970.

[53] ALLEN, RICHARD V., ED. *Yearbook on International Communist Affairs 1968.* [Covers 1967] Stanford: Hoover Institution, 1969.

[54] ALLISON, GRAHAM T. *Essence of Decision: Explaining the Cuban Missile Crisis.* Boston: Little, Brown, 1971.

[55] ALLOT, ANNA. *See* 199.

[56] AL'PEROVICH, M. S. "Soviet Historiography of the Latin American Countries." *LARR* 1970 5(1): 63-70.

[57] ALPROVITS, K. *Atomnaia diplomatiia—Khirosima i Potsdam* [Atomic diplomacy—Hiroshima and Potsdam]. Moscow: I.M.O., 1968.

[58] ALT'SHULLER, A. B. "Valiutnofinansovoe sotrudnichestvo stran SEV" [Financial currency cooperation of the countries of CMEA]. *SGP* 1969 (1): 81-87.

[59] ———. *Valiutnye otnosheniia vo vneshnei torgovle SSSR* [Currency relations in the foreign trade of the USSR]. Moscow: I.M.O., 1968.

[60] ALTUG, YILMAZ. *Problems of China, Vietnam, Czechoslovakia and the Middle East.* Istanbul: Sermet Matbaasi, 1970.

[61] AMALRIK, ANDREI. *Will the Soviet Union Survive Until 1984?* New York: Harper, 1970.

[62] AMBROZ, OTON. "The Doctrine of Limited Sovereignty: Its Impact on East Europe." *EE* 1969 18(5): 19-24.

[63] ———. "Moscow Summit Conference." *EE* 1969 18(8-9): 15-20.

[64] ———. "Outer Mongolia: Sino-Soviet Prize." *EE* 1971 20(11): 32-33.

[65] AMERICAN SECURITY COUNCIL. *USSR vs. USA: The ABM and the Changed Strategic Military Balance.* Washington, D.C.: Acropolis Books, 1969.

[66] AMES, KENNETH. "Reform and Reaction [Czechoslovakia]." *PoC* 1968 17(6): 38-49.

[67] AMETISTOV, E. M. *Mezhdunarodnoe trudovoe pravo i rabochii klass* [International labor law and the working class]. Moscow: I.M.O., 1970.

[68] AMME, CARL H., JR. "Seapower and the Superpowers." *USNI,P* 1968 94(10): 26-35.

[69] ———. "The Soviet Navy in the Mediterranean Sea." *NWCR* 1969 21(10): 154-159.

[70] ANAN'EV, M. *Mezhdunarodnyi turizm* [International tourism]. Moscow: I.M.O., 1968.

[71] ANCKAR, DAG. "Finnish Foreign Policy Debate: The Saimaa Canal Case." *CaC* 1970 5: 201-223.

[72] ANDERSON, STEPHEN S. "East Europe: The Politics of Recovery." *CH* 1969 56: 207-213, 241.

[73] ———. "Soviet Russia and the Two Europes." *CH* 1967 52: 203-207, 241-242.

[74] ———. "The United States and Soviet Russia." *CH* 1968 55: 281-287, 304.

[75] ———. "Yugoslavia: The Diplomacy of Balance." *CH* 1969 56: 212-217, 243.

[76] ANDRAS, CHARLES. "The Slow Drift to Danubian Cooperation." *EE* 1968 17(12): 19-25.

[77] ANDREASIAN, R. "Soviet Experience and the Developing Countries." *IA(M)* 1967 (8): 17-22.

[78] ANDREEV G. "Lenin and Peaceful Soviet Foreign Policy." *IA(M)* 1970 (5): 3-14.

[79] ANDREEV, I. "Sovetskoe oborudovanie na rynkakh stran Afriki" [Soviet equipment in the markets of the countries of Africa]. *VT* 1968 (10): 7-10.

[80] ANDRONOV, I. "Defenders of the Caucasian Black Sea Coast." *NT* 1971 (20): 18-25.

[81] ———. "Lenin's Ambassador in America (Ludwig Mertens)." *NT* 1970 (17): 28-32.

[82] ———. "Soviet Russia and Turkey." *NT* 1967 (38): 19-22.

[83] ———. "The 25th Anniversary of V-J Day." *NT* 1970 (35): 26-29.

[84] ANDRUSIAK, NICHOLAS "Soviet Anti-Americanism." *UQ* 1970 26: 270-276.

[85] "Anglo-Franco-Soviet Talks in Moscow, 1939 (a Documentary Survey)." *IA(M)* 1969 (11): 78-88.

[86] ANSBERRY, W. F. *Arms Control and Disarmament: Success or Failure.* Berkeley, California: McCutchan Publishing Corporation, 1969.

[87] ANTHERN, THOMAS. "Balkan Cockpit." *CR* 1969 214: 117-121.

[88] ———. "Russia in the Mediterranean." *CR* 1968 212: 132-137.

[89] *Antikommunizm i antisovetiszm—professiia Sionistov* [Anti-Communism and anti-Sovietism—the occupation of the Zionists]. Moscow: Politizdat, 1971.

[90] APALIN, G. " 'New Period' in Peking's Foreign Policy?" *IA(M)* 1969 (2): 7-13.

[91] APPATOV, S. J. *Novyi tip mezhdunarodnykh otnoshenii (vneshnepoliti-cheskaia deiatel'nost' stran sotsializma)* [A new type of international relations (the foreign policy activity of the socialist countries)]. Kiev: Znanie USSR, 1971.

[92] APRÓ, ANTAL. "Hungarian Economy and Cooperation Within the CMEA." *IA(M)* 1967 (7): 27-33.

[93] ———. "A New Type of Inter-State Economic Relations." *WMR* 1968 (2): 53-58.

[94] ———. *Sotrudnichestvo stran chlenov SEV v ekonomicheskikh orga-nizatsiiakh sotsialisticheskikh stran* [Cooperation of the member countries of CMEA in the economic organization of the socialist countries]. Moscow: Ekonomika, 1969.

[95] ABRABADZHIAN, A. Z. "O Sovetsko-Iranskom ekonomicheskom so-trudnichestve" [On Soviet-Iranian economic cooperation]. *NAA* 1968 (2): 15-25.

[96] ARALDSEN, O. P. "The Soviet Union and the Arctic." *USNI,P* 1967 93(6): 48-57.

[97] ARBATOV, G. A. *Ideologicheskaia bor'ba v sovremennykh mezh-dunarodnykh otnosheniiakh. Doktrina, metody i organizatsiia vneshnepoliticheskoi propagandy imperializma* [Ideological strug-gle in contemporary international relations. Doctrine, methods and the organization of the foreign policy propaganda of imperialism]. Moscow: Politizdat, 1970.

[98] ARISMENDI, RODNEI. "Marks, Engels i Lenin o 'putiakh revoliutsii'" [Marx,Engels,and Lenin on "paths of revolution"]. *Komm* 1970 (2): 24-46.

[99] ARKAD'EV, E. "International Human Rights Year." *IA(M)* 1968 (4): 8-11.

[100] ARKAD'EV, G. P. *Diplomatiia i industrializatsiia* [Diplomacy and in-dustrialization]. Moscow: I.M.O., 1967.

[101] ARKAD'EV, N. "Contribution to International Security." *NT* 1970 (52): 4-5.

[102] ———. "Nuclear Disarmament: Five Power Conference." *NT* 1971 (27): 4.

[103] ———. "A Quarter-Century of Struggle for Disarmament." *NT* 1971 (5): 18-20.

[104] ———. "The Soviet Union and Disarmament." *NT* 1971 (26): 18-19.

[105] ARMSTRONG, JOHN A. *The Soviet Union: Toward Confrontation or Co-existence?* New York: Foreign Policy Association Serial 2, cci, 1970.

[106] ARMSTRONG, WILLIS. "The Economic Balance of Power." *StNCE* 1968-9 2(4): 243-247.

[107] ARNAUTOV, L. "Discovery of a World: Early Workers' Delegations to Soviet Russia." *NT* 1967 (44): 5-7.

[108] ARTSIBASOV, I. N. *Germanskaia Demokraticheskaia Respublika—sub"ekt mezhdunarodnogo prava* [The German Democratic Republic—a subject of international law]. Moscow: Iuridicheskaia Literatura, 1969.

[109] ASCHERSON, NEAL. "Poland's Place in Europe." *WT* 1969 25(12): 520-529.

[110] ASLAN'IAN, R. "50-letie Mezhdunarodnoi Organizatsii Truda" [The 50th anniversary of the International Organization of Labor]. *SGP* 1970 (2): 140-142.

[111] ASPATURIAN, VERNON V. "The Aftermath of the Czech Invasion." *CH* 1968 55: 263-267, 305-310.

[112] ——. "East European Relations with the USSR." In *The Changing Face of Communism in Eastern Europe,* edited by Peter A. Toma. Tucson: The University of Arizona Press, 1970.

[113] ——. "Moscow's Foreign Policy." *Sur* 1967 (65): 35-60.

[114] ——.*Process and Power in Soviet Foreign Policy.* Boston: Little, Brown, 1971.

[115] ——. "Soviet Aims in East Europe." *CH* 1970 57: 206-211.

[116] ——. "Soviet Foreign Policy." In *Foreign Policy in World Politics,* 3d ed., edited by Roy C. Macridis. Englewood Cliffs, New Jersey: Prentice-Hall, 1967.

[117] ——. "Soviet Foreign Policy at the Crossroads: Conflict and/or Cooperation." *IO* 1969 23: 589-620.

[118] ——. "Soviet Foreign Policy Perspectives in the Sixties." In *Soviet Politics Since Khrushchev,* edited by Alexander Dallin and Thomas B. Larson. Englewood Cliffs, New Jersey: Prentice-Hall, 1969.

[119] ASTAF'EV, G. V., ED. *Vneshniaia politika KNR. O sushchnosti vnesh-nepoliticheskogo kursa sovremennogo Kitaiskogo rukovodstva* [The foreign policy of the People's Republic of China. On the nature of the foreign policy course of the present Chinese leadership]. Moscow: I.M.O., 1971.

[120] ATHAY, ROBERT E. *The Economics of Soviet Merchant-Shipping Policy.* Chapel Hill: University of North Carolina Press, 1971.

[121] ATWOOD, WILLIAM. *The Reds and the Blacks [Africa].* New York: Harper and Row, 1967.

[122] AUERSPERG, P. "Czechoslovakia in the Struggle for Peace and European Security." *NT* 1971 (17): 12-14.

[123] AUSCH, S. "International Division of Labour and the Present Forms of Economic Mechanism in the CMEA Countries." In *Reform of the Economic Mechanism in Hungary,* pp. 223-246, edited by Istvan Friss. Budapest: Akademiai Kiado, 1971.

[124] AUSTIN, DENNIS. "Russia and China in Central Asia." *WT* 1967 23: 89-93.

[125] "Autumn for Czechoslovakia." *Ag* 1969 12(October): 38-41.

10

[126] AUTY, PHYLLIS. "Popular Front in the Balkans: Yugoslavia." *JCH* 1970 5: 51-68.

[127] AVDEEVA, L. "K voprosu o metodakh rascheta effektivnosti vneshnei torgovli" [On the question of methods of raising the effectiveness of foreign trade]. *VE* 1970 (3): 130-133.

[128] AVTORKHANOV, ABDURAKHMAN. "The New Phase of Soviet Expansionist Policy." *B,ISUSSR* 1971 18(12): 13-31.

[129] AYOOB, MOHAMMED. "Pakistan's Trade Relations With the Soviet Union." *IS* 1969 2(1).

[130] AZOVTSEV, N., AND S. GUSAREVICH. "Lenin's Exposure of Militarism." *IA(M)* 1970 (4): 19-23.

[131] BAGDASH, KHALID. "Lenin and Struggle Against Opportunism and Revisionism in National Liberation Movement." *WMR* 1970 (4): 92-97.

[132] ———. "Leninizm o natsional'nom voprose i proletarskom internatsionalizme" [Leninism on the national question and on proletarian internationalism]. *Komm* 1969 (8): 14-24.

[133] BAGLAI, M. "Profsoiuzy protiv monopolii, protiv imperializma" [Labor unions against monopoly, against imperialism]. *Komm* 1970 (3): 106-117.

[134] BAGRAMOV, E. A. "Dialektika natsional'nogo i internatsional'nogo v usloviiakh sotsializma" [The dialectic of the national and the international in the conditions of socialism]. *VF* 1970 (4): 121-133.

[135] BAILEY, CLINTON. "America and the Soviet Involvement in Azerbaijan in 1946: Some Parallels for 1970." *IP* 1970 9(3-4): 20-24.

[136] BAILEY, GERALD, ED. *The Great Britain-USSR Handbook.* London: Great Britain-USSR Association, 1968.

[137] BAILEY, SYDNEY D. "Veto in the Security Council." *IC* 1968 (566): 5-66.

[138] BAKER, ROSS, K. "Soviet Military Assistance to Tropical Africa." *MR* 1968 48(7): 76-81.

[139] BAKOTIC, B. *See* 1404.

[140] BALLIS, WILLIAM B. "Soviet Foreign Policy Toward Developing States: The Case of Egypt." *B,ISUSSR* 1968 15(3): 84-113.

[141] BARATASHVILI, D. I. "Ekonomicheskaia nezavisimost' osvobodivshikhsia stran i mezhdunarodnoe pravo" [The economic independence of the liberated countries and international law]. *SGP* 1970 (8): 65-72.

[142] ———. "Lenin's Doctrine on the Self-Determination of Nations and the National Liberation Struggle." *IA(M)* 1970 (12): 9-15.

[143] BARCHAK, A. "Za dal'neishie uspekhi Chekhoslovatsko-Sovetskoi torgovli" [For further successes of Czechoslovak-Soviet trade]. *VT* 1971 (8): 2-5.

[144] BARDIN, B. "All-European Conference—A Pressing Need." *NT* 1971 (22): 4-6.

[145] ———. "In the Interests of Europe's Future." *NT* 1970 (48): 20-22.

[146] BARGHOORN, FREDERICK C. "Soviet Cultural Effort [in the Middle East]." *APS,P* 1969 29: 156-169.

[147] ———. *The Soviet Image of the United States: A Study in Distortion.* Reprint of 1950. Port Washington, New York: Kennikat, 1970.

[148] BARINOV, N. "U istokov stanovleniia Sovetskoi vneshnei torgovli" [At the sources of the growth of Soviet foreign trade]. *VT* 1970 (11): 4-6.

[149] BARITZ, JOSEPH J. "The Soviet Strategy of Flexible Response." *B,ISUSSR* 1969 16(4): 25-34.

[150] ———. "The Warsaw Pact and the Kremlin's European Strategy." *B,ISUSSR* 1970 17(5): 15-28.

[151] BARK, DENNIS L. "Changing East-West Relations in Europe: The Bonn-Moscow Treaty of August 1970." *Orb* 1971 15: 625-642.

[152] BARNETT, A. DOAK. "The New Multipolar Balance in East Asia: Implications for the United States Policy." *A,AAPSS* 1970 390: 73-86.

[153] BARNETT, FRANK R. "Overview of Soviet Strategy." *NWCR* 1971 22(10): 16-21.

[154] BAROCH, CHARLES T. "The Soviet Doctrine of Sovereignty." *B,ISUSSR* 1971 18(8): 7-25.

[155] ———. *The Soviet Doctrine of Sovereignty (the So-Called Brezhnev Doctrine).* Chicago: American Bar Association, 1970.

[156] BARRETT, RAYMOND J. "Geography and Soviet Strategic Thinking." *MR* 1970 50(1): 17-25.

[157] BARROS, JAMES. *The League of Nations and the Great Powers.* New York: Oxford University Press, 1971.

[158] BARSEGOV, IU. G. "Mir mezhdu narodami i territorial'nyi vopros" [Peace between peoples and the territorial question]. *SGP* 1971 (3): 78-84.

[159] BART, P. H. "Two World Systems Today and Tomorrow." *WMR* 1971 14(1): 64-76.

[160] BARTOW, BARRY G. "Sino-Soviet Relations With Yugoslavia and Its Relationship to the Sino-Soviet Dispute, 1956-1962." *MA* 1967 5(3): 19.

[161] BASHEV, IVAN. "Bulgaria's Foreign Policy." *IA(M)* 1969 (9): 3-11.

[162] ———. "Minister Bashev on Bulgaria's Foreign Policy." *NT* 1969 (36): 2-4.

[163] BASHKIROV, A. "Iran i strany SEV" [Iran and the countries of CMEA]. *AAS* 1968 (12): 12-13.

[164] BATOWSKI, HENRYK. "Diplomatic Events in East-Central Europe in 1944." *EEQ* 1971 5: 313-324.

[165] BAUTINA, N. V. *Ekonomicheskie problemy razvitiia mirovoi sistemy sotsializma* [Economic problems of development of the world socialist system]. Moscow: Izd. Mosk. UNIV-A, 1967.

[166] ———. "O mezhdunarodnykh sotsialisticheskikh proizvodstvennykh otnosheniiakh" [On international socialist production relations]. *MEMO* 1968 (4): 64-71.

[167] ———. "The World Socialist Market and Economic Integration." *IA(M)* 1970 (1): 16-20.

[168] BAVRIN, E. "Sovetsko-Mongol'skaia torgovl'ia na pod"eme" [Soviet-Mongolian trade on the rise]. *VT* 1968 (5): 13-18, (6): 7-9.

[169] BEACH, EDWARD L. "An Appraisal of Soviet Maritime-Naval Capabilities." *NWCR* 1969 21(10): 15-25.

[170] BEATON, LEONARD. "Nuclear Fuel-for-All." *FA* 1967 45: 662-669.

[171] BECKER, A. S., AND A. L. HORELICK. *Soviet Policy in the Middle East.* Santa Monica, California: RAND Corporation, 1970.

[172] BEER, FRITZ. "Ten Weeks That Shook Czechoslovakia." *Sur* 1968 10: 56-66.

[173] BEILLARD, JEAN-MICHAEL. "International Economic Integration in the EEC and COMECON: A Comparison." *DAI* 1971 32: 609-A.

[174] BEKAREVICH, A. D. "SSSR-Kuba: Leninskie printsipy proletarskogo internatsionalizma" [USSR-Cuba: Leninist principles of proletarian internationalism]. *LA* 1970 (1): 20-31.

[175] BEKAREVICH, G. "Ekonomicheskoe i tekhnicheskoe sotrudnichestvo s Turtsei" [Economic and technical cooperation with Turkey]. *VT* 1968 (7): 28-30.

[176] BELEN'KII, A. "Lenin i osvoboditel'noe dvizhenie v Indonezii" [Lenin and the liberation movement in Indonesia]. *AAS* 1969 (11): 5-8.

[177] BELIAEV, IU. N. "CMEA Cooperation Today." *IA(M)* 1968 (12): 5-11.

[178] ———.*CMEA Countries' Economic Cooperation.* Moscow: Novosti, 1970.

[179] ———. Council for Mutual Economic Aid. Moscow: Novosti, 1969.

[180] ———. "Ekonomicheskie interesy i sotrudnichestvo stran-chlenov SEV" [Economic interests and the cooperation of the member countries of CMEA]. *VE* 1970 (12): 93-101.

[181] ———.*Strany SEV v mirovoi ekonomike* [The countries of CMEA in world economics]. Moscow: I.M.O., 1967.

[182] ———, AND IU. SHIRIAEV. "SEV: Novyi etap sotrudnichestva" [CMEA: A new level of cooperation]. *Komm* 1970 (11): 61-71.

[183] BELOFF, MAX. "Russia's Foreign Policy: The Cycle of Mistrust." *IP* 1971 4(2): 9-13.

[184] BENDER, PETER (TRANSLATED BY S. Z. YOUNG). *East Europe in Search of Security.* London: Institute for Strategic Studies, 1971.

[185] ———. "Inside the Warsaw Pact." *Sur* 1970 74-75: 253-269.

[186] ———. "The Special Case of Germany." *StCC* 1969 2(2): 14-33.

[187] BENN, DAVID WEDGWOOD. "New Thinking in Soviet Propaganda." *SSt* 1969 21: 52-63.

[188] BENNETT, EDWARD M. *Polycentrism: Growing Dissidence in the Communist Bloc?* Pullman: Washington State University Press, 1967.

[189] ———.*Recognition of Russia: An American Foreign Policy Dilemma.* Waltham, Massachusetts: Blaisdell, 1970.

[190] BENSON, DAVID V. *Christianity, Communism, and Survival.* Glendale, California: G/L Regal Books, 1967.

[191] BERANEK, ROBERT E. "The Second Berlin Crisis and the Foreign Ministers' Conference at Geneva (1959): A Case Study in Soviet Foreign Diplomacy." *DAI* 1967 27: 4307-A.

[192] BEREZHKOV, V. M. *Gody diplomaticheskoi sluzhby (1940-1944)* [Years of diplomatic service (1940-1944)]. Moscow: I.M.O., 1972.

[193] ———. "The Teheran Meeting: From the Diplomatic History of World War II." *NT* 1967 (49): 27-32, (50): 30-34.

[194] BEREZOWSKI, Z. "Poland and the Emerging New Europe." *PG* 1968 12(1-2): 3-9.

[195] BERKI, R. N. "On Marxian Thought and the Problem of International Relations." *WP* 1971 24: 80-105.

[196] BERMAN, HAROLD J., AND PETER B. MAGGS. *Disarmament Inspection Under Soviet Law.* Dobbs Ferry, New York: Oceana Publications, 1967.

[197] BERNER, WOLFGANG W. "Soviet Strategy Toward Cuba, Latin America and the Third World." *B,ISUSSR* 1968 15(7): 3-12.

[198] BERTON, PETER. "The Border Issue. China and the Soviet Union: The Territorial Issue." *StCC* 1969 2(3-4): 131-149.

[199] _____, ALVIN Z. RUBINSTEIN, AND ANNA ALLOT. *Soviet Works on Southeast Asia: A Bibliography of Non-Periodical Literature, 1946-1965.* Los Angeles: University of Southern California Press, 1967.

[200] BERZINS, ALFRED. *The Two Faces of Co-Existence.* New York: Robert Speller and Sons, 1967.

[201] BESKURNIKOV, D. "Novyi shag v razvitii Sovetsko-Shvedskikh ekonomicheskikh otnoshenii" [A new step in the development of Soviet-Swedish economic relations]. *VT* 1970 (12): 10-12.

[202] BESTUZHEV-LADA, I., AND D. ERMOLENKO. "The Scientific Forecast of International Relations in the Light of Lenin's Teaching." *IA(M)* 1970 (2-3): 93-100.

[203] BETHEL, PAUL D. *The Losers: The Definitive Report by Our Eyewitness of the Communist Conquest of Cuba and the Soviet Penetration in Latin America.* New Rochelle, New York: Arlington House, 1969.

[204] BEYME, KLAUS VON. "The Ostpolitik in the West German 1969 Elections." *GO* 1970 5(2): 193-217.

[205] BEZYMENSKII, L. "The International Communist Forum." *NT* 1969 (25): 3-5.

[206] _____. "One Year After (the Soviet FRG Treaty)." *NT* 1971 (33): 9-10.

[207] _____. "A Task for All Europe (European Security Conference)." *NT* 1970 (27): 4-6.

[208] _____. "UNESCO and the Lenin Year." *NT* 1970 (3): 10-12.

[209] BIALER, SEWERYN. *See* 918.

[210] _____, ED. *Stalin and His Generals: Soviet Military Memoirs of World War II.* New York: Pegasus, 1969.

[211] BIDDER, RICHARD B. "East-West Trade Boycotts: A Study in Private Labor Union, State, and Local Interference With Foreign Policy." *UPLR* 1970 118: 841-938.

[212] BIHARI, OTTO. "International Relations—Hungary." *CSISt,BS* 1968 2(1): 63-64.

15

[213] BILIAK, VASIL. "Chekhoslovatsko-Sovetskie otnosheniia—osnova razvitiia Chekhoslovatskoi gosudarstvennosti" [Czechoslovak-Soviet relations—the basis of the development of the Czechoslovak state system]. *Komm* 1970 (7): 106-111.

[214] ———. "From Dresden to Bratislava: From the History of the Czechoslovak Events." *NT* 1969 (37): 17-23.

[215] ———. "Internatsionalizm-osnovnoi printzip vzaimootnoshenii bratskikh stran" [Internationalism—the basic principle of mutual relations of fraternal countries]. *PS* 1971 (6): 54-59.

[216] BILLINGTON, JAMES H. "Force and Counterforce in Eastern Europe." *FA* 1968 47: 26-35.

[217] BIRNBAUM, KARL E. *Peace in Europe: East-West Relations 1966-1968 and the Prospects for a European Settlement.* London: Chathane House, 1970.

[218] ———. "Soviet Policy in Northern Europe." *Surv* 1970 12: 227-232.

[219] ———. "Ways Toward European Security." *Surv* 1968 10: 193-199.

[220] BIRO, I. "Vengero-Sovetskoe ekonomicheskoe sotrudnichestvo na novom pod"eme" [Hungarian-Soviet economic cooperation on the rise anew]. *VT* 1961 (6): 9-15.

[221] BIRRENBACH, KURT. "The West and German Ostpolitik—The German Opposition View." *ACQ* 1971 9(2): 196-204.

[222] BITZER, RONALD. "Soviet Policy on German Unification in 1952." *WAf* 1969 132: 245-256.

[223] BJOL, ERLING. "The USSR, Détente and the Future of NATO." *Orb* 1969 13: 223-236.

[224] BLACKABY, FRANK, ET AL. *Arms Trade With the Third World.* Stockholm: Almquist and Wicksell, 1971.

[225] BLACKMER, DONALD L. M. *Unity in Diversity: Italian Communism and the Communist World.* Cambridge: Massachusetts Institute of Technology Press, 1968.

[226] BLACKSTOCK, PAUL W. *Agents of Deceit [Espionage].* Chicago: Quadrangle Books, 1967.

[227] ———. *The Secret Road to World War Two: Soviet Versus Western Intelligence, 1921-1939.* Chicago: Quadrangle Books, 1969.

[228] BLACKWELL, VERA. "Czechoslovakia at the Crossroads." *Sur* 1969 (68): 67-79.

[229] BLAGOVIĆ, BOŽICA. "International Relations—Yugoslavia." *CSISt,BS* 1969 3(1): 162-171, 1970 4(1): 64-72.

[230] Blinov, E. "Diplomacy and Social Progress." *IA(M)* 1971 (3): 3-22.

[231] Blishchenko, I. P. *Antisovetizm i mezhdunarodnoe pravo* [Anti-Sovietism and international law]. Moscow: I.M.O., 1968.

[232] _____.*Sovetskoe gosudarstvo i mezhdunarodnaia zakonnost'* [The Soviet state and international legality]. Moscow: Znanie, 1968.

[233] _____, and A. Piradov. "The Soviet Union and Diplomatic Law." *IA(M)* 1967 (1): 86-90.

[234] _____.*See* 1454.

[235] Blixt, Melvin P. "Soviet Objectives in the Eastern Mediterranean." *NWCR* 1969 21(7): 4-26.

[236] Bloemer, Klaus. "Eastern European Politics and Reunification." *ACQ* 1967 5: 219-222.

[237] Bloomfield, Lincoln P. "The United States, the Soviet Union, and the Prospects for Peacekeeping." *IO* 1970 24: 548-565.

[238] Blumenfeld, Yorick. "World Communist Summit." *ERR* 1969 (May 28): 393-410.

[239] Bobrov, R. L. *Osnovnye problemy teorii mezhdunarodnogo prava* [Basic problems of the theory of international law]. Moscow: I.M.O., 1967.

[240] *Boevaia solidarnost', bratskaia pomoshch'. (Sbornik razhneishikh dokumentov SSSR po V'etnamskomu voprosu)* [Fighting solidarity, fraternal assistance (a collection of documents of the USSR on the Vietnam question)]. Moscow: Progress, 1970.

[241] "Boevoi avangard bor'by protiv imperializma" [The fighting vanguard of the struggle against imperialism]. *Komm* 1969 (10): 8-19.

[242] Bogdanov, O. V. "Khimicheskoe i bakteriologicheskoe oruzhie—vne zakona" [Chemical and bacteriological weapons are illegal]. *SGP* 1970 (6): 80-89.

[243] _____.*Razoruzhenie-garantiia mira* [Disarmament is the guarantee of peace]. Moscow: I.M.O., 1972.

[244] _____.*See* 411.

[245] _____.*See* 412.

[246] Bogomolov, Oleg. "Economic Integration of Socialist Countries." *WMR* 1970 13(11): 63-68.

[247] _____. "Leninizm i nekotorye problemy sotrudnichestva stran sotsializma" [Leninism and some problems of the cooperation of the socialist countries]. *Komm* 1970 (8): 14-25.

[248] ———. "Nekotorye problemy spetsializatsii i kooperirovaniia proizvodstva mezhdy stranami SEV" [Some problems of specialization and of production cooperation among the countries of CMEA]. *MEMO* 1967 (5) 73-81.

[249] ———. "Rastushchie vozmozhnosti ekonomicheskogo sotrudnichestva" [Extended possibilities of economic cooperation]. *Komm* 1968 (5): 82-91.

[250] ———. "Razvitie stran SEV po puti ekonomicheskoi integratsii" [Development of the countries of CMEA on the path of economic integration]. *Komm* 1971 (16): 72-84.

[251] ———. "Teoreticheskoe nasledie V. I. Lenina i ekonomicheskaia integratsiia stran sotsializma" [The theoretical legacy of V. I. Lenin and the economic integration of the socialist countries]. *MEMO* 1970 (4): 55-66.

[252] ———, AND V. TEREKHOV. "Lenin i razvitie mirovogo sotsialisticheskogo sodruzhestva" [Lenin and the development of world socialist collaboration]. *VE* 1970 (2): 3-15.

[253] ———, ED. *Ekonomika stran sotsializma 1969 god* [The economy of the socialist countries, 1969]. Moscow: Ekonomika, 1970.

[254] BOGUSH, E. IU. *Maoizm i politika raskola v natsional'no-osvoboditel'nom dvizhenii* [Maoism and the policy of splitting in the national liberation movement]. Moscow: Mysl', 1969.

[255] ———. "Sources of Working Class's International Policy." *IA(M)* 1968 (5): 7-12.

[256] ———. *Sovetskaia vneshniaia politika i mirovoi revoliutsionnyi protsess* [Soviet foreign policy and the world revolutionary process]. Moscow: I.M.O., 1967.

[257] BOGUSLAVSKII, M. M. *Pravovoe regulirovanie mezhdunarodnykh khoziaistvennykh otnoshenii* [The legal regulation of international economic relations]. Moscow: Nauka, 1970.

[258] BOLE, ROBERT D. *Summit at Holly Bush.* Glassboro, New Jersey: Glassboro State College, 1969.

[259] BOLGARANOV, B. "Peaceful Coexistence—Struggle Against Imperialist Aggression, for Peace." *WMR* 1968 11(8): 3-10.

[260] BOLL, MICHAEL M. "The Dilemma of the Warsaw Pact." *MR* 1969 49(7): 89-98.

[261] ———. "Soviet Policy in Eastern Europe." *EE* 1969 18(2): 20-24.

[262] BOLSHAKOV, V. *Anti-Sovietism—Profession of Zionists.* Moscow: Novosti, 1971.

[263] BOLTHO, ANDREA. *Foreign Trade Criteria in Socialist Economies.* London and New York: Cambridge University Press, 1971.

[264] BOLTIN, E. "Vneshniaia politika SSSR nakanune i v gody Velikoi Otechestvennoi Voiny" [The foreign policy of the USSR on the eve of and during the Great Patriotic War]. *Komm* 1970 (7): 112-122.

[265] "The Border Issue. China and the Soviet Union March-October 1969: Documents." *StCC* 1969 2(3-4): 150-382.

[266] BORGESE, ELIZABETH MANN. "Last Days of the Superpowers." *CM* 1970 (4): 2-7.

[267] BORISOV, A. "U.S. Anti-Communism." *IA(M)* 1970 (11): 54-58.

[268] BORISOV, IU. V. "USSR-France: 45 Years of Diplomatic Relations." *IA(M)* 1969 (10): 71-77.

[269] ———, ET AL. *Vneshniaia politika Sovetskogo Soiuza. Aktual'nye problemy* [The foreign policy of the Soviet Union. Actual problems]. Moscow: I.M.O., 1967.

[270] BORISOV, O. B., AND BORIS T. KOLOSKOV. "Antisovetskii kurs gruppy Mao Tsee-duna" [The anti-Soviet course of the group of Mao Tse-tung]. *Komm* 1969 (7) 86-97.

[271] ———, AND BORIS T. KOLOSKOV. *Kratkii ocherk istorii Sovetsko-Kitaiskikh otnoshenii, 1949-1968* [A short sketch of the history of Soviet-Chinese relations, 1949-1968]. Moscow: Mysl', 1970.

[272] ———, AND BORIS T. KOLOSKOV. *Sovetsko-Kitaiskie otnosheniia 1945-1970* [Soviet-Chinese relations 1945-1970]. Moscow: Mysl', 1970.

[273] BORKO, IU. "Bor'ba za internatsional'noe edinstvo rabochego klassa" [The struggle for the international unity of the working class]. *Komm* 1971 (12): 93-104.

[274] BORNSTEIN, MORRIS. "Communist Chinese Society in Soviet Perspective." *CSSH* 1968 10: 221-229.

[275] BOROB'EV, A. I. *Ukrainskaia SSR na mezhdunarodnoi arene. (Nekotorye voprosy vneshnepoliticheskoi deiatel'nosti')* [The Ukrainian SSR in the international arena. (Some questions of foreign policy activity)]. Kiev: Znanie, USSR, 1970.

[276] BORODAEVSKII, A. *See* 1296.

[277] BORODIN, NIKOLAI. "The Soviet Union and the Middle East—Facts and Fiction." *NME* July 1971 (34): 14-17.

[278] BOSE, TARUN CHANDRA. "American and Soviet Interests in Asia: Conflict and Co-operation." *IS* July-October 1968 10(1-2): 48-108.

[279] _____.*American-Soviet Relations, 1921-1933.* Calcutta: K. L. Muk-hopodhyay, 1967.

[280] BOSKY, BENNETT, AND MASIC WILRICH, EDS. *Nuclear Proliferation: Prospects for Control.* New York: Dunellen, 1970.

[281] BOTTOME, EDGAR M. *The Balance of Terror: A Guide to the Arms Race.* Boston: Beacon Press, 1971.

[282] BOUCEK, J. ALEX. "Conflict in Czechoslovakia: The Developing Crisis." *CSIP* 1968 10: 479-501.

[283] BOWLES, CHESTER. "America and Russia in India." *FA* 1971 49: 636-651.

[284] BOYCHUK, STEPHAN. "Mongolia and Sino-Soviet Competition." *UQ* 1967 23: 264-272.

[285] BOYD, ANDREW. "The Role of the Great Powers in the United Nations System." *IJ* 1970 25: 356-369.

[286] BOYD, R. G. "Soviet and Chinese Involvement in Southern Asia." *CSIP* 1970 12: 175-194.

[287] BRACKMAN, ARNOLD C. "Indonesia: Another Communist Disaster." *CH* 1969 56(March): 156-160.

[288] BRADA, JOSEF C. "The Allocative Efficiency of Czechoslovakian Foreign Trade." *DAI* 1971 32: 1134-A.

[289] BRADLEY, JOHN. *Allied Intervention in Russia.* New York: Basic Books, 1968.

[290] BRANDHORST, CARL G. "Soviet Activity with Third World—A Threat to United States National Security." *MA* 1971 9: 38.

[291] BRANDT, WILLY, WALTER SCHEELS, KURT GEORGE KISSINGER, AND FRANZ JOSEF STRAUS. "The German-Soviet Treaty." *CEJ* 1970 18: 399-403.

[292] *Bratskaia druzhba—vsestoronnee sotrudnichestvo (Sovetsko-Bolgarskie otnosheniia)* [Fraternal friendship is comprehensive cooperation (Soviet-Bulgarian relations)]. Moscow: Politizdat, 1969.

[293] BRAY, WILLIAM G. "The Pattern of U.S.-Soviet Relations." *EE* 1971 3: 25-27.

[294] BREGEL', E. "Leninskaia kritika antimarksistskikh teorii imperializma i sovremennost'" [The Leninist critique of anti-Marxist theories of imperialism and the present]. *Komm* 1969 (6): 93-104.

[295] _____. "O metode Leninskogo issledovaniia imperializma" [On the method of Leninist research on imperialism]. *VE* 1971 (7): 104-114.

[296] BREGMAN, ALEXANDER. "The USSR and Eastern Europe." *PoC* 1967 16(3): 50-54.

[297] BRETHOLZ, WOLFANG. "The Czechoslovak Crisis Has Not Yet Ended." *CEJ* 1969 117: 231-240.

[298] BREYER, SIEGFRIED. *Guide to the Soviet Navy.* rev. ed. Annapolis: United States Naval Institute, 1970.

[299] BREZHNEV, LEONID I. "The Cause of Lenin Lives on and Triumphs: Address by L. I. Brezhnev at the Joint Lenin Centenary Session of the CC CPSU, the Supreme Soviet of the USSR and the Supreme Soviet of the Russian Federation, April 21, 1970." *NT* 1970 (17): 3-20. Russian version appears in *Komm* 1970 (7): 3-38.

[300] ———. "Kommunisticheskoe dvizhenie vstuplo v polosu novogo pod"ema" [The communist movement has entered the zone of a new upsurge]. *Komm* 1969 (11): 3-16.

[301] ———. "Otchetnyi doklad Tsentral'nogo Komiteta KPSS XXIV S"ezdu Kommunisticheskoi Partii Sovetskogo Soiuza—mezhdunarodnoe polozhenie SSSR. Vneshnepoliticheskaia deiatel'nost' KPSS" [Report of the Central Committee of the CPSU to the 24th Congress of the Communist Party of the Soviet Union—international position of the USSR. Foreign policy activity of the CPSU]. *Komm* 1971 (5): 3-81.

[302] ———. "Piat'desiat let velikikh pobed sotsializma. Doklad General'nogo Sekretaria tsk KPSS tovarishcha L. I. Brezhneva na sovmestnom torzhest vennom zasedanii Tsentral'nogo Komiteta KPSS, verkhovnogo Soveta Soiuza SSR, verkhovonogo Soveta RSFSR, posviashchennom 50-letiiu Velikoi Oktiabr'skoi Sotsialisticheskoi Revoliutsii. Part IV: Velikii Oktiabr' i mirovoe revoliutsionnoe dvizhenie; Part V: Leninskaia vneshniaia politika Sovetskogo Soiuza" [50 Years of great victories of socialism. Speech of General Secretary of the CC of the CPSU comrade L. I. Brezhnev at the joint ceremonial meeting of the Central Committee of CPSU, the Supreme Soviet of the USSR, the Supreme Soviet of the RSFSR, devoted to the 50th anniversary of the Great October Socialist Revolution. Part IV: The Great October and the world revolutionary movement; Part V: Leninist foreign policy of the Soviet Union]. *Komm* 1967 (16): 24-41.

[303] BRINKLEY, G. A. "The Soviet Union and the UN: The Changing Role of the Developing Countries." *RP* 1970 32: 91-123.

[304] BRISCH, HANS. *See* 1210.

[305] BROMKE, ADAM. "Aftermath of Czechoslovakia." *CSIP* 1969 11: 23-30.

[306] ———. "Czechoslovakia and the World: 1968." *CSIP* 1968 10: 581-591.

[307] ———. "Eastern Europe on the Threshold of the 1970's." *SlEER* 1969 14: 31-48.

[308] ———. "Ideology and National Interest in Soviet Foreign Policy." *IJ* 1967 22: 547-562.

[309] ———, AND HAROLD VON RIEKHOFF. "The West German-Polish Treaty." *WT* 1971 27: 124-130. *EE* 20(2): 2-8.

[310] ———, AND PHILIP E. UREN, ED. *The Communist States and the West.* New York: Praeger, 1967.

[311] ———, ED. *The Communist States at the Crossroads.* New York: Praeger, 1967.

[312] BROSIO, MANLIO. "Soviet Policy: Weakness Yes, but Danger Too." *ACQ* 1968 6: 493-500.

[313] BROSIO, MANLIO. "Will NATO Survive Détente?" *WT* 1971 27: 231-240.

[314] BROVKA, IU. *Mezhdunarodnaia pravosub"ektnost' BSSR* [The international legal personality of the Belorussian SSR]. Minsk: Nauka i tekhnika, 1967.

[315] BROWER, DANIEL R. "The Soviet Union and the German Invasion of 1941: A New Soviet View." *JMH* 1969 41(3): 327-334.

[316] BROWN, ALAN A., AND PAUL MARER. "New Options for the United States in East-West Trade." *StCC* 1971 4: 119-145.

[317] ———, AND EGON NEUBERGER, EDS. International Trade and Central Planning: An Analysis of Economic Interactions. Berkeley: University of California Press, 1968.

[318] BROWN, J. F. "Rumania Today II: The Strategy of Defiance." *PoC* 1969 18: 32-38.

[319] BROWN, NEVILLE. "American and Soviet Weapons in Israeli and Arab Hands." *NME* 1970 (20): 11-15.

[320] ———. "The Balance Between the Superpowers: Into Strategic Deadlock." *MR* 1967 47(3): 71-79.

[321] ———. "Soviet Naval Expansion as a Factor in the New Power Politics." *NME* 1971 (30): 17-21.

[322] ———. "An Unstable Balance of Terror?" *WT* 1970 26(1): 38-46.

[323] BRUTENTS, K. "Epokha sotsializma i natsional'noe osvobozhdenie narodov" [The epoch of socialism and the national liberation of peoples]. *Komm* 1967 (18): 91-102.

[324] ———. "O revoliutsionnoi demokratii" [On revolutionary democracy]. *MEMO* 1968 (3): 15-28, (4): 24-35.

[325] BRYANT, CHRISTOPHER. "Prague Summer: 1968." *EE* 1968 17(9): 7-11.

[326] BRZEZINSKI, ZBIGNIEW K. "The Changing Nature of the Challenge." *CSIP* 1967 9: 50-59.

[327] ———. "Communist State Relations: The Effect on Ideology." *EE* 1967 16(3): 2-7.

[328] ———. "East-West Relations After Czechoslovakia." *EE* 1969 18(11-12): 2-10.

[329] ———. "The Framework of East-West Reconciliation." *FA* 1968 46: 256-275.

[330] ———. *Ideology and Power in Soviet Politics.* New York: Praeger, 1967.

[331] ———. "Peace and Power." *Surv* 1968 10: 386-396.

[332] ———. *The Soviet Bloc: Unity and Conflict.* 3d ed. Cambridge, Massachusetts: Harvard University Press, 1967.

[333] ———, MICHAEL KASER, LEOPOLD LABEDZ, KLAUS MEHNERT, JOHN M. MONTIAS, MICHEL TATU, ET AL. *The Atlantic Community and Eastern Europe: Perspectives and Policy.* New York: The Dunnellen Company, 1970.

[334] BUCK, TIM. "Lenin and New Problems of Struggle for Peace, Democracy and Socialism." *WMR* 1970 13(7): 7-13.

[335] "Budapest Consultative Meeting of Representatives of Communist and Workers' Parties (February 26-March 5, 1968)." *WMR* 1968 (5-6-7): 3-187, (8): 18-71.

[336] BUDRAJ, VIJAY SEN. "The Evolution of Russia's Pakistan Policy." *AJPH* 1970 16: 343-360.

[337] BUKH, M., AND IU. SHINTIAPIN. "Intensifikatsiia sel'skogo khoziaistva v Evropeiskikh stranakh-chlenakh SEV" [The intensification of agriculture in the European member countries of CMEA]. *VE* 1971 (1): 86-97.

[338] BUL'BA, T., AND A. N. BYKOV. "Konsolidatsiia stran sotsializma" [The consolidation of the socialist countries]. *PS* 1970 (3): 57-65.

[339] "Bulgaria-Byelorussia-Czechoslovakia-Hungary-Mongolia-Poland-Rumania-Union of Soviet Socialist Republics Draft Convention." *ILM* 1970 9: 386-391.

[340] BURGESS, W. RANDOLPH, AND JAMES ROBERT HUNTLEY. "The Outlook for East-West Accomodations." *ACQ* 1971 8: 447-460.

[341] BURGUCHEV, G., AND M. ROZENBERG. "Komissiia OON po Pravu Mezhdunarodnoi Torgovli" [The UN Commission on the Law of International Trade]. *VT* 1971 (4): 45-51.

[342] _____, AND M. ROZENBERG. "Obshchie usloviia postavok SEV 1968 GODA"[The general conditions of deliveries of CMEA in 1968]. *VT* 1969 (5): 30-37.

[343] BURKEMPER, RAYMOND G. "Soviet Disarmament Policy—What Lies Ahead?" *NWCR* 1967 20(4): 29-59.

[344] BURKS, RICHARD V. "The Communist Politics of Eastern Europe." In *Linkage Politics,* pp. 275-303, edited by James N. Rosenau. New York, 1969.

[345] _____, ED. *The Future of Communism in Europe.* Detroit, Michigan: Wayne State University Press, 1968.

[346] BURNETT, JOHN H. "Soviet-Egyptian Relations During the Khrushchev Era: A Study in Soviet Foreign Policy." *DAI* 1967 27: 2187-A.

[347] BURNHAM, C. "Czechoslovakia. Thirty Years After Munich." In *Year Book of World Affairs.* London, 1969.

[348] BURTIKE, K. "Rumyno-Sovetskoe ekonomicheskoe sotrudnichestvo" [Rumanian-Soviet economic cooperation]. *VT* 1971 (10): 12-14.

[349] BUSH, KEITH. "The Soviet Position at the Second UN Conference on Trade and Development." *B,ISUSSR* 1968 15(3): 38-41.

[350] BUSS, ROBIN. "Wary Partners: The Soviet Union and Arab Socialism." *AP* 1970 (73): 1-28.

[351] BUTAKOV, D. "Finansovye voprosy khoziaistvennykh reform v stranakh-chlenakh SEV" [Financial questions of economic reform in the member countries of CMEA]. *VE* 1970 (11): 105-114.

[352] BUTENKO, A. "The International and the National in the Socialist World." *NT* 1969 (41): 2-4.

[353] _____. "Nekotorye teoreticheskie problemy razvitiia mirovoi sistemy sotsializma"[Some theoretical problems of the development of the world socialist system]. *MEMO* 1971 (9): 99-108.

[354] BUTLER, WILLIAM E. "American Research on Soviet Approaches to Public International Law." *CLR* 1970 70: 218-235.

[355] _____.*The Law of Soviet Territorial Waters.* New York: Praeger, 1967.

[356] _____. "The Legal Regime of Russian Territorial Waters." *AJIL* 1968 62: 51-77.

[357] ———. "Self-Determination in Soviet International Law." *SAIS* 1967 12(1): 32-39.

[358] ———. " 'Socialist International Law' or 'Socialist Principles of International Relations'?" *AJIL* 1971 65: 796-804.

[359] ———. "The Soviet Union and the Continental Shelf." *AJIL* 1969 63: 103-107.

[360] ———. *The Soviet Union and the Law of the Sea.* Baltimore and London: Johns Hopkins Press, 1971.

[361] ———, AND JOHN B. QUIGLEY, JR. *The Merchant Shipping Code of the USSR (1968).* Baltimore, Maryland: Johns Hopkins Press, 1970.

[362] BYKHOVSKII, B. E. "Sophistries of Anti-Marxism." *NT* 1970 (7): 21-23.

[363] BYKOV, A. N. *Nauchno-tekhnicheskie sviazi stran Sotsializma.* [The scientific-technical ties of the socialist countries]. Moscow: Mysl', 1970.

[364] ———. "Science, Technology and Socialist Integration." *NT* 1971 (4): 22-23.

[365] ———. *See* 338.

[366] BYKOV, O. "Détente and Stance of Western Politologists [European Security]." *WMR* 1971 (14): 97-102.

[367] BYRNES, ROBERT F. *International Negotiation: Eastern Europe—The Unstable Element in the Soviet Empire. Report to Subcommittee on National Security and International Operations, Senate Committee on Government Operations.* Washington, D.C.: United States Government Printing Office, 1970.

[368] ———. "Russia in Eastern Europe: Hegemony Without Security." *FA* 1971 49: 682-697.

[369] ———, ED. *The United States and Eastern Europe.* Englewood Cliffs, New Jersey: Prentice-Hall, 1967.

[370] CALDWELL, LAWRENCE T. "Soviet Attitudes to SALT." *AP* 1971 75: 1-28.

[371] CALZINI, PAOLO, ED. *Italo-Jugoslav Relations.* Rome: Instituto Affari Internazionali, 1970.

[372] CAMBON, JULES, ET AL. *The Foreign Policy of the Powers: France, Germany, Great Britain, Italy, Japan, Russia and the United States.* Freeport, New York: Books for Libraries Press, 1970.

[373] CAMPBELL, JOHN C. "Czechoslovakia: American Choices, Past and Present." *CSIP* 1969 11: 10-22.

[374] ———. "Hungary and Central Europe: An American View." *StNCE* 1971-72 3(1): 49-57.

[375] ———. "Soviet-American Relations." *CH* 1971 60: 193-197.

[376] ———. "Soviet-American Relations: Conflict and Cooperation." *CH* 1967 52: 193-202, 241.

[377] ———. "The Soviet Union and the Middle East." *RR* 1970 29: 143-153, 247-261.

[378] ———. "The Soviet Union in the International Environment." In *Prospects for Soviet Society,* pp. 473-496, edited by Allen Kassof. New York, 1968.

[379] ———. *Tito's Separate Road: America and Yugoslavia in World Politics.* New York: Harper and Row, 1967.

[380] CAMPBELL, WILLIAM R. *See* 1693.

[381] CARELL, PAUL. *Scorched Earth: The Russian-German War, 1943-1944.* Boston and Toronto: Little, Brown, 1970.

[382] CARLTON, ROBERT G., ED. *Soviet Image of Contemporary Latin America: A Documentary History, 1960-1968.* Austin: University of Texas Press, 1970.

[383] DE CARMOY, GUY. "France, Algeria and the Soviet Penetration of the Mediterranean." *Int* 1969 3(3): 23-26.

[384] ———. "Soviet Penetration in the Mediterranean." *MR* 1970 50(3): 83-90.

[385] CARPOZI, GEORGE. *Red Spies in Washington.* New York: Trident, 1968.

[386] CARTER, JAMES RICHARD. *The Net Cost of Soviet Foreign Aid.* New York: Praeger Publishers, 1971.

[387] CEAUSESCU, NICOLAE. "Romania's Foreign Policy." *EE* 1971 20(1): 4-6.

[388] ———. "Rumania and European Security." *WMR* 1969 11(6): 27-32.

[389] CECIL, ROBERT. "Potsdam and Its Legends." *IA(L)* 1970 44: 455-465.

[390] CHAKOVSKII, A. "V pogone za mifami: O nekotorykh novykh tendentsiiakh v strategii antikommunizma" [Running after myths: On some new tendencies in the strategy of anti-Communism]. *Komm* 1970 (11): 95-109.

[391] CHANDLER, TREVOR. "Paradigms of Development in World Perspective: The Applicability of Modified Marxist Models to Developing Areas." *DAI* 1970 31.

[392] CHANDRA, BIPAN. "Lenin on the National Liberation Movement." *IQ* 1971 27 1): 40-56.

[393] *Changing Trends in East Central Europe and Implications for U.S. Security.* 3 vols. Philadelphia: Foreign Policy Research Institute, University of Pennsylvania, 1967.

[394] CHAO, KANG. "Sino-Soviet Exchange Rates." *CQ* 1971 47: 546-551.

[395] CHARY, FRED B. "International Relations—Bulgaria." *CSISt,BS* 1967 1(4): 84; 1968 2(1): 63, 2(2): 68-69, 2(4): 129.

[396] CHEKHOVICH, O. S. "Zadachi Sredneaziatskoi diplomatiki" [The tasks of Central Asian diplomacy]. *NAA* 1969 (6): 75-82.

[397] CHEKLIN, V. "Torgovye otnosheniia s Angliei" [Trade relations with England]. *VT* 1970 (6): 9-13.

[398] CHEPRAKOV, V. "Lenin o sushchnosti i natsional'nykh tipakh imperializma" [Lenin on the nature and national types of imperialism]. *MEMO* 1968 (9): 16-26.

[399] CHEPROV, I. I. *Novye problemy mezhdunarodnogo prava* [New problems of international law]. Moscow: I.M.O., 1969.

[400] ———.*See* 1721.

[401] CHEREPANOV, A. "The Soviet Union and the Chinese Revolution (Reminiscences of a Military Advisor)." *NT* 1967 (11): 18-20.

[402] CHERKASSKII, L. IA. *See* 890.

[403] CHERNIAVSKII, V. *Ot U-2 do "Pueblo." Shpionazh i drugie podryvnye deistviia imperialisticheskikh razvedok protiv sotsialisticheskikh stran* [From the U-2 to the "Pueblo." Espionage and other subversive activities of the imperialist intelligence services against the socialist countries] Moscow: Znanie, 1970.

[404] CHERNICHENKO, S. V. *Mezhdunarodnopravovye voprosy grazhdanstva* [International legal questions of citizenship]. Moscow: I.M.O., 1968.

[405] ———. "Status podsudimykh v mezhdunarodnykh sudebnykh organakh" [The status of the accused in international judicial organs]. *SGP* 1971 (7): 63-68.

[406] CHERNOV, L. N. *Pod znamenem proletarskogo internatsionalizma* [Under the banner of proletarian internationalism]. Moscow: Mysl, 1967.

[407] CHESHKOV, M. A. "Iz istorii pervykh Sovetskogo-Vietnamskikh revoliutsionnykh sviazei" [From the history of the first Soviet-Vietnamese revolutionary ties]. *NAA* 1967 (5): 84-89.

[408] CHEW, ALLEN F. *The White Death (Soviet-Finnish War).* East Lansing: Michigan State University Press, 1971.

[409] CHICHVARIN, V. A. *Okhrana prirody i mezhdunarodnye otnosheniia* [The protection of nature and international relations]. Moscow: I.M.O., 1970.

[410] CHIN-YAO, YUNI. "Soviet Imperialism and China." *AO* 1967 2(11): 17-22, 2(12): 13-16.

[411] CHKHIKVADZE, V., AND O. V. BOGDANOV. "Definition of Aggression—An Important Instrument in the Struggle for Peace." *IA(M)* 1969 (7): 27-32.

[412] _____, AND O. V. BOGDANOV. "Who is Hindering Progress in the Definitions of Aggression?" *IA(M)* 1971 (10): 22-28.

[413] _____, AND IA. OSTROVSKII. "International Human Rights Conference." *IA(M)* 1968 (8): 16-21.

[414] CHISTIAKOV, N. "Sovetsko-Finskie nauchno-tekhnicheskie sviazi" [Soviet-Finnish scientific-technical relations]. *VT* 1969 (3): 34-39.

[415] CHO-HSUAN, JEN. "The Introduction of Marxism-Leninism into China: The Early Years, 1919-1924." *StST* 1970 10: 138-166.

[416] CHOPRA, MAHARAJ K. "East German Security." *MR* 1971 51(10): 12-20.

[417] CHOSSUDOVSKY, EVGENY. "Commentary on Documentation on Co-Existence: Soviet-Canadian Protocol on Consultation." *Co* 1971 8: 185-188.

[418] "Chronicle of Soviet Major Foreign Policy Acts Between the 23rd and the 24th Party Congresses." *IA(M)* 1971 (2): 93-100, (3): 106-112, (4): 114-120.

[419] CHUBAR'IAN, A. O. "V. I. Lenin i nekotorye voprosy Sovetskoi vneshnei politiki" [V. I. Lenin and some questions of Soviet foreign policy]. *NNI* 1967 (5) 57-68.

[420] CHUEVA, I. P. *Lenin ob ideinykh istokakh antikommunizma* [Lenin on the ideological sources of anti-Communism]. Leningrad: Lenizdat, 1969.

[421] CHUKANOV, O. "Nauchno-tekhnicheskoe sotrudnichestvo stran chlenov SEV na novom etape" [The scientific-technical cooperation of the member countries of CMEA at a new stage]. *Komm* 1970 (13): 46-55.

[422] _____. "Sotsialisticheskaia ekonomicheskaia integratsiia i nauchno-tekhnicheskaia revoliutsiia" [Socialist economic integration and the scientific technical revolution]. *Komm* 1971 (13): 80-92.

28

[423] CHUNG, CHIN O. "North Korea's Attitude in the Sino-Soviet Dispute 1958-1967." *DAI* 1970 30: 3073-A.

[424] CHUNG-KIANG, TING. "Russia in the Mediterranean: A Report to the Council of NATO Foreign Ministers." *AO* 1970 (August): 14-17.

[425] CHURAKOV, IU. "Razvitie ekonomiki Evropeiskikh stran—chlenov SEV v tekushchei piatiletke" [The development of the economy of the European members of CMEA in the current five-year plan]. *VE* 1967 (6) 78-87.

[426] CHURBA, JOSEPH. *Soviet Penetration into the Middle East.* Maxwell Air Force Base, Alabama: Documentary Research Division, Aerospace Studies Institute, 1968.

[427] CHURCH, FRANK. "The United States and the USSR: Two Sentinels of the Status Quo." *Prog* 1969 33(October): 14-19.

[428] CIOLKOSZ, ADAM. "The Bolshevik Revolution: Its Impact in Eastern Europe." *EE* 1967 16(11): 3-8.

[429] CIORANESCU, GEORGE. "Rumania After Czechoslovakia: Ceausescu Walks the Tightrope." *EE* 1969 18(6): 2-7.

[430] CLABAUGH, SAMUEL F., AND EDWIN G. FEULNER, JR. *Trading With the Communists: A Research Manual.* Washington, D.C.: Center for Strategic Studies, Georgetown University, 1968.

[431] CLARK, CAL. "Foreign Trade as an Indicator of Political Integration in the Soviet Bloc." *IStQ* 1971 15: 259-298.

[432] CLARK, CLAIRE. "Soviet and Afro-Asian Voting in the General Assembly, 1946-1965." *AO* 1970 24: 296-308.

[433] CLARK, DONALD L. "Soviet Strategy for the Seventies." *AUR* 1971 22(1): 2-18.

[434] CLARK, JOHN L. "The Encircling Sea [Russia's Maritime Strategy]." *USNI,P* 1969 95(703): 26-35.

[435] CLARKSON, STEPHEN. "Manicheism Corrupted: The Soviet View of Aid to India." *IJ* 1967 22: 253-264.

[436] ———. "Peaceful Coexistence: Gaullist Style." *CH* 1968 53: 160-165, 178.

[437] ———. "Soviet Theory and Indian Reality." *PoC* 1967 16(1): 11-20.

[438] CLAVIER, PHILIPPE A. "Soviet Nuclear Defense Policy." *MR* 1967 47(1): 72-77.

[439] CLEMENS, DIANE SHAVER. *Yalta: A Study in Soviet-American Relations.* New York: Oxford University Press, 1970.

[440] CLEMENS, WALTER C., JR. *The Arms Race and Sino-Soviet Relations.* Stanford: Hoover Institution, 1968.

[441] ———. "The Changing Warsaw Pact." *EE* 1968 17(6): 7-12.

[442] ———. "Czechoslovakia and U.S. Policy: All or Nothing at All?" *W/PR* 1970 10(1): 14-19.

[443] ———. "The Future of the Warsaw Pact." *Orb* 1968 11: 996-1033.

[444] ———. "Maintaining the Status Quo in East Central Europe." *WA* 1970 133: 98-105.

[445] ———. "Shift in Soviet Arms Control Posture." *MR* 1971 51(7): 28-36.

[446] ———. "The Soviet Alliance After Czechoslovakia." *MR* 1970 50(10): 20-29.

[447] ———. "Soviet European Policy in the 1970's." *MR* 1970 50(4): 52-64.

[448] ———. "Soviet Policy in the Third World in the 1970's: Five Alternative Futures." *Orb* 1969 13: 476-501.

[449] ———. "The Soviet World Faces West." *IA(L)* 1970 46: 475-489.

[450] ———.*See* 1382.

[451] CLIFF, DONALD K. "Soviet Naval Infantry: A New Capability?" *NWCR* 1971 23(10): 90-101.

[452] CLISSOLD, STEPHEN, ED. *Soviet Relations With Latin America, 1918-1968: A Documentary Survey.* London, New York, Toronto: Oxford University Press, 1970.

[453] CLUBB, O. EDMUND. *Russia and China: The Great Game.* New York: Columbia University Press, 1971.

[454] COFFEY, J. I. "The Soviet ABM and Arms Control." *BAS* 1970 26: 39-43.

[455] ———. "Soviet ABM Policy: The Implications for the West." *IA(L)* 1969 45: 205-222.

[456] ———. "Strategic Arms Limitations and European Security." *IA(L)* 1971 47: 692-707.

[457] ———. "Strategic Superiority, Deterrence and Arms Control." *Orb* 1970 13: 991-1107.

[458] COGNIOT, GEORGES. "Internationalism and the National Tasks of the Communist Parties." *WMR* 1968 11(6): 4-11.

[459] ———. "Lenin and France." *NT* 1969 (39): 7-10.

[460] _____. "Lenin and the Communist Parties of the West." *NT* 1967 (17): 13-16.

[461] COHEN, BERNARD C. "National-International Linkages: Superpolitics." In *Linkage Politics,* pp. 125-146, edited by James N. Rosenau. New York, 1969.

[462] COHN, HELEN D. "Soviet Theories of African Development: A Focus on National Integration." *DAI* 1971 32: 2150-A.

[463] COLLINS, EDWARD M. "The Evolution of Soviet Strategy Under Khrushchev." *DAI* 1967 27: 2584-A.

[464] COLM, PETER W. *See* 1382.

[465] COMBS, RICHARD E., JR. "The Role of Ideology in Postwar Soviet Policy Determination." *DAI* 1967 28: 1106-A.

[466] "Communiqué of Conferences of European Communist and Workers' Parties, Karlovy Vary." *WMR* 1967 (6): 3-10.

[467] "Communiqué of Conference of Ministers of Foreign Affairs of Warsaw Treaty Member-States." *ACQ* 1971 9: 267-269.

[468] *Comprehensive Programme for the Further Extension and Improvement of Co-operation and the Development of Socialist Integration by the CMEA Member-Countries.* Moscow: Progress, 1971.

[469] CONDON, WILLIAM R. "The Moscow Parenthesis: A Study of Finnish-German Relations, 1940-1941." *DAI* 1969 30: 2456-A.

[470] "Conference of Communist and Workers' Parties: Documents Adopted by the International Conference of Communist and Workers' Parties (Moscow June 5-17, 1969)." *IA(M)* 1969 (8): 3-31.

[471] CONOLLY, VIOLET. "Soviet-Japanese Economic Cooperation in Siberia." *PC* 1970 2: 55-65.

[472] _____. "The Soviet Pacific Bastion." *Sur* 1969 (70/71): 178-192.

[473] CONQUEST, ROBERT. "Czechoslovakia: The Soviet Outlook." *StCC* 1968 1: 7-16.

[474] _____. "The Limits of Détente." *FA* 1968 46: 733-742.

[475] _____. "Stalin's Successors." *FA* 1970 48: 509-524.

[476] "Consideration of Measures for the Strengthening of International Security." *IA(M)* 1970 (12): 66-67.

[477] *Contemporary International Law.* Moscow: Progress Publishers, 1969.

[478] COOK, DON. "Towards a New Congress of Vienna? Salt in Old Wounds." *Enc* 1970 25(3): 53-60.

[479] COOPER, ORAH. "Soviet Economic Assistance to the Less Developed Countries of the Free World." In *Economic Performance and the Military Burden in the Soviet Union, U.S. Congress, Joint Economic Committee,* pp. 117-122. Washington, D.C., 1970.

[480] COSTELLO, MICHAEL. "Bulgaria's Cautious Balkan Policy." *EE* 1968 17(8): 2-5.

[481] COTTRELL, ALVIN J. "Soviet-Egyptian Relations." *MR* 1969 49(12): 69-76.

[482] ———. "The Soviet Union in the Middle East." *Orb* 1970 14: 588-598.

[483] COUHAT, J. LABAYLE. *See* 1720.

[484] COULMAS, PETER. "The Rumanian Balancing Act." *IP* 1970 3(14): 23-32.

[485] COWDEN, M. H. "Soviet and Comintern Policies Toward British Labor, 1917-1921." *DAI* 1968 28: 4238-A.

[486] COX, D. R. "Sea Power and the Soviet Foreign Policy." *USNI,P* 1969 96(6): 32-44.

[487] COX, FREDERICK J. "The Russian Presence in Egypt." *NWCR* 1970 22(6): 44-55.

[488] COX, IDRIS. "Prospects of Aid to Developing Countries." *WMR* 1968 11(10-11): 63-68.

[489] CRANE, ROBERT D. "The Structure of Soviet Military Thought." *StST* 1967 7(1): 28-34.

[490] CRANKSHAW, EDWARD. *The New Cold War: Moscow vs. Peking.* Reprint of 1963 ed. Freeport, New York: Books for Libraries, 1970.

[491] CROAN, MELVIN. "Czechoslovakia, Ulbricht and the German Problem." *PoC* 1969 18(1): 1-7.

[492] CROWLEY, EDWARD L., ED. *The Soviet Diplomatic Corps, 1917-1967.* Metuchen, New Jersey: Scarecrow Press, 1970.

[493] CROZLER, BRIAN. *Since Stalin.* New York: Coward McCann, 1970.

[494] CSABAFI, I. *See* 1404.

[495] CUNHAL, A. "Proletarianism—A Policy and Outlook." *WMR* 1970 13(5): 70-77.

[496] CURREY, VIRGINIA A. "Soviet-Turkish Relations, 1917-1922." *DAI* 1968 29: 1939-A.

[497] CURTIS, MICHAEL. "Soviet-American Relations and the Middle East Crisis." *Orb* 1971 15: 403-427.

[498] CZECHANOWSKI, S. "Eastern European Policy Unchanged [of FRG]." *PG* 1967 11(39-40): 3-6.

[499] *Czechoslovakia: Lessons of the Crisis.* Moscow: Progress, 1971.

[500] "Czechoslovakia-Union of Soviet Socialist Republics: Treaty of Friendship, Co-Operation, and Mutual Assistance." *ILM* 1970 9: 655-657.

[501] CZEMPIEL, ERNST-OTTO. "Foreign Policy Issues in the West German Federal Election of 1969." *CP* 1970 2: 605-628.

[502] DABROWSKI, STANISLAU. "The Peace Treaty of Riga, 1921." *DAI* 1969 29: 4420-A.

[503] DAGAN, AVIGDOR. *Moscow and Jerusalem: Twenty Years of Relations Between Israel and the Soviet Union.* New York: Abelard-Schuman, 1970.

[504] DAIM, WILFRIED. *The Vatican and Eastern Europe.* New York: Frederick Ungar, 1970.

[505] DALFEN, C. M. *See* 902.

[506] DALIN, S. "Leninskaia teoriia imperializma i osobennosti tsiklicheskogo razvitiia sovremennogo kapitalizma" [The Leninist theory of imperialism and the features of the cyclical development of contemporary capitalism]. *Komm* 1969 (1): 48-60.

[507] ———. "Leninskaia teoriia imperializma i problemy sovremennogo kapitalizma" [The Leninist theory of imperialism and the problems of contemporary capitalism]. *Komm* 1970 (7): 67-79.

[508] DALLIN, ALEXANDER. "Soviet Foreign Policy and Domestic Politics: A Framework for Analysis." *JIA* 1969 23: 250-265.

[509] ———. "The USSR and World Communism." In *The Soviet Union Under Brezhnev and Kosygin,* edited by John W. Strong. New York: Van Nostrand Reinhold, 1971.

[510] ———, AND THOMAS B. LARSON, EDS. *Soviet Politics Since Khrushchev.* Englewood Cliffs, New Jersey: Prentice-Hall, 1968.

[511] DALLIN, DAVID J. *Soviet Russia and the Far East.* Reprint of 1948 ed. Hamden, Connecticut: Archon Books, 1971.

[512] DAMIEN, GEORGE D. "On the Philosophy of Contradictions: The Sino-Soviet Dispute as a Case Study in Communist Conflict Thinking." *Orb* 1968 11: 1208-1232.

[513] DANELIUS, G. "Leninism—Sharp Weapon of All Revolutionary Forces of Our Time." *WMR* 1970 13(4): 9-13.

[514] DANKEWYCH, MICHAEL. "Siberia in Global Power Politics: Economic, Strategic, and Geopolitical Factors." *DAI* 1970 30: 4507-A.

[515] DANSHINA, V., AND V. KAIE. "Ekonomicheskoe sotrudnichestvo Chekhoslovakii so Sovetskim Soiuzom" [The economic cooperation of Czechoslovakia with the Soviet Union]. *VE* 1969 (4): 116-124.

[516] DAPONTES, ANDREW. *The Cuban Crisis and the Chinese-Indian Border War.* New York: Vantage Press, 1969.

[517] DARBY, J. J. "Soviet Trade With a Member of the Common Market: A Survey With Special Reference to the Commercial Aspects of Private International Law." *DAI* 1968 28: 3743-A.

[518] DARISHEV, B. *V. I. Lenin v bor'be za svobodu kolonial'nykh narodov* [V. I. Lenin in the struggle for the freedom of colonial peoples]. Alma Alta: Kazakhstan, 1968.

[519] DARLY, WILBUR D. "The Consular Convention With the United States." *MA* 1968 6: 147.

[520] DASBACH, ANITA MALLINCKRODT. "Propaganda Behind the Wall—A Case Study in the Use of Propaganda as a Tool of Foreign Policy by Communist Governments." *DAI* 1969 29: 2331-A.

[521] DAU, MARY. "The Soviet Union and the Liberation of Denmark." *Sur* 1970 76: 64-81.

[522] DAVID, VACLAV. "Czechoslovakia's Foreign Policy Today." *IA(M)* 1967 (6): 7-11.

[523] DAVIS, DONALD EDWARD. "Lenin's Theory of War." *DAI* 1970 30: 4908-A.

[524] DAVLETSHIN, T. "Limited Sovereignty: The Soviet Claim to Intervene in the Defense Socialism." *B,ISUSSR* 1969 16(8): 3-9.

[525] DAVYDOV, IU. "Washington's East European Doctrines." *NT* 1969 (31): 8-10.

[526] DAYAN, MOSHE. "Israel's Response to the Russians in Egypt." *NME* 1970 (June): 18-21.

[527] DEAN, ROBERT W. "Czechoslovakia: Consolidation and Beyond." *Sur* 1971 17(3): 98-111.

[528] ———. "The Politics of West German Trade With the Soviet Bloc, 1954-1968." *DAI* 1971 32: 2769-A.

[529] DEBO, RICHARD K. "Dutch-Soviet Relations, 1917-1924: The Role of Finance and Commerce in the Foreign Policy of Soviet Russia and the Netherlands." *CSISt* 1970 4: 199-217.

[530] DEDIJER, VLADIMIR. *The Battle Stalin Lost: Memoirs of Yugoslavia, 1948-1953.* New York: Viking, 1971.

[531] DEGTIABR', D. "Ekonomicheskoe i tekhnicheskoe sotrudnichestvo SSSR so stranami Afriki" [Economic and technical cooperation of the USSR with the countries of Africa]. *VT* 1968 (9): 2-6.

[532] ———. "Ekonomicheskoe sodeistvie SSSR razvivaiushchimsia stranam" [Economic assistance of the USSR to the developing countries]. *VT* 1969 (6): 14-16.

[533] DEGTIAR', L. S. *Trudovye resursy i ikh ispol'zovanie v zarubezhnykh sotsialisticheskikh stranakh-chlenakh SEV* [Labor resources and their utilization in foreign socialist member countries of CMEA]. Moscow: Nauka, 1969.

[534] DEGTIAREV, V. "Doktrina EKLA o putiakh resheniia problem vneshnei torgovli" [The doctrine of the ECLA on ways of solving the problems of foreign trade]. *VT* 1970 (6): 32-34.

[535] DEICHSEL, CHRISTINE. "Yugoslav Ideology and Its Importance to the Soviet Bloc: An Analysis." *MA* 1968 6: 52.

[536] "Deistvennost' Leninskoi vneshnei politiki—mezhdunarodnoe znachenie XXIV S ezda KPSS" [The effectiveness of Leninist foreign policy—the international meaning of the 24th Congress of the CPSU]. *Komm* 1971 (14): 73-81.

[537] DEKMEJIAN, R. H. "Soviet-Turkish Relations and Politics in the Armenian SSR." *SSt* 1968 19 510-525.

[538] DELIUSIN, L. P. "Oktiabr'skaia Revoliutsiia i Kitai. (Otkliki nachala 20-kh gg.)" [The October Revolution and China. (Responses of the beginning of the 20's.)]. *NAA* 1967 (6): 32-39.

[539] DELLIN, L. A. D. "Political Factors in East-West Trade." *EE* 1969 18(8): 8-14; reprinted in corrected form (9): 25-30.

[540] DEMAITRE, EDMUND. "The Origins of National Communism." *StCC* 1969 2: 1-20.

[541] DENNIS, M. WAYNE. *See* 2355.

[542] DERNBERG, S., ET AL. *Sovetsko-Germanskie otnosheniia. Ot peregovorov v Brest-Litovske do podpisaniia Rapall'skogo Dogovora. Sbornik dokumentov* [Soviet-German relations. From the negotiations at Brest-Litovsk to the signing of the Treaty of Rapallo. A collection of documents]. Vol. I 1917-1918, Vol. 2 1918-1922. Moscow: Politizdat, 1968.

[543] DE TOLEDANO, RALPH. *Spies, Dupes, and Diplomats.* New Rochelle, New York: Arlington House, 1967.

[544] DEUTSCHER, ISAAC. *Russia, China and the West 1953-1966.* Baltimore, Maryland: Penquin Books, Incorporated, 1971.

[545] DEVLIN, KEVIN. "Czechoslovakia and the Crisis of Austrian Communism." *StCC* 1969 2(3-4): 9-37.

[546] _____. "Interparty Relations: Limits of 'Normalization.'" *PoC* 1971 20(4): 22-35.

[547] _____. "The New Crisis in European Communism." *PoC* 1968 17(6): 57-68.

[548] _____. "Which Side Are You On?" *PoC* 1967 16(1): 52-59.

[549] D'IACHENKO, K. "Dva podkhoda k ekonomicheskomu sotrudnichestvu s Tseilonom" [Two approaches to economic cooperation with Ceylon]. *VT* 1968 (12): 24-27.

[550] DIAKIN, B., AND G. KHARAKHASH'IAN. "Problemy sotsialisticheskoi internatsionalizatsii proizvodstva" [Problems of socialist international production]. *VE* 1971 (5): 93-104.

[551] _____.*See* 1423.

[552] DINERSTEIN, HERBERT S. *Fifty Years of Soviet Foreign Policy.* Baltimore, Maryland: Johns Hopkins Press, 1968.

[553] _____. "The Future of Ideology in Alliance Systems." *JIA* 1971 25(2): 238-265.

[554] _____.*Intervention Against Communism.* Baltimore, Maryland: Johns Hopkins Press, 1967.

[555] _____. "Moscow and the Third World." *PoC* 1968 17(1): 52-56.

[556] _____. "Soviet and Cuban Conceptions of Revolution." *StCC* 1971 4: 3-22.

[557] _____. "Soviet Policy in Latin America." *APSR* 1967 61: 80-90.

[558] _____. "The Soviet Union and China." In *Conflict in World Politics,* pp. 78-98, edited by Steven L. Speigel and Kenneth N. Waltz. Cambridge, Massachusetts: Winthrop, 1971.

[559] "Diplomatic History of the Opening of the Second Front in Europe, 1941-1944." *IA(M)* 1970 (4): 70-76,(7): 68-72, (12): 71-77.

[560] DIRSCHERL, DENIS, L. J., ED. *The New Russia: Communism in Evolution.* Dayton, Ohio: Pflaum Press, 1968.

[561] DIUMULEN, I. "Sdvigi v tovarnoi strukture mezhdunarodnoi torgovli" [Changes in the commodity structure of international trade]. *VT* 1969 (5): 24-28.

[562] DIVINE, ROBERT A., ED. *The Cuban Missile Crisis.* Chicago: Quadrangle Books, 1971.

[563] DIAZ, JUAN. "Leninism and Some Aspects of the Ideological Struggle." *WMR* 1970 13(3): 22-25.

[564] DMITRIEV, B. "Likvidatsiia ochagov voiny—nasushchnaia problema sovremennosti" [The liquidation of the breeding grounds of war—the urgent problem of the present]. *PS* 1971 (7): 70-77.

[565] ———. "Policy of Détente." *NT* 1971 (43): 7-8.

[566] DMITRIEV, E. "Soviet-Arab Friendship: A New Stage." *IA(M)* 1971 (8): 66-68.

[567] DOBRIANSKY, LEV E. "Trade With the Red Empire." *UQ* 1967 23: 141-160.

[568] ———. *U.S.A. and the Soviet Myth.* Old Greenwich, Connecticut: Devin-Adair, 1971.

[569] "Documents Adopted by the International Conference of Communist and Workers' Parties." *WMR* 1969 12(7): 3-53. Russian language version appeared in *Komm* 1969 (9): 3-78.

[570] "Documents: Anglo-Franco-Soviet Talks in Moscow on the Eve of War." *IA(M)* 1969 (8): 87-95.

[571] "Documents: From the History of Soviet Foreign Policy. Soviet Diplomats Urge for the Signing of the Soviet-French Non-Aggression Pact, 1932." *IA(M)* 1969 (3): 131-140.

[572] "Documents of the Meeting of the Warsaw Treaty Political Consultative Committee." *NT* 1970 (50): 28-32.

[573] "Documents on Talks Between Communist and Workers' Parties of Socialist Countries." *WMR* 1968 11(9): 3-8.

[574] "Documents on the Comintern and the Chinese Revolution." *CQ* 1971 45: 100-115.

[575] DOHAN, MICHAEL R. *Soviet Foreign Trade in the NEP Economy and Soviet Industrialization Strategy.* Cambridge: Massachusetts Institute of Technology, 1969.

[576] *Doing Business With the USSR.* New York: Business International, 1971.

[577] *Dokumenty Konferentsii Evropeiskikh Kommunisticheskikh i Rabochikh Partii v Karlovykh Varakh (24-26 Aprelia 1967 g.)* [Documents of the Conference of European Communist and Workers' Parties at Karlovy Vary (24-26 April, 1967)]. Moscow: Politizdat, 1967.

[578] *Dokumenty vneshnei politiki SSSR (1917-1967)* [Documents of the foreign policy of the USSR (1917-1967)]. Moscow: Progress, 1967.

[579] DOMDEY, K. H. "Economic Aspects of the Foreign Policy of the G.D.R." *Co* 1971 8: 161-168.

[580] DONALDSON, CHARLIE B., JR. "Soviet Consular Conventions: Post Vienna." *HILJ* 1969 10: 360-373.

[581] DONALDSON, LORAINE. "The Underdeveloped Countries and the Soviet Bloc Trade." *EEQ* 1969 2: 439-460.

[582] DÖNHOFF, MARION. "Bonn Looks Eastward." *Int* 1970 3: 13-15.

[583] DOUGHERTY, JAMES E. "A Nuclear Arms Agreement: What Shape Might It Take?" *W/PR* 1969 9: 8-11.

[584] DOUGLAS, WILLIAM A. "West German Communism as an Aid to Moscow." *WA* 1970 132: 318-331.

[585] DOUGLAS-HOME, ALEC, ET AL. "Red Fleet Off Suez." *ACQ* 1969 7: 78-89.

[586] DOWNS, MICHAEL C. "A Study of Soviet Participation in the International Labor Organization With Emphasis on the Period 1960-1964." *DAI* 1971 32: 2770-A.

[587] DRACHKOVITCH, MILORAD M., ED. *Yearbook on International Communist Affairs, 1966.* Stanford: Hoover Institution, 1967.

[588] DRACHMAN, EDWARD. *See* 1046.

[589] DROBYSHEVA, L., AND A. TELEFUS. "Ekonomicheskoe stimulirovanie tekhnicheskogo progressa v stranakh-chlenakh SEV" [The economic stimulation of technical progress in the member countries of CMEA]. *VE* 1969 (8): 51-63.

[590] DROZDOV A. "Uspekhi Sovetsko-Iranskikh ekonomicheskikh otnoshenii" [The successes of Soviet-Iranian economic relations]. *VT* 1970 (1): 18-22.

[591] DRUKS, HERBERT. "Dealing With the Russians: The Eisenhower Era." *EE* 1971 20(12): 9-16.

[592] _____. "Dealing With the Russians: The Truman Experience." *EE* 1971 20(8): 2-8.

[593] _____. *Harry S. Truman and the Russians, 1945-1953.* New York: Robert Speller and Sons, 1967.

[594] _____. "The Soviet Role in the Middle East." *EE* 1971 20(2): 19-27.

[595] DUBINSKII, L. "Leninskaia teoriia imperializma i gosudarstvenno-monopoliticheskii kapitalizm" [The Leninist theory of imperialism and state-monopoly capitalism]. *Komm* 1971 (1): 45-56.

[596] DÜCHENE, FRANÇOISE. "SALT, the Ostpolitik and the Post-Cold War Context." *WT* 1970 16: 500-511.

[597] DUCLOS, JACQUES. "Komintern i bor'ba za edinstvo revoliutsionnykh sil" [The Comintern and the struggle for the unity of revolutionary forces]. *Komm* 1969 (4): 18-30.

[598] ———. "Proletarskii internatsionalizm i patriotizm" [Proletarian internationalism and patriotism]. *PS* 1971 (6): 107-111.

[599] DUDINSKII, I. V. "Economic Integration—Law of Development of the Socialist Community." *IA(M)* 1970 (11): 3-10.

[600] ———. "Idei Lenina i nekotorye problemy sotsialisticheskogo sodruzhestva" [The ideas of Lenin and some problems of socialist concord]. *MEMO* 1969 (11): 3-13.

[601] ———. "Nauchno-teknicheskiia revoliutsiia i razvitie ekonomiki stran SEV" [The scientific-technical revolution and the development of the economies of the countries of CMEA]. *VE* 1971 (1) 121-131.

[602] ———. "The Road of Economic Advance (CMEA)." *IA(M)* 1971 (11): 3-11.

[603] ———. "Sotsialisticheskoe soobshchestvo i revoliutsionnoe obnovlenie mira" [Socialist cooperation and the revolutionary renewal of international relations]. *MEMO* 1967 (9): 13-25.

[604] ———. "Vozniknovenie mirovoi sistemy sotsializma i novye tendentsii v mirovom revoliutsionnom protsesse" [The rise of the world socialist system and new tendencies in the world revolutionary process]. *VI* 1971 (1): 21-43.

[605] ———. "The World Socialist System and International Development." *IA(M)* 1969 (11): 58-65.

[606] ———, ED. *Resursy i mezhdunarodnoe sotrudnichestvo* [Resources and international cooperation]. Moscow: I.M.O., 1968.

[607] DUEVEL, CHRISTIAN. "Eighty-Six Foreign Parties Report to the Twenty-fourth Soviet Party Congress." *B,ISUSSR* 1971 18(5): 3-25.

[608] DUKES, P. *The Emergence of the Superpowers: A Short Comparative History of the U.S.A. and the USSR.* London: Macmillan, 1970.

[609] DULLES, ELEANOR LANSING. *One Germany or Two: The Struggle at the Heart of Europe.* Stanford: Hoover Institution, 1970.

[610] DUMOGA, J. *Africa Between East and West.* London: Bodley Head, 1969.

[611] DUNCAN, W. RAYMOND. "Soviet Policy in Latin America Since Khrushchev." *Orb* 1971 15: 643-669.

[612] _____, ED. *Soviet Policy in Developing Countries.* Waltham, Massachusetts: Blaisdell, 1970.

[613] DUNCANSON, DENNIS J. "Vietnam and Foreign Powers." *IA(L)* 1969 45: 413-423.

[614] DUNN, DENNIS JOHN. "Stalinism and the Vatican." *DAI* 1971 31: 4082-A.

[615] DUPUY, T. N., ET AL. *The Almanac of World Military Power.* Dunn Loring, Virginia: T. N. Dupuy Associates in association with Stackpole Books, 1971.

[616] DUTT, GARGI. "Peking, the Indian Communist Movement and International Communism, 1962-1970." *AsS* 1971 11: 984-991.

[617] DUTT, R. PALME. "Marxism and Internationalism." *WMR* 1968 11(5): 3-11.

[618] "XXIV S'ezd KPSS i problemy natsional'no-osvoboditel'nogo dvizheniia" [The 24th Congress of the CPSU and the problems of the national liberation movement]. *NAA* 1971 (3): 3-14.

[619] DYCK, HARVEY L. "German-Soviet Relations, 1926-1933: A Study in the Diplomacy of Instability." *DAI* 1967 28: 586-A.

[620] DZASOKHOV, A., AND G. KIM. "Leninist Theory on the Unity of Revolutionary Currents." *IA(M)* 1969 (11): 45-49.

[621] DZHALOGONIIA, V. *See* 1276.

[622] DZIAK, JOHN J. "The Soviet Union and National Liberation Movements: An Examination of the Development of a Revolutionary Strategy." *DAI* 1971 32: 2024-A.

[623] DZIEWANOWSKI, M. KAMIL. "The Aftermath of the Czechoslovak Crisis." *StNCE* 1968-9 2(3): 54-66.

[624] _____. "Communist China and Eastern Europe." *Sur* 1970 77: 59-74.

[625] _____. "The Pattern of Rumanian Independence." *EE* 1969 18(6): 8-12.

[626] _____. "Peking and Eastern Europe." *Sur* 1970 77: 59-74.

[627] DZIUBKO, I. S., ED. *Ukrainskoi SSR v nauchno-kul'turnoe sotrudnichestvo Sovetskogo Souiza s Evropeiskimi sotsialisticheskimi stranami* [The Ukranian SSR in the scientific-technical cooperation of the Soviet Union with the European Socialist countries]. Kiev: Izd. Kievskogo Un-ta, 1970.

[628] EAGLES, KEITH D. "Ambassador Joseph E. Davies and American-Soviet Relations, 1937-1941." *DAI* 1967 27: 2981-A.

[629] "East-West Détente: The European Debate." *JIA* 1968 22(1): 1-120.

[630] "East-West European Trade in 1968 and Early 1969." *EBE* 1970 21(1): 33-41.

[631] "East-West Relations in Europe: A Yugoslav Perspective." *AO* 1970 24: 227-237.

[632] EBEL, ROBERT E. *Communist Trade in Oil and Gas: An Evaluation of the Future Export Capability of the Soviet Bloc.* New York, Washington, London: Praeger, 1970.

[633] ECCLES, HENRY E. "The Russian Maritime Threat: An Approach to the Problem." *NWCR* 1969 21(10): 4-14.

[634] ECKHARDT, W., AND RALPH K. WHITE. "Test of the Mirror Image Hypothesis: Kennedy and Khrushchev." *JCR* 1967 11: 325-332.

[635] EDMONDS, MARTIN, AND JOHN SKITT. "Current Soviet Maritime Strategy and NATO." *IA(L)* 1969 45: 28-43.

[636] EDWARDS, DAVID V. *Arms Control in International Politics.* New York: Holt, Rinehart and Winston, 1969.

[637] EFREMOV, A. E. *Evropa i iadernoe oruzhie* [Europe and nuclear armaments]. *Moscow: I.M.O., 1972.*

[638] EGOROV, V. N. *Mirnoe sosushchestvovanie i revoliutsionnyi protsess* [Peaceful coexistence and the revolutionary process]. Moscow: I.M.O., 1971.

[639] EHRLICH, WOLFF. "Leninism and Struggle Against Chauvinism and for Proletarian Internationalism." *WMR* 1970 13(3): 56-58.

[640] EIDUS, KH. "Lenin i Iaponskii imperializm" [Lenin and Japanese imperialism]. *AAS* 1969 (8): 10-13.

[641] EISENBERG, RAFAEL. *The East-West Conflict: Psychological Origin and Resolution.* New York: Diplomatic Press, 1967.

[642] *Ekonomicheskie osnovy mirovoi sotsialisticheskoi sistemy* [The economic foundations of the world socialist system]. Moscow: Mysl', 1968.

[643] *Ekonomicheskii mezhanizm sotrudnichestva stran Sotsializma. (Voprosy teorii i metodologii)* [The economic mechanism of the cooperation of the socialist countries. (Questions of theory and methodology)]. Moscow: Mysl', 1970.

[644] "Ekonomicheskoe i tekhnicheskoe sotrudnichestvo SSSR so stranami Afriki" [Economic and technical cooperation of the USSR with the countries of Africa]. *VT* 1968 (9): 2-5.

[645] *Ekonomicheskoe sotrudnichestvo SSSR so stranami Afriki* [Economic cooperation of the USSR with the countries of Africa]. Moscow: Nauka, 1969.

[646] *Ekonomika stran sotsializma. Ezhegodnik* [The economics of the socialist countries. Annual]. Moscow: Ekonomika, published annually.

[647] *Eksportno-importnye operatsii* [Export-import operations]. Moscow: I.M.O., 1970.

[648] ELAGIN, V. "Towards the All-European Conference." *NT* 1969 (49): 9-11.

[649] ELDRIDGE, P. J. *The Politics of Foreign Aid in India.* New York: Schocken, 1970.

[650] EMEL'IANOV, V. S. *Atom i mir* [The atom and peace]. Moscow: Atomizdat, 1967.

[651] ENTHOVEN, ALAIN C. "Arms and Men: The Military Balance in Europe." *Int* 1969 2(10): 11-14.

[652] ENTIN, L. M. "Natsional'noe demokraticheskoe gosudarstvo i ekonomicheskoe razvitie" [The national democratic state and economic development]. *SGP* 1968 (1): 83-89.

[653] _____, AND S. A. SOSNA. *Natsional'no demokraticheskoe gosudarstvo i ekonomicheskii progress* [The national democratic state and economic progress]. Moscow: I.M.O., 1968.

[654] EPSTEIN, JULIUS. "The Beginning of the Cold War II." *CEJ* 1969 17: 81-90.

[655] _____. "Forced Reparations [of the Soviet Union in Eastern Europe]: Some Unanswered Questions." *RR* 1970 29: 209ff.

[656] _____. "President Kennedy, Détente, and the Rapacki Plan." *CEJ* 1970 (special issue): 1-16.

[657] EPSTEIN, WILLIAM. *Disarmament: Twenty Five Years of Effort.* Toronto: Canadian Institute of International Affairs, 1971.

[658] ERAN, ODED, AND JEROME E. SINGER. "Soviet Policy Towards the Arab World, 1955-1971." *Sur* 1971 17(4): 10-29.

[659] ERASOV, B. S. "Marksizm i ideologiia natsionalizma v stranakh Afriki" [Marxism and the ideology of nationalism in the countries of Africa]. *AsS* 1968 (11): 6-8.

[660] ERB, THEODORE HENRY. "The Sino-Soviet Conflict and its Impact on the Sovereignties of Eastern Europe." *DAI* 1969 30: 2104-A.

[661] ERICKSON, JOHN. "The Fly in Outer Space: The Soviet Union and the Anti-Ballistic Missile." *WT* 1967 23: 106-114.

[662] _____. "A Framework for Soviet Foreign Policy." *StSU* 1967 6(3): 108-128.

[663] _____. "The World Strategic Balance." *Year Book of World Affairs* London, 1969.

[664] ERMARTH, FRITZ W. *Internationalism, Security and Legitimacy: The Challenge to Soviet Interests in East Europe, 1964-1968.* Santa Monica, California: RAND Corporation, 1969.

[665] ERMARTH, FRITZ W. "The Soviet Union in the Third World: Purpose in Search of Power." *A,AAPSS* 1969 386: 31-40.

[666] ERMOLENKO, D. "Sociology and International Relations." *IA(M)* 1967 (1): 14-19.

[667] _____. *See* 202.

[668] ERMONSKII, A. "The Dynamism of Socialist Diplomacy." *IA(M)* 1967 (7): 6-12.

[669] ESGAIN, ALBERT E. "The position of the United States and the Soviet Union on Treaty Law and Treaty Negotiation." *MR* 1969 46(October): 31-76.

[670] ESPOSITO, BRUCE J. "The Comintern and the Canton Commune." *DAI* 1968 29: 1491-A.

[671] EUDIN, XENIA JOUKOFF, AND ROBERT M. SLUSSER, EDS. *Soviet Foreign Policy 1928-1934: Documents and Materials, II.* University Park: The University of Pennsylvania Press, 1967.

[672] "European Security." *NT* 1968 (33): 4-6.

[673] "European Security and Relations Between States of the Two Systems. From International Seminar on European Security and Relations Between States of the Two Systems, Moscow, April 23-25, 1968." *IA(M)* 1968 (6): 68-76; 1968 (7): 68-75.

[674] "European Security System: Content and Ways of Ensuring It, Discussion Organized by the Editorial Board." *IA(M)* 1971 (11): 64-88.

[675] EVANS, HUBERT. "Recent Soviet Writing on Afghanistan." *CAR* 1967 15: 316-330.

[676] _____. "Recent Soviet Writing on India." *CAR* 1968 16: 110-121, 135.

[677] _____. "Recent Soviet Writing on the Mongolian PR." *CAR* 1968 16: 26-39.

[678] EVRON, YAIR. "The Soviet Union in Egypt." *Surv* 1970 12: 259-262.

[679] _____. *See* 2356.

[680] *Evropeiskaia bezopasnost' i otnosheniia gosudarstv dvukh sistem* [European security and the relations of states of the two systems]. Moscow: I.M.O., 1968.

[681] "Evropeiskaia bezopasnost' i otnosheniia gosudarstv dvukh sistem. Mezhdunarodnaia nauchnaia konferentsiia, sostoiavshaiasia v Moskve 23-25 Aprelia 1968 g" [European security and the relations of states of the two systems. An international scientific conference held in Moscow, 23-25 April, 1968]. *MEMO* 1968 (7): 102-121; 1968 (8): 72-81.

[682] "Exposing Anti-Sovietism." *WMR* 1971 14(2): 132-136.

[683] EZERGAILIS, ANDREW. "'Monolithic' versus 'Crumbling' Communism." *PoC* 1970 19: 1-7.

[684] ———.*See* 918.

[685] EZHOV, V. "Kommunisty v avangarde antiimperialisticheskoi bor'bi" [Communists in the vanguard of the anti-imperialist struggle]. *Komm* 1971 (4): 94-102.

[686] FADDEEV, N. V. "CMEA: Cooperation of Equal Nations." *IA(M)* 1967 (4): 7-12.

[687] ———. "Leninskie idei i ekonomicheskoe sotrudnichestvo sotsialisticheskikh stran" [Leninist ideas and the economic cooperation of the socialist countries]. *MEMO* 1967 (12): 3-13.

[688] ———. "Objective: Socialist Integration." *WMR* 1970 13(8): 50-52.

[689] ———. "Pod flagom ekonomicheskogo sotrudnichestva" [Under the banner of economic cooperation]. *SDT* 1970 (3): 102-109.

[690] ———.*Sovet Ekonomicheskoi Vzaimopomoshchi, 1949-1969* [The Council for Mutual Economic Assistance, 1949-1969]. Moscow: Ekonomika, 1969.

[691] FAINSOD, MERLE. "Some Reflections on Soviet-American Relations." *APSR* 1968 62: 1093-1103.

[692] ———. "Through Soviet Eyes." *PoC* 1970 19(6): 59-64.

[693] FAIRHALL, DAVID. *Russian Sea Power.* Boston: Gambit, 1971.

[694] FALK, RICHARD A. "Plan for U.S.-USSR Cooperation on Environment." *University: A Princeton Quarterly* 1971 48: 19-24.

[695] FALLENBUCHL, ZBIGNIEW M. "The Role of International Trade in the Czechoslovak Economy." *CSIP* 1969 10: 430-449.

[696] FANN, WILLERD R. "Germany and East Europe: Problems of Détente." *CH* 1968 53: 263-267, 305-307.

[697] FARLOW, ROBERT L. "Alignment and Conflict: Romanian Foreign Policy, 1958-1969." *DAI* 1971 32: 1595-A.

[698] ———. "Romanian Foreign Policy: A Case of Alignment." *PoC* 1971 20(6): 54-63.

[699] FARNSWORTH, BEATRICE. *William C. Bullitt and the Soviet Union.* Bloomington: Indiana University Press, 1967.

[700] FARRELL, JOHN T. *See* 1443.

[701] FARRELL, R. BARRY. "East European Foreign Policy Leadership." *StCC* 1971 4: 80-96.

[702] _____. "Foreign Policy Formation in the Communist Countries of Eastern Europe." *EEQ* 1967 1: 39-74.

[703] FARSHI, K. KHOSBAFE. "Sir Winston Churchill's Attitude Toward Communism." *DAI* 1968 28: 3730-A.

[704] "Federal Republic of Germany-Union of Soviet Socialist Republics: Non-Aggression Treaty." *ILM* 1970 9: 1026-1027.

[705] FEDERENKO, NIKOLAI. "Diplomacy of Peace and Progress." *NT* 1967 (45): 11-114.

[706] FEDLAM, FRUZSINA H. "Communist Doctrines Concerning Under-developed Countries." *MA* 1967 5(4): 21.

[707] FEDOROV, V. "The Driving Forces of the National-Liberation Revolution." *IA(M)* 1968 (1): 66-72.

[708] _____. "Marks, kolonializm sovremennost'" [Marx, colonialism, the present]. *AAS* 1968 (4): 2-4.

[709] _____. "OON i mezhdunarodnaia bezopasnost'" [The U.N. and international security]. *MEMO* 1971 (3): 78-81.

[710] FEDOSEEV P. "Marksizm i Maotseedunizm" [Marxism and Mao Tse-tungism]. *Komm* 1967 (5): 107-122.

[711] _____. "Marxism and Internationalism." *IA(M)* 1969 (3): 3-8.

[712] FEDOSEEV, P. N., ET AL. Komintern i ego revoliutsionnye traditsii; Materialy nauchnoi sessii, posviashchennye 50-letiiu obrazovaniia Kommunisticheskogo Internatsionala [The Comintern and its revolutionary tradition: Materials of a scientific session devoted to the 50th anniversary of the formation of the Communist International]. Moscow: Politizdat, 1969.

[713] _____, ED. *Mezhdunarodnoe znachenie Velikoi Oktiabr'skoi Sotsialisticheskoi Revoliutsii* [The international meaning of the Great October Socialist Revolution]. Moscow: Nauka, 1968.

[714] FEDYSHYN, OLEH S. *Germany's Drive to the East and the Ukrainian Revolution, 1917-1918.* New Brunswick, New Jersey: Rutgers University Press, 1971.

[715] _____. "Soviet Foreign Policy Toward Western Europe and the United States." *StNCE* 1968-9 2(3): 81-87.

[716] FEINBERG, E. I. "Ustanovlenie Russko-Japanskikh diplomaticheskikh i torgovykh otnoshenii" [The establishment of Russian-Japanese diplomatic and trade relations]. *VI* 1969 (3): 73-89.

[717] FEIS, HERBERT. *From Trust to Terror: The Onset of the Cold War, 1945-1950.* New York: Norton, 1970.

[718] FEJTO, FRANÇOIS. *The French Communist Party and the Crisis of International Communism.* Cambridge: Massachusetts Institute of Technology Press, 1967.

[719] ———. "Moscow and Its Allies." *PoC* 1968 17(6): 29-37.

[720] FELD, WERNER J. "National-International Linkage Theory: The East European Communist System and the EEC." *JISt* 1968 22: 107-120.

[721] ———. "The Utility of the EEC Experience for Eastern Europe." *JCMSt* 1970 8: 236-261.

[722] FEL'DMAN, D.I., AND M. V. IANOVSKII. *General'naia Assambleia OON i voprosy razvitiia mezhdunarodnogo prava* [The General Assembly of the UN and the question of international law]. Kazan': Izdatel'stvo Kazan'skogo Universiteta, 1968.

[723] FELDT, B. T., G. W. GREENWOOD, G. W. RATHJENS, AND S. WEINBERG, EDS. *Impact of New Technologies on the Arms Race.* Cambridge: Massachusetts Institute of Technology Press, 1971.

[724] FELLER, ALBERT. "Security and East-West Trade." *B,ISUSSR* 1967 14(1): 3-16.

[725] FERGUSON, MICHAEL L. "The Soviet Union's Place in de Gaulle's Foreign Policy: An Inquiry into French-Russian Relations With Emphasis on the Period of the Fifth Republic." *MA* 1967 5(1): 18.

[726] FERRING, R. L. "Austrian State Treaty of 1955 and the Cold War." *WPQ* 1968 21: 651-667.

[727] FESSLER, LOREN. "A Russian-Chinese American Dilemma in Cold War Relations." *American University Field Staff Reports, East Asia Series.* 1970 17(6): 1-14.

[728] FEULNER, EDWIN G., JR. *See* 430.

[729] FIC, MIROSLAV VICTOR. "The Origins of the Conflict Between the Czechoslovak Legion and the Bolsheviks: A Study of the Background. March-May 1918." *DAI* 1969 30: 787-A.

[730] FIEDLER, PETER C. "The Pattern of Super-Power Crisis." *IR* 1969 3: 498-510.

[731] FILENE, PETER G. *Americans and the Soviet Experiment, 1917-1933.* Cambridge, Massachusetts: Harvard University Press, 1967.

[732] FILIPPOVOI, M. M., ED. *Bor'ba za mir. Materialy Trekh Internatsionalov. Sbornik* [The struggle for peace. Materials of the Third International. A collection]. Moscow: "Vysshaia shkola," 1967.

[733] "Finland-Union of Soviet Socialist Republics: Agreement on Fishing and Sealing." *ILM* 1970 9: 507-510.

[734] FINLEY, DAVID D. *See* 2858.

[735] FINOGENOV, V. *Internatsionalizm v deistvii* [Internationalism in action]. Leningrad: Leniizdat, 1967.

[736] FIRMAGE, EDWIN B. "The Treaty on the Non-Proliferation of Nuclear Weapons." *AJIL* 1969 63: 711-746.

[737] FISCHER, LOUIS. *Russia's Road from Peace to War: Soviet Foreign Relations: 1917-1941.* New York: Harper & Row, 1969.

[738] FISCHER-GALATI, STEPHEN. "France and Rumania: A Changing Image." *EEQ* 1968 1: 107-121.

[739] FITHIAN, F. J. "Dollars Without the Flag: The Case of Sinclair and Sakhalin Oil." *PHR* 1970 39: 205-222.

[740] FITZGERALD, C. P. "The Sino-Soviet Border Conflict." *PC* 1970 1 271-283.

[741] ———. "Tension on the Sino-Soviet Border." *FA* 1967 45: 683-693.

[742] FLEMING, DENNA FRANK. *The Cold War and Its Origins, 1917-1960.* Garden City, New York: Doubleday, 1970.

[743] FLERON, JR., FREDERIC J. *See* 1042.

[744] FLOOD, DANIEL J. "U.S. Policy and Soviet Objectives in the Panama Canal." *EE* 1971 20(9): 13-22.

[745] FLORIN, PETER. "State Secretary Peter Florin on G.D.R. Foreign Policy." *NT* 1969 (40): 10-12.

[746] FLOROV, L. "Novye rubezhi bratskogo sotrudnichestva stran SEV" [New boundaries of fraternal cooperation of the countries of CMEA]. *VT* 1969 (7): 7-11.

[747] FÖLDI, T., AND T. KISS, EDS. *Socialist World Market Prices.* Leyden: A. W. Sijthoff, 1969.

[748] FOMIN, V. V. *"Ekonometricheskie teorii i modeli mezhdunarodnykh ekonomicheskikh otnoshenii"* [Econometric theories and models of international economic relations]. Moscow: Mysl', 1970.

[749] ———. *IUNKTAD: Mezhdunarodnaia organizatsiia po torgovle i razvitiiu* [UNCTAD: International organization for trade and development]. Moscow: Nauka, 1970.

[750] ———. *OON i mezhdunarodnaia torgovlia* [The UN and international trade]. Moscow: I.M.O., 1971.

[751] FONER, PHILIP S. *The Bolshevik Revolution: Its Impact on American Radicals, Liberals, and Labor (a Documentary Study).* New York: International Publishers, 1967.

[752] FONKIN, D. *Vneshniaia torgovlia SSSR: 1918-1966. Stat. sbornik* [Foreign trade of the USSR, 1918-1966. Statistical collection]. Moscow: I.M.O., 1967.

[753] FONTAINE, ANDRÉ. *History of the Cold War: From the Korean War to the Present.* New York: Pantheon Books, 1969.

[754] ———. *History of the Cold War: From the October Revolution to the Korean War, 1917-1950.* New York: Pantheon Books, 1968.

[755] ———. "Potsdam: A French View." *IA(L)* 1970 44: 466-474.

[756] ———. "The Real Divisions of Europe." *FA* 1971 49: 302-314.

[757] *Foreign Policy of the People's Republic of Bulgaria. Vol. 1, 1944-1962; Vol. 2, 1963-1969.* Sofia: Nauka i Izkustvo, 1970-1971.

[758] "Foreign Politics and Ideological Struggle at the Present Stage." *IA(M)* 1968 (6): 3-7.

[759] FORSTER, KENT. "Finland's 1966 Elections and Soviet Relations." *Orb* 1968 12: 774-792.

[760] FORSYTHE, DAVID P. "The Soviets and the Arab-Israeli Conflict." *WA* 1971 134: 132-142.

[761] FORTE, DAVID F. P. "The Response of Soviet Foreign Policy to the Common Market, 1957-1963." *SSt* 1968 19: 373-386.

[762] FOSTER, WILLIAM C. "Prospects for Arms Control." *FA* 1969 47: 413-421.

[763] "France-Union of Soviet Socialist Republics: Consular Convention." *ILM* 1970 9: 365-376.

[764] "France-Union of Soviet Socialist Republics: Protocol and Declaration on Political Cooperation." *ILM* 1970 9: 1165-1172.

[765] "France-Union of Soviet Socialist Republics-United Kingdom-United States: Agreement and Notes on Berlin." *ILM* 1971 10: 895-903.

[766] FRANCK, THOMAS M. *The Johnson-Brezhnev Doctrines: Verbal Behavior Analysis of Superpower Confrontrations.* New York: New York University, Center for International Studies, 1970.

[767] ———, AND EDWARD WEISBAND. *The Johnson-Brezhnev Doctrines.* New York: New York University, 1970.

[768] _____, AND EDWARD WEISBAND. "The Role of Reciprocity and Equivalence in Systemic Superpower Interaction." *NYUJIL* 1970 3: 363-377.

[769] FRANK, ELKE. "East and West Germany." In *Conflict in World Politics,* pp. 179-198, edited by Steven L. Spiegel and Kenneth N. Waltz. Cambridge, Massachusetts: Winthrop, 1971.

[770] *Franko-Russkie ekonomicheskie sviazi. Sbornik* [French-Russian economic ties. A collection]. Moscow: Nauka, 1970.

[771] FRANTSOV, IU. P. *Mezhdunarodnoe znachenie Velikoi Oktiabr'skoi Sotsialisticheskoi Revoliutsii* [The international meaning of the Great October Socialist Revolution]. Moscow: Mysl', 1967.

[772] FREDERICKS, EDGAR J. "Soviet-Egyptian Relations, 1955-1965, and Their Effects on Communism in the Middle East and the International Position of the Soviet Union." *DAI* 1968 29: 1265-A.

[773] FREEDMAN, ROBERT O. *Economic Warfare in the Communist Bloc—A Study of Soviet Economic Pressure Against Yugoslavia, Albania, and Communist China.* New York: Praeger, 1970.

[774] _____. "The Soviet Union's Utilization of Economic Pressure as an Instrument of Its Foreign Policy Toward Other Communist Nations." *DAI* 1971 31: 1866-A.

[775] FRELEK, RYSZARD. "Poland and the All-European Conference." *IA(M)* 1971 (7): 31-33.

[776] FRUMKIN, A. *Sovremennye teorii mezhdunarodnykh ekonomicheskikh otnoshenii* [The contemporary theories of international economic relations]. Moscow: Progress, 1969.

[777] GADDIS, JOHN L. *The United States and the Origins of the Cold War.* New York: Columbia University Press, 1971.

[778] _____. "The United States and the Origins of the Cold War: 1943-1946." *DAI* 1970 30: 5377-A.

[779] GAFUROV, B. G. "Lenin and the Liberation of the Peoples of the East." *IA(M)* 1970 (5): 35-40.

[780] _____. "Leninizm i probuzdenie Vostoka" [Leninism and the awakening of the East]. *AAS* 1970 (4): 4-10.

[781] _____. *Oktiabr'skaia Revoliutsiia i natsional'no-osvoboditel'noe dvizhenie* [The October Revolution and the national-liberation movement]. Moscow: Mysl', 1967.

[782] ———. "Sovetskaia Rossiia i natsional'no-osvoboditel'naia bor'ba narodov Srednego i Blizhnogo Vostoka" [Soviet Russia and the national-liberation struggle of the peoples of the Middle and Near East]. *VI* 1967 (10): 37-53.

[783] ———. "The Soviet Union and the National Liberation Movement." *IA(M)* 1971 (7): 17-21.

[784] ———. "Velikii Oktiabr' i natsional'no-osvoboditel'noe dvizhenie" [The Great October and the national liberation movement]. *NAA* 1967 (5): 5-20.

[785] ———, ET AL., EDS. *Lenin i natsional'no-osvoboditel'noe dvizhenie v stranakh Vostoka* [Lenin and the national-liberation movement in the countries of the East]. Moscow: Nauka, 1970.

[786] GAIDAENKO, I. "Franko-Sovetskaia Torgovaia Palata" [Franco-Soviet Chamber of Commerce]. *VT* 1968 (6): 47-51.

[787] GAILAR, JOANNE L. "Seven Warning Signals: A Review of Soviet Defense." *BAS* 1969 25(10): 18-22.

[788] GALAY, NIKOLAI. "The Geo-Political and Strategic Significance of Soviet Central Asia." *StSU* 1968 7(4): 45-61.

[789] ———. "The Record of Soviet Diplomacy." *StSU* 1967 6(3): 91-107.

[790] ———. "The Soviet Armed Forces' First Half Century: Legends and Reality." *B,ISUSSR* 1968 15(3): 5-19.

[791] GALLAGHER, MATTHEW P. "The Uneasy Balance: Soviet Attitudes Towards Missile Talks." *Int* 1969 3(5): 21-25.

[792] ———.*See* 1382.

[793] GALLANT, GEORGE W. "Limited Sovereignty: The Political Doctrine of the Warsaw Treaty Organization." *DAI* 1971 32: 2163-A.

[794] CALLUS, EDWARD. "The Possibility of a Neutralized Zone in Central Europe." *StNCE* 1967-68 2(1): 9-14.

[795] GALTING, JOHN, ED., AND SVERRE LODGAARD. *Cooperation in Europe.* Stockholm: Almqvist and Wiksell, 1970.

[796] GAMARNIKOW, MICHAEL. "Eastern Europe—Light at the End of the Tunnel." *Int* 1968 1(10): 28, 33-35.

[797] ———. "Industrial Cooperation: East Europe Looks West." *PoC* 1971 20(3): 41-48.

[798] ———. "Is COMECON Obsolete?" *EE* 1968 17(4): 12-18.

[799] ———. "Poland's Foreign Trade With East and West." *PG* 1967 11(41-42): 36-53.

[800] GAMBLE, PHILIP L. "Soviet Aid and Trade and Its Threat to the Free World." *NWCR* 1969 21(10): 80-105.

[801] GAMSON, WILLIAM A., AND ANDRÉ MODIGLIANI. "Some Aspects of Soviet-Western Conflict." *P,PRS* 1968 9: 9-24.

[802] ———, AND ANDRÉ MODIGLIANI. *Untangling the Cold War: A Strategy for Testing Rival Theories.* Boston: Little, Brown, 1971.

[803] GAN, CLAUDE C. "Communist Wars of National Liberation and the Sino-Soviet Dispute." *DAI* 1968 28: 3244-A.

[804] GANCHEV, TOGOR. "Natsional'noe i internatsional'noe vo vzaimootno-sheniiakh sotsialisticheskikh stran" [The national and the international in the mutual relations of the socialist countries]. *Komm* 1969 (5): 82-91.

[805] GARDNER, LLOYD C., ARTHUR SCHLESINGER, JR., AND HANS J. MORGEN-THAU. *The Origins of the Cold War.* Waltham, Massachusetts, Toronto, London: Ginn-Blaisdell, 1970.

[806] GAREAU, FREDERICK H. "Cold War Cleavages as Seen From the United Nations General Assembly." *JP* 1970 32: 929-968.

[807] ———. *The Cold War 1947-1967: A Quantitative Study.* Denver: Social Science Foundation and Graduate School of International Studies, Monograph series in World Affairs, 6(1) 1968.

[808] GARETOVSKII, A. "Sovetskii vostok—razvivaiushchimsia stranam" [The Soviet east—to the developing countries]. *AAS* 1967 (11): 26-31.

[809] GARNER, WILLIAM R. "The Sino-Soviet Ideological Struggle in Latin America." *JI-ASt* 1968 10: 244-255.

[810] GARTHOFF, DOUGLAS F. "The Soviet Dilemma in Yemen." *SAIS* 1967 12: 15-22.

[811] GASPARD, J. "The Kremlin Without Abdul Nasser: The Soviet Union and Egypt: A New Relationship." *NME* 1970 (November): 17-19.

[812] GASS, OSCAR. "China, Russia and the U.S." *Comm* 1967 43(3): 65-73, (4): 39-46.

[813] GASTEYGER, CURT. "Moscow and the Mediterranean." *FA* 1968 46: 676-687.

[814] GATI, CHARLES. "Methodology and Soviet Foreign Policy." *CSISt* 1967 1: 660-663.

[815] ———. "Soviet Elite Perception of International Regions: A Research Note." In *The Behavioral Revolution and Communist Studies,* pp. 281-300, edited by Roger E. Kanet. New York: Free Press, 1971.

[816] _____. "Soviet Tutelage in East Europe." *CH* 1971 60: 206-209.

[817] GAVILEVSKII, V. "Soviet-Yugoslav Co-operation." *NT* 1970 (28): 12-13.

[818] _____. "Soviet-Yugoslav Co-operation." *NT* 1970 (28): 16-17.

[819] _____. "Soviet-Yugoslav Co-operation." *NT* 1971 (39): 6-7.

[820] GAVRILOV, A. "Cherez Obshcheevropeiskoe soveshchanie—k bezopasnosti kontinenta" [Through an all-European conference to the security of the continent]. *MEMO* 1969 (6): 3-12.

[821] _____. "Programma bor'by za mir i bezopasnost' narodov" [A program of struggle for the peace and security of peoples]. *MEMO* 1971 (7): 3-11.

[822] GAWOREK, NORBERT HORST. "Allied Economic Warfare Against Soviet Russia From November 1917 to March 1921." *DAI* 1971 31: 5317-A.

[823] GEHLEN, MICHAEL P. *The Politics of Co-Existence: Soviet Methods and Motives.* Bloomington: Indiana University Press, 1967.

[824] GEHLEN, MICHAEL P. "The Integrative Process in East Europe: A Theoretical Framework." *JP* 1968 30: 90-113.

[825] GELBER, HARRY G. "The Sino-Soviet Relationship and the United States." *Orb* 1971 15(1): 118-133.

[826] _____. "Strategic Arms Limitations and the Sino-Soviet Relationship." *AsS* 1970 10: 265-289.

[827] GELLERT, ANDRE. "The Diplomacy of the Czechoslovak Crisis." *StNCE* 1968-69 2(3): 43-49.

[828] GENERALOV, V. E. *Zakonomernosti razvitiia mirovoi sistemy sotsializma* [The regularity of the development of the world socialist system]. Moscow: Izdatel'stvo Moskovskogo universiteta, 1970.

[829] GENIN, S. IA., ED. *SSSR i zarubezhnye strany posle pobedy Vekiloi Oktiabr'skoi Sotsialisticheskoi Revoliutsii. Statisticheskii sbornik* [The USSR and foreign countries after the Great October Socialist Revolution. Statistical collection]. Moscow: Statistika, 1970.

[830] GEORGEVICH, MIODRAG. "An Analysis of Yugoslavia's Policy of Peaceful Coexistence." *DAI* 1970 31: 2467-A.

[831] GEORGIEV, IU. "Iugoslaviia: Novyi variant sotsializma?" [Yugoslavia: A new variant of socialism?]. *Komm* 1968 (15): 82-97.

[832] GERASIMOV, G. "O nekotorykh burzhuaznykh 'kontseptsiiakh' mezhdunarodnykh otnoshenii" [Concerning some bourgeois "conceptions" of international relations]. *MEMO* 1968 (8): 16-27.

[833] GERASIMOV, N. "Rastet Sovetsko-Shvedskaia torgovlia" [Soviet-Swedish trade is growing]. *VT* 1970 (3): 19-21.

[834] GERBER, WILLIAM, AND RICHARD L. WORSNOP. "Czechoslovakia and European Security." *ERR* October 18, 1968: 763-780.

[835] GERLACH, DIETER. "Discrimination Between the USSR and Its Partners." *Inte* 1967 2: 41-43.

[836] GERTSOVICH, G. B. *Sovershenvstvovanie metodov khoziaistvovaniia v Evropeiskikh stranakh-chlenakh SEV* [The perfection of methods of economy in the European member-countries of CMEA]. Moscow: Nauka, 1968.

[837] ———, AND O. TARNOVSKII. "Plata za proizvodstvennye fondy Evropeiskikh stranakh-chlenakh SEV" [Assessments for the production fund of the European members of CMEA]. *VE* 1969 (4) 85-94.

[838] GHAREKHAN, C. R. "Strategic Arms Limitation Talks—II." *IQ* 1970 26: 389-399.

[839] GHOREICHI, AHMAD. "Soviet Foreign Policy in Iran 1917-1960." *DAI* 1969 30: 1219-A.

[840] GHOSH, MANMOHAN. *China's Conflict with India and Soviet Union.* Delhi: UBS Publishers' Distributors, 1969.

[841] GIBERT, STEPHEN P. "Soviet-American Military Aid Competition in the Third World." *Orb* 1970 13: 1117-1137.

[842] ———, AND WYNFRED JOSHUA. *Guns and Rubles: Soviet Aid Diplomacy in Neutral Asia.* New York: American Asian Educational Exchange, 1970.

[843] ———.*See* 1184.

[844] GIBSON, SHERRI. "Sino-Soviet Military Relations, 1946-1966." *JICSt* 1969 2(1) 24-30.

[845] GIFFEN, JAMES HENRY. *The Legal and Practical Aspects of Trade With the Soviet Union.* New York: Praeger, 1969.

[846] GIFT, RICHARD E. "Trading in a Threat System: The US-Soviet Case." *JCR* 1969 13: 418-437.

[847] GILBERG, TROND. "The Relations Between the Soviet Communist Party and the Norwegian Communist Parties, 1917-World War II. (April, 1940)." *DAI* 1970 30(12): 5505-A.

[848] ———. "Soviet Policies in West Europe." *CH* 1971 60: 198-205.

[849] GILBOA, YEHOSHUA A. "Soviet Politics on Palestine." *IP* 1971 10(3-4): 11-19.

[850] GILL, R. ROCKINGHAM. "Europe's Military Balance After Czechoslovakia." *EE* 1968 17(10): 17-21.

[851] GINSBURGS, GEORGE. "A Calendar of Soviet Treaties. Addenda and Corrigenda." *Oe-R* 1970 16: 47-74,118-135.

[852] _____. "The Dynamics of the Sino-Soviet Territorial Dispute: The Case of the River Islands." In *The Dynamics of China's Foreign Policy*, pp. 1-20, edited by Jerome A. Cohen. Cambridge, Massachusetts: Harvard University, East Asian Research Center, 1970.

[853] _____. "The Kremlin and the Common Market: A Conspectus." *SoR* 1970 37: 296-305.

[854] _____. *See* 2334.

[855] GIRITIL, ISMET. "Turkish-Soviet Relations." *IQ* 1970 26(1): 3-19.

[856] GITTINGS, JOHN. "The Great Power Triangle and Chinese Foreign Policy." *CQ* 1969 39: 41-54.

[857] _____. *Survey of the Sino-Soviet Dispute: A Commentary and Extracts From the Recent Polemics, 1963-1967.* London: Oxford University Press, 1968.

[858] _____. "The View From Moscow: The Sino-Soviet Dispute." *FEER* 1967 58: 277-278.

[859] GIVEN, DEAM W. "The Sea of Okhotsk—USSR's Great Lake?" *USNI,P* 96(9): 46-51.

[860] GLAGOLEV, I. S. *Bezopasnost' narodov i razoruzhenie* [The security of the peoples and disarmament]. Moscow: Znanie, 1971.

[861] GLASENAPPS, IGOR O. "Recent Development in Soviet Policy Toward Israel." *B,ISUSSR* 1969 16(4): 35-40.

[862] GLASSMAN, JON D. "Soviet Foreign Policy Decision-Making." In *Columbia Essays in International Affairs: The Dean's Papers, III, 1967.* New York: 1968.

[863] GLAUBITZ, JOACHIM. "Moscow-Peking-Tokyo: A Triangle of Great Power Relations." *B,ISUSSR* 1971 18(6): 20-33.

[864] GLENNY, M. V. "The Anglo-Soviet Trade Agreement, March 1921." *JCH* 1970 5(2): 63-82.

[865] GLINKA-JANCZEWSKI, GEORGE H. "American Policy Toward Poland Under the Truman Administration, 1945-1952." *DAI* 1967 27: 2985-A.

[866] GLINKMAN, PAVEL. "Vneshnie ekonomicheskie sviazi sotsialisticheskikh stran—vazhnyi faktor povysheniia effektivnosti obshchestvennogo proizvodstva" [Foreign economic ties of the socialist countries are an important factor in the rise in effectiveness of social production]. *VE* 1967 (2): 76-85.

[867] GNEDOVETS, P. P., ED. *SSSR v Velikoi Otechestvennoi Voine. 1941-1945* [The USSR in the Great Patriotic War,1941-1945]. Moscow: Voenizdat, 1970.

[868] GNEVUSHEV, N. "Evropeiskii Fond Razvitiia" [The European Development Fund]. *MEMO* 1969 (10): 119-125.

[869] GOLANOV, V., AND A. CHULKOV. "Litsenzii v mezhdunarodnoi torgovle" [Licenses in international trade]. *VT* 1971 (8): 30-31.

[870] GOLDEN, ANNE. "Attitudes to the Soviet Union as Reflected in the American Press, 1944-1948." *DAI* 1971 32: 881-A.

[871] GOLDMAN, MARSHALL I. *Soviet Foreign Aid.* New York: Praeger, 1967.

[872] _____. "Soviet Trade and Foreign Aid to Developing Countries." *NWCR* 1968 20(8): 56-69.

[873] GOLDMAN, STUART D. "The Forgotten War: The Soviet Union and Japan, 1937-1939." *DAI* 1971 31: 3468-A.

[874] GOLIKOV, F. I. "Sovetskaia voennaia missiia v Anglii i SSHA v 1941 g" [The Soviet military mission in England and the USA in 1941]. *NNI* 1969 (3): 100-111.

[875] GOLLAN, J. "Lenin's Analysis of Imperialism and Some Developments of Monopoly." *WMR* 1970 13(3): 71-77.

[876] GOLOSHUBOV, E. "The Northern Countries and European Security." *NT* 1970 (18-19): 37-38.

[877] _____. "Problems of North European Security." *NT* 1971 (4): 20-21.

[878] GOLOVIN, Y. "Nordic Europe: Security and Cooperation." *IA(M)* 1971 (2): 53-59.

[879] GOMULKA, W. "Lenin's Approach to National Question." *WMR* 1970 13(4): 77-84.

[880] GONIONSKII, S. "The Soviet Union and Latin America." *NT* 1971 (7): 20-22.

[881] GONZALES, EDWARD. "Castro's Revolution, Cuban Communist Appeals, and the Soviet Response." *WP* 1968 21: 39-68.

[882] _____. "The Cuban Revolution and the Soviet Union,1959-1960." *DAI* 1967 27: 3502-A.

[883] ———. "Relationships With the Soviet Union." In *Revolutionary Change in Cuba: Polity, Economy, Society,* edited by Carmelo Mesa-Lago. Pittsburgh: University of Pittsburgh Press, 1971.

[884] GOODMAN, ELLIOT R. "Détente." *ACQ* 1969 7: 351-372.

[885] ———. "Détente: The Soviet View." *Sur* 1969 (70-71): 121-148.

[886] ———. "NATO and German Unification." *Sur* 1970 76: 30-40; *RPu* 1970 12: 591-604.

[887] ———. "NATO and German Reunification." *ACQ* 1971 8(4): 538.

[888] GORBACHEV, B. *Mirovaia sistema sotsializma. Uspekhi, problemy i tendentsii sovremennogo etapa* [The world system of socialism. Successes, problems and tendencies of the present stage]. Riga: Liesma, 1967.

[889] GORBATOV, O. M. "SSSR i Arabskie strany (druzhestvennye sviazi)" [USSR and the Arab countries (fraternal ties)]. *NNI* 1969 (2): 78-90.

[890] ———, AND L. IA. CHERKASSKII. *Sotrudnichestvo SSSR so stranami Afriki i Arabskogo vostoka (1917-1967)* [Cooperation of the USSR with the countries of Africa and the Arab East (1917-1967)]. Moscow: Nauka, 1972.

[891] GORENOV, V. P. "Normalizatsiia torgovli-trebovanie vremeni" [The normalization of trade is a requirement of the times]. *VT* 1968 (8): 15-19.

[892] ———. "Torgovye i ekonomicheskie otnosheniia SSSR s razvivaiush-chimisia stranami Azii i Afriki" [The commercial and economic relations of the USSR with the developing countries of Asia and Africa]. *NAA* 1969 (2): 3-14.

[893] GÖRGEY, LASZLO. "New Consensus in Germany's Eastern European Policy." *WPQ* 1968 21: 681-697.

[894] GORIUNOV, V. "Ekonomicheskie otnosheniia SSSR s razvivaiushchimisia stranami i burzhuaznaia propaganda" [The economic relations of the USSR with the developing countries and bourgeois propaganda]. *VT* 1968 (1): 5-10.

[895] GORIZONTOV, B. "Transport i ego rol' v ekonomicheskom sotrudnichestve stran sotsializma" [Transport and its role in the economic cooperation of the socialist countries]. *VE* 1969 (5): 69-78.

[896] GOROKHOV, A. "Leninist Diplomacy: Principles and Traditions." *IA(M)* 1968 (4): 38-44.

[897] ———. "The Struggle of the Soviet Union for the Elimination of War Hotbeds, for International Security." *IA(M)* 1971 (7): 3-10.

[898] ———. "The USSR's Struggle for European Security." *IA(M)* 1971 (1): 3-8.

[899] ———. *G. V. Chicherin—A Diplomat of the Lenin School.* Moscow: Gospolitizdat, 1966.

[900] GORSKII, V. "Torgovaia politika EES—orudie diskriminatsii sotsialisticheskikh stran" [The commercial policy of the EEC—an instrument of discrimination against the socialist countries]. *VT* 1969 (12): 23-27.

[901] GOSHINA, L. "Aid to Developing Countries Under U.N. Auspices." *IA(M)* 1967 (7): 72-76.

[902] GOTLIEB, A. E., AND C. M. DALFEN. "International Relations and Outer Space: The Politics of Co-Operation." *IJ* 1970 25: 285-703.

[903] GRAFSKII, V. G. "Razvivaiushchiesia strany natsional'nyi vopros v svete Leninskogo analiza imperializma" [The developing countries: The national question in the light of the Leninist analysis of imperialism]. *SGP* 1971 (4): 44-50.

[904] GRAIBNER, NORMAN A. "The United States and the Soviet Union: The Elusive Peace." *CH* 1970 59: 193-198.

[905] GRAIVER, B. Z., ED. *Organizatsiia Ob"edinennykh Natsii* [The United Nations]. Moscow: Nauka, 1967.

[906] GRANOV, V. "Nature and Specific Features of Petty-Bourgeois Anticommunism." *IA(M)* 1970 (9): 12-20.

[907] GREAT BRITAIN, CENTRAL OFFICE OF INFORMATION, REFERENCE DIVISION. *Russia, China and the West.* London: H.M.S.O., 1968.

[908] GRECHKO, A. "V. I. Lenin i stroitel'stvo Sovetskikh vooruzhennykh sil" [Lenin and the building of Soviet military forces]. *Komm* 1969 (3): 15-26.

[909] GREGOR, R. "Lenin, Revolution, and Foreign Policy." *IJ* 1967 22: 563-575.

[910] GREGORY, GENE ADRIAN. "The Japanese on the East European Market." *EE* 1971 20(11): 2-5.

[911] GRIAZNOV, E. "SSSR—krupneishii importer Indiiskikh tovarov" [The USSR is the major importer of Indian goods]. *VT* 1968 (5): 13-18.

[912] GRIAZNOV, V. S., AND IU. KOLOSOV. "Mezhdunarodno-pravovoe regulirovanie otvetstvennosti v vozdushnom prave" [The international legal regulation of responsibility in air law]. *SGP* 1968 (11): 62-71.

[913] GRIFFITH, WILLIAM E. *Cold War and Coexistence: Russia, China, and the United States.* Englewood Cliffs, New Jersey: Prentice-Hall, 1971.

[914] _____.*Eastern Europe After the Soviet Invasion of Czechoslovakia.* Santa Monica, California: RAND Corporation, 1968.

[915] _____.*Moscow, Bonn, and European Security.* Cambridge: Massachusetts Institute of Technology, Center for International Studies, 1970.

[916] _____. *The Sino-Soviet-American Relationship. No. I of the Great Globe Transformed.* Cambridge: Massachusetts Institute of Technology Center for International Studies, 1971.

[917] _____. *The Soviet-American Confrontation, 1970: I. The Global Soviet-American Relationship; II. The East-West Confrontation in Europe, 1970; The Soviet-West-German Treaty and European Security; III. The Great Powers and the Middle East in 1970; IV. Sub-Sahara Africa 1970 : The Main Trends.* Cambridge: Massachusetts Institute of Technology, Center for International Studies, 1970.

[918] _____, SEWERYN BIALER, TIBOR SZAMUELY, RENATO MIELI, LEO LABEDZ, AND ANDREW EZERGAILIS. "Myths, Perceptions, and Policy: II." *PoC* 1970 19: 1-13.

[919] _____, AND WALT W. ROSTOW. *East-West Relations: Is Détente Possible?* Rational Debate Seminars, 3(3), American Enterprise Institute, 1969.

[920] _____.*See* 2310.

[921] _____, ED. *Communism in Europe: Continuity Change, and the Sino-Soviet Dispute.* Cambridge: Massachusetts Institute of Technology Press, 1967.

[922] _____, ED. *Sino-Soviet Relations, 1964-1965.* Cambridge: Massachusetts Institute of Technology Press, 1967.

[923] GRIFFITHS, FRANKLYN. "Inner Tensions in the Soviet Approach to 'Disarmament.'" *IJ* 1967 22: 593-617.

[924] GRIGOR'EV, A. *Sovetskii Soiuz -drug i brat Kitaiskogo naroda* [The Soviet Union is the friend and brother of the Chinese people]. Moscow: Novosti, 1971.

[925] GRIGOR'EV, I. "France and the USSR: Fruitful Co-operation." *IA(M)* 1967 (7): 19-24.

[926] GRIGORIAN, S. N., ED. *Ideologiia sovremennogo natsional'no-osvoboditel'nogo dvizheniia* [The ideology of the contemporary national liberation movement]. Moscow: Nauka, 1966.

[927] GRINEV, O. "Soviet Efforts for Disarmament." *IA(M)* 1967 (12): 63-69.

[928] _____, AND B. PAVLOV. "The 23rd U.N. General Assembly: Problems and Prospects." *IA(M)* 1968 (10): 66-70.

[929] GRIUNWAL'D, K. K. *Franko-Russkie Soiuzy* [Franco-Russian councils]. Moscow: I.M.O., 1968.

[930] GROMYKO, ANATOLII. *O mezhdunarodnom polozhenii i vneshnei politike Sovetskogo Soiuza* [On the international position and the foreign policy of the Soviet Union]. Moscow: Novosti, 1968.

[931] _____. "Soviet Foreign Policy and Africa." *IA(M)* 1967 (9): 23-28.

[932] _____. *See* 2143.

[933] GROSS, GEORGE. "Communism Divided: Some Considerations for American Foreign Policy." *RR* 1969 28: 137-151.

[934] GROTE, MANFRED W. H. "A New West German Policy Toward Eastern Europe." *DAI* 1968 28: 3245-A.

[935] GROTH, ALEXANDER J. *Eastern Europe After Czechoslovakia.* New York: Foreign Policy Association, Headline series, (195), 1969.

[936] GROTHE, JOHN P. "Attitude Change of American Tourists in the Soviet Union." *DAI* 1970 31: 1856-A.

[937] GRUB, PHILLIP D., AND KAREL HOLBIK. *American-East European Trade: Controversy, Progress Prospects.* Washington, D.C.: National Press, 1969.

[938] GRUBER, HELMUT, ED. *International Communism in the Era of Lenin.* Greenwich, Connecticut: Fawcett Publications; Ithaca, New York: Cornell University, 1967.

[939] GRUNDY, KENNETH W. "Africa in the World Arena: The Communist World and Africa." *CH* 1967 52: 132-134.

[940] GRZYBOWSKI, KAZIMIERZ. "The Foreign Trade Regime in the COMECON Countries Today." *NYUJIL* 1971 4: 183-211.

[941] _____. *Soviet Public International Law: Doctrines and Diplomatic Practice.* Leyden: A. W. Sijthoff; Durham: North Carolina Rule of Law Press, 1970.

[942] GUBIN, V. F. *Karl Marks i mezhdunarodnoe pravo* [Karl Marx and international law]. Moscow: Znanie, 1969.

[943] GUERIN, ALAIN. "Web of Anti-Communism." *NT* 1970 (4): 29-31.

[944] GULIEV, V. E. *Demokratiia i sovremennyi imperializm* [Democracy and contemporary imperialism]. Moscow: I.M.O., 1970.

[945] GUPTA, SISIR. "The Third World and the Great Powers." *A,AAPSS* 1969 386: 54-63.

[946] GURIEL, BORIS. "The Mediterranean in Soviet Strategic Thinking." *NME* November 1970 (26): 2024.

[947] ———. "Two Hundred Years of Russian Interests in the Mediterranean." *NME* November 1968 (2): 35-41.

[948] GURNEY, RAMSDELL JR. "From Recognition to Munich: Official and Historiographical Soviet Views of Soviet-American Relations, 1933-1938." *DAI* 1969 30: 2459-A.

[949] GURTOV, MELVIN. *Sino-Soviet Relations and Southeast Asia: Recent Developments and Future Possibilities.* Santa Monica, California: RAND Corporation, 1970.

[950] ———. "Sino-Soviet Relations and Southeast Asia: Recent Developments and Future Possibilities." *PA* 1970 63: 491-505.

[951] GUSAREVICH, S. *See* 130.

[952] GUSAROV, V. I., AND N. S. SEMIN. *Strany sotsializma—vernye druz'ia Arabskikh narodov* [The socialist countries are the true friends of the Arab peoples]. Moscow: Politizdat, 1971.

[953] GUSEINOV, K. A. *Internatsional'nye sviazi profsoiuzov SSSR s profsoiuzami stran Azii i Afriki* [The international ties of the Soviet labor unions with the labor unions of the countries of Asia and Africa]. Moscow: Nauka, 1965. English translation, 1967.

[954] GUSEVA, N. "Sodeistvie SSSR v razvitii meditsinskoi promyshlennosti Indii" [The assistance of the USSR in the development of medical facilities in India]. *VT* 1969 (3): 30-31.

[955] GUYOT, R. "International Meeting—Big Success for World Communist Movement." *WMR* 1969 12(10): 15-20.

[956] GVISHIANI, D. "Soviet Scientific and Technical Cooperation With Other Countries." *IA(M)* 1970 (2-3): 46-52.

[957] ———. "The USSR's International Scientific and Technical Ties and the Prospects for Their Development." *IA(M)* 1971 (7): 22-30.

[958] GVISHIANI, L. A. *Sovetskaia Rossiia i SShA, 1917-1920 g* [Soviet Russia and the USA, 1917-1920]. Moscow: I.M.O., 1970.

[959] GYORGY, ANDREW. "Competitive Patterns of Nationalism in Eastern Europe." *CSIP* 1968 10: 557-580.

[960]   ————. "Diversity in Eastern Europe: Cohesion and Disunity." *CSlSt* 1967 1: 24-43; and *NWCR* 1967 19(2): 76-104.

[961]   ————. "Ideological Diversity and Political Nationalism in Eastern Europe." *TSJIA* 1969 4(1): 1-15.

[962]   HAAS, ARLIN. "Soviet Strategic and Political Concepts: An Analysis." *StSU* 1970 10: 1-18.

[963]   HABTER, HELWAN M. "The United Arab Republic's Relations With the USSR Between the Suez, 1956, and the June, 1967, Wars." *MA* 1971 9: 88.

[964]   HADIK, LASZLO. "The Process of Détente in Europe." *Orb* 1970 13: 1008-1028, and *ACQ* 1970 8: 325-334.

[965]   HAGER, DAVID RUSSELL. "Space Law, the United Nations, and the Super Powers: A Study of International Legal Development and Codification, 1957-1969." *DAI* 1971 31: 4866-A.

[966]   HAGERTY, J. "The Soviet Share in the War Against Japan." *B,ISUSSR* 1970 17(9): 5-15.

[967]   HAIGH, PATRICIA. "Reflections on the Warsaw Pact." *WT* 1968 24: 166-172.

[968]   HAITHCOX, JOHN PATRICK. *Communism and Nationalism in India: M. N. Roy and Comintern Policy, 1920-1939.* Princeton, New Jersey: Princeton University Press, 1971.

[969]   HAJENKO, F. "Soviet Criticism of the Convergence Theory." *B,ISUSSR* 1970 17: 49-58.

[970]   HALBROOK, STEPHEN. "'Bakuninist' Chinese Versus 'Marxist' Russians: A Key to the Sino-Soviet Rift." *JCRV* 1971 3(4): 68-73.

[971]   HALLE, LOUIS J. *The Cold War as History.* New York: Harper and Row, 1967.

[972]   ————. "A Multitude of Cold Wars." *IJ* 1968 23: 335-343.

[973]   HALPERIN, MORTON H. "Prospects for SALT." *AJIL* 1970 64: 200-202.

[974]   ————, ED. *Sino-Soviet Relations and Arms Control.* Cambridge: Massachusetts Institute of Technology Press, 1967.

[975]   HAMBURG, ROGER P. "Soviet and Chinese Revolutionary Strategy: Comparison and Evaluation at the Present." *ASt* 1968 6: 340-357.

[976]   ————. "Soviet Foreign Policy: The Church, the Christian Democrats, and Chile." *JI-ASt* 1969 11: 571-604.

[977]   HAMBY, ALONZO L. "Henry A. Wallace, the Liberals, and Soviet-American Relations." *RP* 1968 30: 153-169.

[978] HAMOUZ, F., AND N. NOVIKOV. "Growing Czechoslovak-Soviet Cooperation." *WMR* 1968 11(12): 11-15.

[979] HANRIEDER, WOLFRAM F. "Reunification, Chapter 3." In *Stable Crisis: Two Decades of German Foreign Policy.* New York: 1970 87-128.

[980] ———. "West German Foreign Policy: Background to Current Issues." *Orb* 1970 13: 1029-1049.

[981] HANSON, PHILIP. "The Rise of the Soviet Merchant Marine." *WT* 1970 26: 130-136.

[982] ———. "Soviet Imports of Primary Products: A Case-Study of Cocoa." *SSt* 1971 23: 59-77.

[983] ———. "The Soviet Union and World Shipping." *SSt* 1970 22: 44-60.

[984] HARLE, VILHO. "Actional Distances Between the Socialist Countries in the 1960's." *CaC* 1971 6: 201-222.

[985] HAROCHE, CHARLES. "Europe: From Split to Cooperation." *IA(M)* 1970 (4): 62-69.

[986] HARRIMAN, AVERELL. *America and Russia in a Changing World: A Half Century of Personal Observation.* Garden City, New York: Doubleday, 1971.

[987] HARRIS, DENNIS EARL. "The Diplomacy of the Second Front: America, Britain, Russia and the Normandy Invasion." *DAI* 1971 31: 5985-A.

[988] HARRISON, STANLEY L. "NATO's Role After Czechoslovakia." *MR* 1969 49(7): 12-23.

[989] HART, B. H. LIDDELL, ED. *The Red Army: The Red Army, 1918-1945; The Soviet Army, 1946 to the Present.* Gloucester, Massachusetts: Peter Smith, 1968.

[990] HARTLEY, ANTHONY. "Europe Between the Superpowers." *FA* 1971 49: 271-282.

[991] HARTMANN, FREDERICK H. "The Meaning and Implication of the Sino-Soviet Split." *NWCR* 1967 20(4): 14-28.

[992] ———. "Meaning of the Crisis in Czechoslovakia." *NWCR* 1969 21(6): 43-48.

[993] HARVEY, MOSE L. "Lunar Landing and the U.S.-Soviet Equation." *BAS* 1969 25(7): 28-35.

[994] ———. *See* 1368.

[995] HASAN, ZUBEIDA. "Pakistan's Relations With the USSR in the 1960's." *WT* 1969 25: 26-35.

[996] ———. "Soviet Arms Aid to Pakistan and India." *PH* 1969 21(4): 344-355.

[997] HASHAVIA, ARIE. "The Soviet Fleet in the Mediterranean." *MR* 1967 47(2): 79-81.

[998] HASSNER, PIERRE. "The Implications of Change in Eastern Europe for the Atlantic Alliance." *Orb* 1969 13: 237-255.

[999] HATA, IKUHIKO. *Reality and Illusion: The Hidden Crisis Between Japan and the USSR, 1932-1934.* New York: East Asian Institute, Columbia University, 1967.

[1000] HAUPTMANN, JERZY. "Persistent Communism-Accommodating Democracy." *CEJ* 1970 18: 360-369.

[1001] HAVIGHURST, CLARK C., ED. *International Control of Propaganda.* Dobbs Ferry, New York: Oceana, 1967.

[1002] HAYES, JOHN D. "The Soviet Navy in the Caribbean Sea and Gulf of Mexico." *IP* 1971 4(1): 5-9.

[1003] HAYTER, WILLIAM. *The Kremlin and the Embassy.* New York: Macmillan, 1967.

[1004] ———. *Russia and the World: A Study of Soviet Foreign Policy.* New York: Taplinger Publishing Company, 1970.

[1005] HAZARD, JOHN N. "Marxian Socialism in Africa: The Case of Mali." *CP* 1969 2: 1-16.

[1006] ———. "Renewed Emphasis upon a Socialist International Law." *AJIL* 1971 65: 142-148.

[1007] ———. "The Residue of Marxist Influence in Algeria." *CJTL* 1970 9: 194-225.

[1008] HEALEY, DENIS W. "NATO, Britain and Soviet Military Policy." *Orb* 1969 13: 48-58.

[1009] HEATHCOTE, NINA. "Brandt's Ostpolitik and Western Institutions." *WT* 1970 26: 334-343.

[1010] ———. "Western Integration and German Reunification, 1966-1968." *JCMSt* 1968 7: 102-118.

[1011] HEDLEY, JOHN H. "Moscow's New Look in Western Europe." *YR* 1967 56: 390-396.

[1012] HEDLIN, MYRON WALTER. "Zinoviev, the Comintern and European Revolution, 1919-1926." *DAI* 1971 32: 883-A.

[1013] HEISS, HERTHA W. "The Council for Mutual Economic Assistance—Developments Since the Mid-1960's." In *Economic Developments in Countries of Eastern Europe: A Compendium of Papers, Submitted to the Subcommittee on Foreign Economic Policy of the Joint Economic Committee, Congress of the United States,* pp. 528-542. Washington, D.C.: United States Government Printing Office, 1970.

[1014] HELDMAN, DAN C. "The Sino-Soviet Split and Party Legitimacy." *Sur* 1970 77: 51-58.

[1015] ———. "Soviet Relations With the Developing States: An Application of Correlation Analysis." In *The Behavioral Revolution and Communist Studies,* pp. 339-364, edited by Roger E. Kanet. New York: Free Press, 1971.

[1016] HELIN, RONALD A. "Finland Regains an Outlet to the Sea: The Saimaa Canal." *GM* 1968 58: 5-16.

[1017] HELLMANN, DONALD C. *Japanese Domestic Politics and Foreign Policy: The Peace Agreement With the Soviet Union.* Berkeley: University of California Press, 1969.

[1018] HENTGES, P. "A High Priority: To Invigorate the Anti-Imperialist Front." *WMR* 1971 14(10): 116-119.

[1019] HEN-TOV, JACOB. "The Comintern and Zionism in Palestine: An Inquiry into the Circumstances Surrounding the Comintern's Involvement in the 1929 Riots in Palestine." *DAI* 1969 30: 2460-A.

[1020] HERMANN, RUDOLF. "Can COMECON Integrate?" *EE* 1969 18(5): 15-18.

[1021] HERRICK, ROBERT WARING. *Soviet Naval Strategy: Fifty Years of Theory and Practice.* Annapolis: United States Naval Institute, 1968.

[1022] HEYDEN, G. "Anti-Communism and Its Manifestations." *WMR* 1971 14(6): 123-132.

[1023] HIGGINS, T. *Hitler and Russia: The Third Reich in a Two-Front War, 1937-1943.* London: Collier-Macmillan, 1967.

[1024] HILDNER, ROBERT E. *See* 2343.

[1025] HILTON, RONALD. "Is Cuba a Typical Soviet Satellite?" *Report of the California Institute of International Studies.* 1971 1: 45-54.

[1026] HINTERHOFF, EUGENE. "German Reunification and Poland's Interests." *PG* 1967 11(39-40): 7-13.

[1027] ———. "The Question of German Unification." *PG* 1969 13(1-2): 33-42.

[1028]   ———. "Soviet Penetration into the Middle East." *CR* 1968 212: 61-70.

[1029]   ———. "The Soviet Presence in the Mediterranean." *Orb* 1969 13: 261-269.

[1030]   ———. "The Soviet Threat Since Czechoslovakia." *MR* 1970 50: 68-73.

[1031] HINTON, HAROLD C. "Conflict on the Ussuri: A Clash of Nationalisms." *PoC* 1971 20(1-2): 45-61.

[1032]   ———. "Sino-Soviet Relations in the Brezhnev Era." *CH* 1971 60: 135-141.

[1033] HIRSCHMAN, A. C. *Soviet Bloc—Latin American Relations and United States Policy, RM-2457-1.* Santa Monica, California: RAND Corporation, 1967.

[1034] HIRSCHMANN, IRA. *Red Star Over Bethlehem: Russia Drives to Capture the Middle East.* New York: Simon and Schuster, 1971.

[1035] "Historical Significance of the Great October Socialist Revolution. Papers Delivered at a Seminar Sponsored by Problems of Peace and Socialism in Prague, June 22-24, 1967." *WMR* 1967 10(8): 7-72, (9): 21-62, (10): 37-80, (11): 45-86.

[1036] HITCHCOCK, DAVID I., JR. "Joint Development of Siberia: Decision-Making in Japanese-Soviet Relations." *AsS* 1971 11: 279-300.

[1037] HOAGLAND, JOHN H. "Arms in the Third World." *Orb* 1970 14: 500-504.

[1038] HODGSON, JOHN H. "Soviet Foreign Policy: Mental Alienation or Universal Revolution?" *WPQ* 1971 24: 653-666.

[1039] HODNETT, GREY, AND PETER J. POTICHNYJ. *The Ukraine and the Czechoslovak Crisis. Occasional Paper No. 6 Dept. of Political Science, Research School of Social Sciences.* Canberra: Australian National U.P., 1970.

[1040] HOEFFDING, OLEG. *Recent Structural Changes and Balance of Payment Adjustments in Soviet Foreign Trade.* Santa Monica, California: RAND Corporation, 1967.

[1041]   ———.*Soviet Interdiction Operations, 1941-1945.* Santa Monica, California: RAND Corporation, 1970.

[1042] HOFFMANN, ERIK P., AND FREDERIC J. FLERON, JR., ED. *The Conduct of Soviet Foreign Policy.* Chicago: Aldine-Atherton, 1971.

[1043] HÖHNE, HEINZ. *Codeword: Director: The Story of the Red Orchestra.* New York: Coward, McCann and Geoghegan, 1971.

[1044] HOLBIK, KAREL. "A Comparison of U.S. and Soviet Foreign Aid, 1961-1965." *WA* 1968 100: 320-340.

[1045] ———. *The United States, the Soviet Union, and the Third World.* Hamburg: Verlag Weltarchiv, 1968.

[1046] ———, AND EDWARD DRACHMAN. "Egypt as Recipient of Soviet Aid, 1955-1970." *Zeitschrift für die gesamte Staatswissenschaft* 1971 127: 137-165.

[1047] ———. *See* 937.

[1048] HOLLOWAY, DAVID. "Strategic Concepts and Soviet Policy." *Surv* 1971 13: 364-369.

[1049] ———. "Technology, Management and the Soviet Military Establishment." *AP* 1971 76: 1-44.

[1050] HOLOWATY, LUBA ANASTESIA. "The Soviet Union and Countries of the African Horn: A Case Study of Soviet Perceptions and Policies, 1959-1968." *DAI* 1970 31: 3001-A.

[1051] HOLST, JOHAN J. *Comparative U.S. and Soviet Deployments, Doctrines, and Arms Limitation.* Chicago: University of Chicago, Center for Policy Study, 1971.

[1052] ———. "The Soviet Union and Nordic Security." *CaC* 1971 6: 137-146.

[1053] HOLSTI, OLE R. "Cognitive Dynamics and Images of the Enemy." *JIA* 1967 21: 16-39.

[1054] HOLT, STEPHEN, AND KEN STAPLETON. "Yugoslavia and the European Community, 1958-1970." *JCMSt* 1971 10: 47-57.

[1055] HOLZMAN, FRANKLYN D. "The Ruble Exchange Rate and Soviet Foreign Trade Pricing Policies, 1929-1961." *AER* 1968 58: 803-825.

[1056] ———. "Soviet Trade and Aid Policies." *APS,P* 1969 24: 104-120.

[1057] HOOVER, CALVIN B. "Soviet Economic Policies at Home and Abroad." *APS,P* 1971 30(3): 184-193.

[1058] HOPMANN, PHILIP TERRENCE. "The Effects of International Conflict and Détente on Cohesion in the Communist System." In *The Behavioral Revolution and Communist Studies,* pp. 301-338, edited by Roger E. Kanet. New York: Free Press, 1971.

[1059] ———. "International Conflict and Cohesion in International Political Coalitions: NATO and the Communist System During Postwar Years." *DAI* 1970 30: 3526-A.

[1060] ———. "International Conflict and Cohesion in the Communist System." *IStQ* 1967 11: 212-236.

[1061] HORELICK, A. L. *See* 171.

[1062] HORN, ROBERT C. "Soviet-Indonesian Relations Since 1965." *Sur* 1971 16(1): 216ff.

[1063] HORVATH, JANOS. "A Comparative Appraisal of Economic Aid (U.S. and USSR)." *DAI* 1969 30: 1695-A.

[1064] _____. "Economic Aid Flow from the USSR: A Recount of the First Fifteen Years." *SIR* 1970 29: 613-632.

[1065] _____. "International Grants as Policy Instruments: The Case of the USSR." In *The Grants Economy in an International Perspective,* edited by Kenneth E. Boulding, et al. Belmont, California: Wadsworth, 1971.

[1066] HOWARD, PETER. "Cambodia and the War in Indochina: The Soviet View." *Miz* 1970 12: 80-90.

[1067] _____. "The Cold War—Second Phase: China." *IJ* 1968 23: 421-434.

[1068] _____. "Moscow, Jakarta, and the PKI." *Miz* 1969 11: 105-118.

[1069] _____. "Russia, China, and South-East Asia." *Miz* 1968 10: 156-161.

[1070] _____. "Soviet Policies in Southeast Asia." *IJ* 1968 23: 435-455.

[1071] _____. "Soviet Relations With Malaysia and Singapore." *Miz* 1968 10: 29-34.

[1072] _____. "The Soviet Union and the Philippines: Prospects for Improved Relations." *Miz* 1968 10: 96-102.

[1073] _____. "A System of Collective Security." *Miz* 1969 11: 199-204.

[1074] _____. "The USSR and Indonesia." *Miz* 1967 9: 108-117.

[1075] _____. "The USSR and the Indian Political Crisis." *Miz* 1969 11: 315-320.

[1076] HOWE, JONATHAN T. *Coping with Multicrises: Sea Power and Global Politics in the Missile Age.* Cambridge: Massachusetts Institute of Technology Press, 1970.

[1077] _____. "Soviet Beachhead in the Fluid World." *USNI,P* October 1968 94: 60-67.

[1078] HOYA, THOMAS W. "The COMECON General Conditions—A Socialist Unification of International Trade Law." *CLR* 1970 70: 253-306.

[1079] HUDSON, G. F. *The Hard and Bitter Peace: World Politics Since 1945.* New York: Praeger, 1967.

[1080] HUGHES, BARRY, AND THOMAS VOLGY. "Distance in Foreign Policy Behavior: A Comparative Study of Eastern Europe. *MJPS* 1970 14: 459-492.

[1081] HUGHES, R. D. "Soviet Foreign Policy and Germany, 1945 to 1948." *DAI* 1968 28: 4224-A.

[1082] HULL, HENRY L. "The Holy See and Soviet Russia, 1918-1930: A Study in Full-Circle Diplomacy." *DAI* 1971 31: 4087-A.

[1083] HUMPHREY, HUBERT H. "The Course of Soviet Foreign Policy and Soviet-American Relations in the 1970's." *Orb* 1971 15(1): 65-71.

[1084] HUNCZAK, TARAS. "'Operation Winter' and the Struggle for the Baltic." *EEQ* 1970 4: 40-57.

[1085] HUNTER, ROBERT E. "Are the Russians Really a Mediterranean Threat?" *NME* January 1969 (4): 7-12.

[1086] ———. "The Future of Soviet-American Détente." *WT* 1968 24: 281-289.

[1087] ———. "The Soviet Dilemma in the Middle East." *AP* 1969: 59-60.

[1088] HUNTLEY, JAMES R. *See* 340.

[1089] HUPKA, HERBERT. "European Eastern Policy—Soviet European Policy." *CEJ* 1971 19: 274-276.

[1090] ———. "German-Polish Relations Still Not Normalized." *CEJ* 1971 19: 149-150.

[1091] HUREWITZ, J. C., ED. "Soviet-American Rivalry in the Middle East." *APS,P* 1969 29(3): 1-250. Also published separately by New York: Praeger, 1969.

[1092] HUTCHINGS, RAYMOND. "Soviet Defense Spending and Soviet External Relations." *IA(L)* 47: 518-531.

[1093] HUTTON, C. POWELL. "Changing Soviet Oil Interests: Implications for the Middle East." *NWCR* 1971 24(8): 76-93.

[1094] IAKOVLEV, A. *World Socialist System and National Liberation Movement.* Moscow: Novosti Press Agency, 1968.

[1095] IAKOVLEV, M. D., ED. *Vneshniaia politika Sovetskogo Soiuza. Aktual'nye problemy, 1967-1970* [The foreign policy of the Soviet Union. Actual problems, 1967-70]. Moscow: I.M.O., 1970.

[1096] IAKOVLEV, N. N. "SSSR-SShA: Motivy sotrudnichestva i konflikta (1941-1945)" [USSR-USA: Motives of cooperation and conflict (1941-1945)]. *SShA* 1970 (5): 12-23.

[1097] IAKUBOVSKII, I. "Boevoe sodruzhestvo armii stran sotsializma" [The fighting collaboration of the armies of the socialist countries]. *Komm* 1970 (5): 90-100.

[1098] IAKUSHIN, A. "Sotrudnichestvo stran SEV v reshenii toplivnoi problemy" [The cooperation of the countries of CMEA in the solution of the fuel problem]. *VT* 1971 (1): 5-8.

[1099] IANAEV, G. "Soviet Youth: International Contacts." *NT* 1970 (44): 16-17.

[1100] IANOVSKII, M. V. "Rol' OON v formirovanii norm kosmicheskogo prava" [The role of the UN in the formulation of norms of space law]. *SGP* 1969 (11): 65-68.

[1101] IATRIDES, JOHN O. *Balkan Triangle: Birth and Decline of an Alliance Across Ideological Boundaries.* The Hague and Paris: Mouton, 1968.

[1102] IAZKOVA, ALLA. "Imperialism and Eastern Europe." *NT* 1968 (48): 13-14.

[1103] *Idei Oktiabria i ideologiia natsional'no-osvoboditel'nogo dvizheniia* [The ideas of October and the ideology of the national-liberation movement]. Moscow: Nauka, 1968.

[1104] IGNATEUKO, G. V. *Mezhdunarodnoe pravo i obshchestvennyi progress* [International law and social progress]. Moscow: I.M.O., 1972.

[1105] IGNOTUS, PAUL. "Czechs, Magyars, Slovaks." *PQ* 1969 40: 187-204.

[1106] IGOSHKIN, G. S. *Neitralitet—vozmozhnosti i perspektivy* [Neutrality—possibilities and prospects]. Kiev: Znanie, 1968.

[1107] IKONNIKOV, I. "CMEA's Role in Cooperation Between the Socialist Countries." *IA(M)* 1969 (4): 65-70.

[1108] IL'IN, IU. D. *Osnovnye tendentsii v razvitii konsul'skogo prava* [The basic tendencies in the development of consular law]. Moscow: Iuridicheskaia literatura, 1969.

[1109] IL'IN, V. "Vozmozhnosti i perspektivy torgovli s Islandiei" [The possibility and perspectives of trade with Iceland]. *VT* 1968 (11): 21-22.

[1110] IMAM, ZAFAR. *Colonialism in East-West Relations: A Study of Soviet Policy Toward India and Anglo-Soviet Relations, 1917-1947.* New Delhi: Eastman Publications, 1969.

[1111] *The Impact of the Russian Revolution 1917-1967: The Influence of Bolshevism on the World Outside Russia.* London and New York: Oxford University Press, 1967.

[1112] "India-Union of Soviet Socialist Republics: Treaty of Peace, Friendship and Co-Operation." *ILM* 1971 10(5): 904-908.

[1113] INOKI, MASAMICHI. *See* 2777.

[1114] INOZEMSTEV, A. N. "Sovremennye SShA i Sovetskaia Amerikanistika" [The contemporary United States and Soviet American studies]. *SShA* 1970 (1): 6-14.

[1115] INOZEMTSEV,N. N. "Oktiabr', mezhdunarodnye otnosheniia i sotsial'nyi progress chelovechestva" [October, international relations and the social progress of man]. *MEMO* 1967 (11): 4-23.

[1116] _____, ED. *OON: Itogi, tendentsii, perspektivy* [The UN: Results, tendencies, prospects]. Moscow: I.M.O., 1970.

[1117] "The International Importance of the Ninth Soviet Five-Year Plan." *IA(M)* 1971 (5): 3-8.

[1118] *International Meeting of Communist and Workers' Parties, Moscow, 1969: Official Documents and Complete Speeches of All Delegation Heads.* Moscow: Novosti, 1969.

[1119] *Internationalism. National-Liberation Movement and Our Epoch.* Moscow: Novosti Press, 1967.

[1120] "Internatsional'naia solidarnost' Kommunistov" [The international solidarity of Communists]. *Komm* 1968 (5): 3-11.

[1121] IOFFE, A. E. *Internatsional'nye nauchnye i kul'turnye sviazi Sovetskogo Soiuza, 1928-1932* [International scientific and cultural ties of the Soviet Union, 1928-1932]. Moscow: Nauka, 1969.

[1122] _____. "Mezhdunarodnye nauchnye i kul'turnye sviazi Sovetskogo Soiuza (1917-1932 gg)" [International scientific and cultural ties of the Soviet Union (1917-1932)]. *VI* 1969 (4): 51-66.

[1123] _____. "SSSR i Latinskaia Amerika (kul'turnye sviazi do Vtoroi Mirovoi Voiny)" [The USSR and Latin America (cultural ties before the Second World War)]. *NAA* 1967 (3): 81-89.

[1124] _____. *Vneshniaia politika Sovetskogo Soiuza 1928-1932* [The foreign policy of the Soviet Union 1928-1932]. Moscow: Nauka, 1968.

[1125] IOIRYSH, A. I. *Atomnaia bomba: Istoriia i sovremennost'* [The atom bomb: History and the present]. Moscow: I.M.O., 1970.

[1126] IONESCU, GHITA. "Action and Reaction in the Soviet Bloc." *WT* 1968 24: 179-188.

[1127] _____. "The Austrian State Treaty and Neutrality in Eastern Europe." *IJ* 1968 23: 408-420.

[1128] IRANDOOST, F. J. "Soviet-Iran Relations: Some Long Term Considerations." *Miz* 1969 11: 255-257.

[1129] Iscaro, R. "Peaceful Coexistence and Revolutionary Struggle." *WMR* 1970 13(10): 10-15.

[1130] Iskenderov, A. "The International Working Class and the Anti-Imperialistic Struggle." *IA(M)* 1970 (12): 3-9.

[1131] Iskra, Wieslaw. "Vital Aspects of Socialist Integration." *WMR* 1971 14(11): 87-92.

[1132] Iskrov, M. V., ed. *V. I. Lenin i mezhdunarodnoe Kommunisticheskoe dvizhenie* [V. I. Lenin and the international Communist movement]. Moscow: I.P.L., 1970.

[1133] Israelian, V. "International Security and the United Nations." *IA(M)* 1970 (11): 72-77.

[1134] ———. "The Leninist Science of International Relations and Foreign Policy Reality." *IA(M)* 1967 (6): 46-51.

[1135] ———.*Mezhdunarodnoe znachenie Velikoi Pobedy* [The international meaning of the Great Victory]. Moscow: Politizdat, 1970.

[1136] ———. "The October Revolution and Foreign Policy." *IA(M)* 1967 (9): 3-9.

[1137] ———, et al. *Soviet Foreign Policy: A Brief Review, 1955-65*. Moscow: Progress, 1967.

[1138] ———, et al. *Vneshniaia politika Sovetskogo Soiuza* [The foreign policy of the Soviet Union]. Moscow: Progress, 1967.

[1139] Istiagin, L. "The G.D.R. and Its Place in Europe." *NT* 1967 (41): 4-6.

[1140] *Istoricheskii opyt bratskogo sodruzhestva KPSS i MNRP v bor'be za sotsializm* [The historical task of fraternal collaboration of the CPSU and Mongolian NRP in the struggle for socialism]. Moscow: Politizdat, 1971.

[1141] Isupov, V. "Torgovlia SSSR s GDR" [Trade of the USSR with the GDR]. *VT* 1969 (2): 14-17.

[1142] Iugov, L. "USSR-Italy: Growing Links." *IA(M)* 1971 (7): 51-55.

[1143] Iur'ev, N. "European Security: A Dictate of Our Times." *IA(M)* 1970 (8): 3-7.

[1144] ———. "Imperialism—Source of Violence, Aggression, and Wars." *IA(M)* 1969 (10): 54-60.

[1145] ———.*See* 2480.

[1146] ———.*See* 2481.

[1147] Iur'ev, P. "Socialist Economic Integration." *NT* 1971 (33): 6-8.

[1148] IURKOV, S. "Peking's Policy Towards the Socialist Countries." *IA(M)* 1971 (11): 17-24.

[1149] IUSUPOV, I. A. *Ustanovlenie i razvitie Sovetsko-Iranskikh otnoshenii (1917-1927gg)* [The establishment and development of Soviet-Iranian relations (1917-1927)]. Tashkent: FAN, 1969.

[1150] IVANOV, A., AND IU. SEMONOV. "Socialist Countries' Industrial Cooperation and Progress." *IA(M)* 1968 (8): 34-40.

[1151] IVANOV, K. "Founder of Soviet Foreign Policy." *NT* 1970 (16): 4-7.

[1152] _____. "Lessons for the Future (on Czechoslovakia)." *IA(M)* 1968 (10): 3-10.

[1153] IVANOV, N. I. *Mezhdunarodnye ekonomicheskie otnosheniia novogo tipa* [International economic relations of a new type]. Moscow: Ekonomika, 1968.

[1154] IVANOV, V. E. "Regulirovanie mezhdunarodnogo turizma" [The regulation of international tourism]. *SGP* 1969 (12): 126-130.

[1155] IVANOVA, I. "Antikommunizm i kontseptsiia 'Antlanticheskogo Soobshchestva'" [Anti-Communism and the conception of an "Atlantic Community"]. *MEMO* 1970 (6): 3-10.

[1156] IVANOVA, M. "U istokov Sovetsko-Iranskikh otnoshenii." [At the sources of Soviet-Iranian relations]. *AAS* 1969 (11): 9-11.

[1157] *Iz istorii Kommunisitcheskogo Internatsionala. O II Kongresse Kominterna. Sbornik* [From the history of the Communist International. Concerning the Second Congress of the Comintern. A collection]. Moscow: Politizdat, 1971.

[1158] JACKSON, D. BRUCE. *Castro, the Kremlin, and Communism in Latin America.* Baltimore, Maryland: Johns Hopkins Press, 1969.

[1159] JACKSON, HENRY M. "Czechoslovakia and Western Security." *BAS* 1969 25(1): 36-38.

[1160] JACKSON, W. A. D. *The Russo-Chinese Borderlands.* 2nd edn. Princeton, New Jersey: Van Nostrand, 1968.

[1161] JACOBS, DAN N. "Recent Russian Material on Soviet Advisers in China." *CQ* 1970 41(12): 103-112.

[1162] _____, ED. *The New Communisms.* New York: Harper and Row, 1969.

[1163] JACOBS, WALTER DARNELL. "Brezhnev's New Doctrine." *MR* 1970 50: 3-10.

[1164] _____. "Soviet View of Wars of National Liberation." *MR* 1967 47(10): 59-66.

[1165] JAMES, ROBERT R. "International Crisis, the Great Powers, and the United Nations." *IJ* 1970 25: 245-255.

[1166] JAMGOTCH, NISH A., JR. "Eastern Europe as a Soviet Core Interest." *DAI* 1968 28: 4238-A.

[1167] ———.*Soviet-East European Dialogue: International Relations of a New Type?* Stanford: Hoover Institution, 1968.

[1168] JANCAR, BARBARA. "The Great Purges and 'The Prague Spring.'" *Orb* 1971 15: 609-624.

[1169] JAROSINSKI, W. "Imperialist War Policy and Unity of the World Communist Movement." *WMR* 1968 11(7): 33-37.

[1170] JASTER, ROBERT S. "Foreign Aid and Economic Development: The Shifting Soviet View." *IA(L)* 1969 45: 452-464.

[1171] JASZCZUK, B. "CMEA and Integration of Socialist Countries." *WMR* 1969 12(9): 44-48.

[1172] JASZI, OSCAR. *Revolution and Counter Revolution in Hungary.* New York: Fertig, 1969.

[1173] JEDRYCHOWSKI, STEFAN."Minister Jedrychowski on Polish-Soviet Relations." *NT* 1969 (9): 1-3.

[1174] JESSUP PHILIP C. "The Berlin Blockade and the Use of the United Nations." *FA* 1971 50: 163-173.

[1175] JIJON, MILTON. "Lenin's Teaching on Imperialism and Our Time." *WMR* 1970 13(3): 59-62.

[1176] JIRANEK, SLAVOMIR. "Economic Relations Between Socialist Countries." *Co* 1971 8: 23-26.

[1177] JOHNSON, A. ROSS. "Franco-Polish Relations." *Surv* 1967 9: 387-392.

[1178] "Joint Soviet-Egyptian Communiqué." *NT* 1971 (43): 4-6.

[1179] JONES, ROBERT HUHN. *The Roads to Russia: United States Lend Lease to the Soviet Union.* Norman: University of Oklahoma Press, 1969.

[1180] JORDAN, LLOYD. "Scientific and Technical Relations Among European Communist Systems." *Min* 1970 8: 376-395.

[1181] JORDAN, ROBERT S. *Europe and the Superpowers.* Boston, Massachusetts: Allyn and Bacon, Incorporated, 1971.

[1182] JOSHUA, WYNFRED. "Arms for Love of Allah." *USNI,P* 1970 96(3): 30-39.

[1183] ———.*Soviet Penetration in the Middle East.* Washington, D.C.: National Strategy Information Center, 1970.

[1184] _____, AND STEPHEN P. GILBERT. *Arms for the Third World: Soviet Military Aid Diplomacy.* Baltimore, Maryland: Johns Hopkins Press, 1969.

[1185] _____.*See* 842.

[1186] JOWITT, KENNETH. "The Romanian Communist Party and the World Socialist System: A Redefinition of Unity." *WP* 1970 23: 38-60.

[1187] JOYCE, JAMES A. "Toward Ending the Cold War in Europe." *W/PR* 1970 10(5): 8-11.

[1188] JUKES, GEOFFREY. "The Soviet Union and the Indian Ocean." *Surv* 1971 13: 370-375.

[1189] JULIAN, THOMAS A. "Operation Frantic and the Search for American-Soviet Military Collaboration, 1941-1944." *DAI* 1968 29: 1193-A.

[1190] JUVILER, PETER. "Soviet Motivation for the Invasion [of Czechoslo-vakia], and Domestic Support." *StNCE* 1968-9 2(3): 93-100.

[1191] "K izucheniiu materialov XXIV S"ezda KPSS: Mezdunarodnoe po-lozhenie SSSR; vneshnepoliticheskaia deiatel'nost' KPSS" [The study of materials of the 24th Congress of the CPSU: The interna-tional position of the USSR; foreign policy activities of the CPSU]. *PS* 1971 (6): 78-84.

[1192] *K sobytiiam v Chekoslovakii. Fakty, dokumenty, svidetel'stva pressy i ochevidtsev* [Events in Czechoslovakia. Facts, documents, evidence of the press and eye-witness accounts]. Moscow: Press-gruppa sov. zhurnalistov, 1968.

[1193] "K 100-letiiu so dnia rozhdeniia Vladimira Il'icha Lenina. Tesisy Tsentral'nogo Komiteta Kommunisticheskoi Partii Sovetskogo Soi-uza" [Commemorating the 100th anniversary of the birth of Vladi-mir Ilich Lenin. The theses of the Central Committee of the Communist Party of the Soviet Union]. *Komm* 1970 (1): 3-37.

[1194] KACHANOV, V. *Piat'desiat let kursom mira* [Fifty years on the path of peace]. Moscow: Novosti, 1967.

[1195] KAHAN, JEROME H. "Strategies for SALT." *WP* 1971 23: 171-188.

[1196] KAIE, V. *See* 515.

[1197] KAISER, KARL. *German Foreign Policy in Transition: Bonn Between East and West.* New York: Oxford University Press, 1968.

[1198] _____. "The Interaction of Regional Subsystems: Some Preliminary Notes on Recurrent Patterns and the Role of Superpowers." *WP* 1968 21: 84-107.

[1199] _____. "Two Germanys Between Two Worlds." *Int* October 1968 2: 25-28.

[1200] KALEVAINEN, URHO. "Soviet Non-Interference: Finland's Current Political Horizon and Finno-Soviet Relations." *IPUB* 1969 19 (January-May): 26-30.

[1201] KALIADIN, A. *Nuclear Energy and International Security.* Moscow: Novosti, 1970.

[1202] ———. "Organichenie iadernykh vooruzhenii i mezhdunarodnaia bezopasnost' " [The arrangement of nuclear weapons and international security]. *MEMO* 1968 (4): 14-23.

[1203] ———. "Razvitie atomnoi tekhniki i mezhdunarodnaia bezopasnost' " [The development of atomic technology and international security]. *MEMO* 1967 (5): 39-50.

[1204] KALININ, B. "Sovetskie mashiny i oborudovanie v Pakistane" [Soviet machinery and equipment in Pakistan]. *VT* 1968 (5): 34-36.

[1205] KALINKIN, G. F. "Dogovor o nerasprostranenii iadernogo oruzhiia—effektivnyi instrument mira i bezopasnosti narodov" [The treaty concerning the nonproliferation of nuclear weapons—an effective instrument of peace and security of peoples]. *SGP* 1968 (10): 54-64.

[1206] ———. "Military Use of the Sea-Bed Should be Banned." *IA(M)* 1969 (2): 45-48.

[1207] KALTAKHCHIAN, S. T. *Leninizm o sushchnosti natsii i puti obrazovaniia internatsional'noi obshchnosti liudei* [Leninism on the nature of the nation and the ways of forming an international community of peoples]. Moscow: Izdatel'stvo Moskovskogo universiteta, 1969.

[1208] KANET, ROGER E. "African Youth: The Target of Soviet African Policy." *RR* 1968 27: 161-175.

[1209] ———. "The Implications of the Occupation of Czechoslovakia for Soviet Foreign Policy." *ISp* 1969 23: 1731-1747.

[1210] ———. "International Relations—Soviet Union." *CSISt* each issue from 1(3) (1967) to 5(4) (1971). Various issues co-authored with Hans Brisch, J. Russell Mills, Jr., and Faria Vahdat.

[1211] ———. "The Recent Soviet Reassessment of Developments in the Third World." In *RR* 1968 27: 27-41. Also in *From Underdevelopment to Affluence: Western, Soviet and Chinese Views,* pp. 132-142, edited by Harry G. Shaffer and Jan S. Prybyla. New York: Appleton-Century-Crofts, 1968. Also in *The Conduct of Soviet Foreign Policy,* pp. 398-408, edited by Eric Hoffmann and Frederic Fleron, Jr. Chicago: Aldine-Atherton, 1971.

[1212] ———. "Soviet Attitudes Toward the Search for National Identity and Material Advancement in Africa." *Vierteljahresberichte der Forschungsinstitut der Friedrich-Ebert-Stiftung.* 1969 36: 143-156. Also in *Communism and Nationalism,* edited by Jan S. Prybyla. University Park: The Pennsylvania State University, Center for Continuing Liberal Education and Slavic and Soviet Language and Area Center, 1969.

[1213] ———. "Soviet Economic Policy in Sub-Saharan Africa." *CSISt* 1967 1: 566-586.

[1214] ———. "The Soviet Union and Sub-Saharan Africa: Communist Policy Toward Africa, 1917-1965." *DAI* 1967 27: 3915-A.

[1215] ———. "The Soviet Union and the Middle East: The Arab-Israeli War and Its Aftermath." *QQ* 1968 75: 731-736.

[1216] ———. "The Soviet Union and the Third World: A Case of Ideological Revision." *RMSSJ* 1969 6(1): 109-116.

[1217] ———, ED. *The Behavioral Revolution and Communist Studies; Applications of Behaviorally Oriented Political Research on the Soviet Union and Eastern Europe.* New York: The Free Press, 1971.

[1218] KANISHCHEV, O. "Spetsializatsiia i kooperirovanie proizvodstva v stranakh SEV" [Specialization and production cooperation in the countries of CMEA]. *VT* 1970 (10): 4-9.

[1219] KAPCHENKO, N. I. "The 'Cultural Revolution' and the Mao Group's Foreign Policy." *IA(M)* 1968 (2): 14-22.

[1220] ———. "Engels on Working-Class Foreign Policy." *IA(M)* 1970 (12): 16-23.

[1221] ———. "Foreign Policy and Ideology." *IA(M)* 1970 (11): 78-85.

[1222] ———. "The Heart of Maoism and Its Policies." *IA(M)* 1969 (5): 10-17.

[1223] ———. "The Leninist Theory and Practice of Socialist Foreign Policy." *IA(M)* 1968 (9): 53-60.

[1224] ———. *Pekin: Politika, chuzhdaia sotsializmu* [Peking: Politics alien to socialism]. Moscow: I.M.O., 1967.

[1225] ———. "The Scientific Principles of Socialist Foreign Policy." *IA(M)* 1970 (5): 41-47.

[1226] ———. *See* 2377.

[1227] ———, ED. *Leninskie printsipy vneshnei politiki SSSR* [Leninist principles of the foreign policy of the USSR]. Moscow: Kniga, 1970.

[1228] KAPELINSKII, IU. N. *Torgovlia SSSR s kapitalisticheskimi stranami posle Vtoroi Mirovoi Voiny* [The trade of the USSR with the capitalist countries after the Second World War]. Moscow: I.M.O., 1970.

[1229] KAPITSA, M. "National Liberation and the Mao Group's Splitting Activity." *IA(M)* 1968 (7): 10-17.

[1230] ———. "Soviet-Mongolian Treaty." *IA(M)* 1971 (2): 12-15.

[1231] KAPLAN, MORTON A. "Changes in United States Perspectives on the Soviet Union and Détente." In *Great Issues of International Politics,* pp. 177-186. Chicago: Aldine, 1970.

[1232] ———. "The Nuclear Non-Proliferation Treaty." *JPL* 1969 18: 1-20.

[1233] ———. "The Nuclear Non-Proliferation Treaty: Its Rationale, Prospects, and Possible Impact on International Law." In *Great Issues of International Politics,* pp. 154-176. Chicago: Aldine, 1970.

[1234] ———. "Weakness of the Non-Proliferation Treaty." *Orb* 1969 12(4): 1042-1057.

[1235] KAPLIN, A. "Lenin on the Principles of Socialist Diplomacy." *IA(M)* 1969 (6): 51-55.

[1236] KAPUR, HARISH. "India and the Soviet Union." *Sur* 1971 16: 189-215.

[1237] ———.*Soviet Russia and Asia 1917-1927: A Study of Soviet Policy Towards Turkey, Iran and Afghanistan.* New York: Humanities Press, 1967.

[1238] KARAL, HALIL I. "Turkish Relations With Soviet Russia During the National Liberation War of Turkey, 1918-1922: A Study in the Diplomacy of Kemalist Revolution." *DAI* 1967 28: 2316-A.

[1239] KARAMANOV, M. O. *Internatsionalizm i natsionalizm* [Internationalism and nationalism]. Moscow: Mosk. rabochii, 1971.

[1240] KARIM, AHMED. "Leninism and Some Problems of National Liberation Movement." *WMR* 1970 13(3): 62-65.

[1241] KARLIER, PHILLIP A. "Czechoslovakia: A Scenario of the Future?" *MR* 1969 49(2): 11-21.

[1242] KARNIN, A. "The Soviet Union and Cuba." *NT* 1971 (44): 12-13.

[1243] KARPICH, V. "CMEA Countries' Plan to Develop Integration." *IA(M)* 1970 (8): 8-13.

[1244] ———. "An Important Milestone in CMEA Cooperation." *IA(M)* 1969 (6): 6-9.

[1245] ———. "Mezhdunarodnaia organizatsiia 'Interkhim' " [The international organization 'InterChem']. *VT* 1969 (11): 23-24.

[1246] ———. "Programme of Socialist Integration." *IA(M)* 1971 (10): 3-8.

[1247] ———. "Razvitie valiutnofinansovykh otnoshenii stran SEV" [The development of currency relations of the CMEA countries]. *VE* 1969 (7): 97-108.

[1248] ———, AND L. LUKIN. "Growing Cooperation of the Socialist Countries." *IA(M)* 1971 (5): 19-24.

[1249] KARPOV, N. "Sovetsko-Iranskaia torgovlia" [Soviet-Iranian trade]. *VT* 1968 (5): 18-21.

[1250] KARTUNOVA, A. I. "Lenin and the National Liberation Movement." *NT* 1969 (33): 13-15.

[1251] ———. "Oktiabr'skaia Sotsialisticheskaia Revoliutsiia i Natsional'no-Osvoboditel' noe Dvizhenie v Kitae (1917-1927 gg.)" [The October Socialist Revolution and the National-Liberation Movement in China (1917-1927)]. *NNI* 1967 (6): 16-31.

[1252] KASER, MICHAEL C. *COMECON: Integration Problems of the Planned Economies.* London: Oxford University Press, 1967.

[1253] ———. "Current Problems in East-West Trade." In *Jahrbuch der Wirtschaft Osteuropas, Vol. 1,* edited by Hans Raupach. Munich-Vienna; Günter Olzog Verlag, 1971.

[1254] ———. "East European Development Aid: Comparative Record and Prospects." *WT* 1970 26: 467-477.

[1255] ———. "The East European Economic Reforms and Foreign Trade." *WT* 1967 23: 512-522.

[1256] ———. "A Volume Index of Soviet Foreign Trade." *SSt* 1969 20: 523-526.

[1257] ———. *See* 333.

[1258] KASHIN, ALEXANDER. "A New Phase in Sino-Soviet Relations." *B,ISUSSR* 1967 14(6): 3-14.

[1259] ———. "The October Revolution and Communism in Southeast Asia." *StSU* 1967 6(3): 48-72.

[1260] KATZ, ZEV. "Soviet Attitudes to the Middle East Crisis—One Year After." *BSJA* 1968 (2).

[1261] KAUFMAN, A. S. *See* 1308·

[1262] ———. *See* 1309.

[1263] KAUFMAN, EDY. "A Comparative Analysis of the Foreign Policies of the United States and the Soviet Union in Latin America and Eastern Europe." *Co* 1971 8: 123-138.

[1264] KAUSHIK, DEVENDRA. *Soviet Relations With India and Pakistan.* Delhi: Vikas Publications, 1971.

[1265] KAUTSKY, JOHN. *Communism and the Politics of Development.* New York: Wiley, 1968.

[1266] KAZHINSKAIA, E. N., AND V. P. SERGEEV. "Sotrudnichestvo stranchlenov SEV i ego burzhuaznye kritiki" [Cooperation of the member countries of CMEA and its bourgeois critics]. *NNI* 1969 (2): 91-97.

[1267] KEBSCHULL, DIETRICH. "FRG and GDR in the Third World." *Inte* 1971 5: 158-160.

[1268] KEEP, JOHN. "The Soviet Union and the Third World." *Sur* 1969 72: 19-38.

[1269] KEINEMAN, PITER. "Oktiabr' i natsional'no-osvoboditel'noe dvizhenie" [October and the national liberation movement]. *Komm* 1967 (16): 108-116.

[1270] KELIN, V. N. *Vneshniaia politika i ideologiia. Rol' ideologii vo vneshnei politike imperializma* [Foreign policy and ideology. The role of ideology in the foreign policy of imperialism]. Moscow: I.M.O., 1969.

[1271] KELLEHER, CATHERINE. "The Non-Proliferation Treaty and European Security." *StNCE* 1968-9 2(4): 298-301.

[1272] KEMENSKAIA, E. "Sovetsko-Vengerskoe ekonomicheskoe sotrudnichestvo" [Soviet-Hungarian economic cooperation]. *VT* 1970 (3): 16-18.

[1273] KEMP, GEOFFREY. "Arms Traffic and Third World Conflicts." *IC* 1970 (577): 5-70.

[1274] ———. "Strategy and Arms Levels, 1945-1967." *APS,P* 1969 29(3): 21-36.

[1275] KENNAN, GEORGE. *Memoirs 1925-1950.* Boston: Little, Brown, 1967.

[1276] KERIMOV, A., AND V. DZHALOGONIIA. *Na meridiane druzhby. Dekada AZSSR na Kube* [On the meridian of friendship. A decade of the Azerbaijan SSR in Cuba]. Baku: Azerneshr, 1968.

[1277] KHAITSMAN, V. M. *SSSR i problema razoruzheniia, 1945-1969. Istoriia mezhdunarodnykh peregovorov* [The USSR and the problem of disarmament, 1945-1969. The history of international negotiations]. Moscow: Nauka, 1970.

[1278] ———, ED. *50 let bor'by SSSR za razoruzhenie. Sbornik dokumentov* [50 years of struggle of the USSR for disarmament. Collection of documents]. Moscow: Nauka, 1967.

[1279] KHALIL, HOUSSAM. "The Making of Soviet Foreign Policy Towards Egypt, 1954-1964." *DAI* 1971 31: 6134-A-6135-A.

[1280] KHARAKHASH'IAN, G. *See* 550.

[1281] KHARLAMOV, M. A., ED. *Leninskaia vneshniaia politika Sovetskoi Strany 1917-1924* [Leninist foreign policy of the Soviet Union 1917-1924]. Moscow: Nauka, 1969.

[1282] KHARMIS, S., AND Y. ROZALIEV. "Lenin and National Liberation Movement." *WMR* 1969 12(12): 20-25.

[1283] KHEIFETS, A. N. "Leninskaia vneshniaia politika i natsional'no-osvoboditel'noe dvizhenie" [Leninist foreign policy and the national liberation movement]. *NAA* 1970 (2): 44-55.

[1284] _____.*Sovetskaia diplomatiia i narody Vostoka, 1921-1927 gg* [Soviet diplomacy and the peoples of the East, 1921-1927]. Moscow: Nauka, 1968.

[1285] KHLEBNIKOV, A. B. "Sovetsko-Amerikanskie otnosheniia: Nekotorye nazrevshie voprosy" [Soviet-American relations: Some unresolved questions]. *SShA* 1970 (3): 3-8.

[1286] KHLESTOV, O. N. "Mezhdunarodno-pravovyi voprosy na XXII sessii General'noi Assamblei OON" [International legal questions at the 22nd session of the UN General Assembly]. *SGP* 1968 (5): 79-85.

[1287] _____. "New Soviet-Czechoslovak Treaty." *IA(M)* 1970 (7): 9-14.

[1288] _____. "Pravo mezhdunarodnykh dogovorov (Venskaia Konferentsiia OON)" [The Law of international treaties (the Vienna Conference of the UN)]. *SGP* 1969 (12): 62-69.

[1289] KHOLMOGOROV, A. I. *Internatsional'nye cherty Sovetskikh Natsii* [International boundaries of the Soviet Nation]. Moscow: Mysl', 1970.

[1290] KHOMUTOV, N. *See* 1962.

[1291] KHRABSKOV, V. "Development of Socialist States' Customs Ties." *IA(M)* 1970 (9): 71-74.

[1292] KHROMUSHIN, G. B. "Sharpening of World Ideological Struggle." *IA(M)* 1968 (12): 60-66.

[1293] _____, ED. *Antikommunisticheskaia propaganda imperializma (teorii, doktriny, apparat)* [Anti-Communist propaganda of imperialism (theories, doctrines, apparatus]. Moscow: I.M.O., 1971.

[1294] *Khronika mezhdunarodnykh sobytii. 1967 g.* [Chronicle of international events, 1967]. Moscow: I.M.O., 1968.

[1295] KHRUSHCHEV, N. S. *Krushchev Remembers*. Boston: Little, Brown, 1970.

[1296] KHVOINIK, P., AND A. BORODAEVSKII. "Ot Zhenevy k Deli (Navstrechu vtoroi konferentsii po torgovle i razvitiiu)" [From Geneva to Delhi: Toward the second conference on trade and development]. *MEMO* 1967 (12): 53-66.

[1297] KHVOSTOV, V. "International Significance of the German Democratic Republic." *IA(M)* 1969 (7): 22-26.

[1298] ————. "Sovetskaia vneshniaia politika i ee vozdeistvie na khod istorii" [Soviet foreign policy and its influence on the course of history]. *Komm* 1967 (10): 79-90.

[1299] ————. "The USSR and European Security." *IA(M)* 1969 (2): 3-7.

[1300] ————. "V. I. Lenin o printsipakh vneshnei politiki Sovetskogo Gosudarstva" [V. I. Lenin on the principles of foreign policy of the Soviet State]. *Komm* 1969 (9): 79-89.

[1301] ————. *See* 2143.

[1302] KIERNAN, BERNARD P. "The Nature of Communism in the Emergent World." *YLJ* 1970 49: 321-332.

[1303] KILMARX, ROBERT A. "Challenge of the Mediterranean—Crossroads of United States-Soviet Relations." *MR* 1970 50(11): 81-89.

[1304] ————. *Soviet Sea Power.* Washington, D.C.: Georgetown University, The Center for Strategic and International Studies, Special Report Series, 10, 1969.

[1305] KIM, G. F. "Antikommunizm—sredstvo bor'by protiv natsional'no-osvoboditel'nogo dvizheniia" [Anti-Communism as a means of struggle against the national-liberation movement]. *AAS* 1970 (3): 5-8.

[1306] ————. *Leninism and the National Liberation Movement.* Moscow: Novosti, 1970.

[1307] ————. "Nekotorye problemy natsional'no-osvoboitel'nykh revoliutsii v svete Leninskikh idei"[Some problems of the national-liberation revolution in the light of Leninist ideas]. *NAA* 1969 (5): 3-17.

[1308] ————, AND A. S. KAUFMAN. "Leninskie printsipy Soiuza Sotsializma s natsional'no-osvobitel nym dvizheniem" [Leninist principles of the Union of Socialism with the National-Liberation movement]. *NAA* 1970 (2): 3-13.

[1309] ————, AND A. S. KAUFMAN. "Non-Capitalist Development: Achievements and Difficulties." *IA(M)* 1967 (12): 70-76.

[1310] ————, AND F. I. SHABSHINA. *Proletarskii internatsionalizm i revoliutsii v stranakh Vostoka* [Proletarian internationalism and the revolutions in the countries of the East]. Moscow: Nauka, 1967.

[1311] _____, ED. *Marksizm i strany Vostoka* [Marxism and the countries of the East]. Moscow: Nauka, 1970.

[1312] _____. *See* 620.

[1313] KIM, JOUNGWON ALEXANDER. "Soviet Policy in North Korea." *WP* 1970 22: 237-254.

[1314] KIM, UOONG JACK. "Sino-Soviet Dispute and North Korea." *DAI* 1967 28: 1879-A.

[1315] KIM, YOUNG HAM, ED. *Twenty Years of Crises: The Cold War Era.* Englewood Cliffs, New Jersey: Prentice-Hall, 1968.

[1316] KIM, YOUN-SOO. "North Korea's Relationship to the USSR: A Political and Economic Problem." *B,ISUSSR* 1971 18(6): 34-38.

[1317] KIMBALL, LORENZO K. "Iraq and the Major Powers." *EE* 1971 20(11): 18-25.

[1318] KINDLEBERGER, CHARLES P. "The Marshall Plan and the Cold War." *IJ* 1968 23: 369-382.

[1319] KINTNER, WILLIAM R., AND WOLFGANG KLAIBER. *Eastern Europe and European Security.* New York: The Dunellen Co., 1971.

[1320] _____, AND WOLFGANG KLAIBER. "Eastern Europe in Flux." *Orb* 1968 12: 415-440.

[1321] _____, AND ROBERT L. PFALTZGRAFF. *Soviet Military Trends: Implications for U.S. Security. No. 6 Special Analyses.* Washington, D.C.: American Enterprise Institute for Public Policy Research, 1971.

[1322] _____, AND HARRIET FAST SCOTT, TRANSLATORS AND EDS. *The Nuclear Revolution in Soviet Military Affairs.* Norman: University of Oklahoma Press, 1968.

[1323] KIRALY, BELA K. "Budapest: 1956—Prague: 1968; Parallels and Contrasts." *PoC* 1969 18(4-5): 52-59.

[1324] _____. "Why the Soviets Need the Warsaw Pact." *EE* 1969 18(4): 8-18.

[1325] KIRBY, RICHARD P. "Tito and Khrushchev: Harmony and Discord." *MA* 1967 5(1): 19.

[1326] KIRILLOV, A. "Voprosy dal'neishego povysheniia effektivnosti Sovetskogo eksporta" [Questions on the further rise in effectiveness of Soviet exports]. *VT* 1970 (12): 31-35.

[1327] KIRKPATRICK, LYMAN B. JR. "Cold War Operations: The Politics of Communist Confrontation. I. Marx and His Followers." *NWCR* 1967 20(4): 3-11. "II. A Brief History of the Cold War." *NWCR* 1967 20(5): 50-59. "III. The Sino-Soviet Split." *NWCR* 1968 20(6): 44-54. "IV. The Communist Control System." *NWCR* 1968 20(7): 12-21. "V. The Cuban Case History." *NWCR* 1968 20(8): 30-42. "VI. Vietnam." *NWCR* 1968 20(9): 40-47. "VII. The Intelligence Organization." *NWCR* 1968 20(10): 61-70. "VIII. Communism in Latin America." *NWCR* 1968 20(11): 3-10. "IX. Communism in Africa." *NWCR* 1968 21(1): 33-42. "X. Communism in the Near East and South Asia." *NWCR* 1968 21(2): 110-115. "XI. Communism in Asia." *NWCR* 1968 21(3): 57-63. "XII. Communism in World Affairs." *NWCR* 1968 21(4): 16-26.

[1328] ———.*Russian Espionage: Communist and Imperialist.* New York: National Strategy Information Center, Incorporated, 1970.

[1329] KIRSANOV, T. "Ekonomicheskoe sodeistvie SSSR Respublike Sudan" [The economic assistance of the USSR to the Republic of Sudan]. *VT* 1969 (12): 18-19.

[1330] KIRSCH, MARIAN P. "Soviet Security Objectives in Asia." *IO* 1970 24: 451-478.

[1331] KISELEV, K. "At the San Francisco Conference and the First General Assembly." *IA(M)* 1970 (8): 79-85.

[1332] KISHCH, T. *Problemy sotsialisticheskoi integratsii stran SEV* [Problems of socialist integration of the countries of CMEA]. Moscow: Progress, 1971.

[1333] KISSINGER, KURT G. *See* 291.

[1334] KIUZADZHAN, L. *Proletarskii internatsionalizm i melkoburzhuaznyi natsionalizm* [Proletarian internationalism and petty bourgeois nationalism]. Moscow: Politizdat, 1968.

[1335] KLAGES, WALTER J. "Soviet Economic Thought and Economic Development: The Case of Foreign Aid." *CSIP* 1970 12: 417-430.

[1336] KLAIBER, WOLFGANG. "East European Relations With the West." In *The Changing Face of Communism in Eastern Europe,* edited by Peter A. Toma. Tucson: The University of Arizona Press, 1970.

[1337] ———. "Security Priorities in Eastern Europe." *PoC* 1970 19: 32-44.

[1338] ———.*See* 1319.

[1339] ———.*See* 1320.

[1340] KLEOPIN, I. "Pribrezhnaia torgovlia s Iaponiei" [Coastal trade with Japan]. *VT* 1968 (9): 48-49.

[1341] KLIEMAN, AARON S. *Soviet Russia and the Middle East.* Baltimore, Maryland: Johns Hopkins Press, 1970.

[1342] KLIMOV, A., AND V. LAPTEV. "On the Policy of Non-Alignment." *IA(M)* 1969 (3): 14-19.

[1343] KLIMOV, V. "Sotsialisticheskii internatsionalizm—osnova vzaimootnoshenii stran sotsializma" [Socialist internationalism—the basis of mutual relations of the socialist countries]. *PS* 1971 (4): 84-91.

[1344] _____. "Unity of the Socialist States' International and National Tasks." *IA(M)* 1968 (8): 10-15.

[1345] KLIMOVICH, D. "Socialist Integration and Management." *NT* 1971 (38): 18-19.

[1346] KLINGHOFFER, ARTHUR JAY. "Mao or Che? Some Reflections on Communist Guerrilla Warfare." *Miz* 1969 11: 94-99.

[1347] _____. "Moscow, the CPI and the Indian Congress Party Before 1942." *Miz* 1970 12: 26-42.

[1348] _____. "Pretext and Context: Evaluating the Soviet Role in the Middle East." *Miz* 1968 10: 86-93.

[1349] _____. *Soviet Perspectives on African Socialism.* Rutherford, New Jersey; Madison, Wisconsin; Teaneck, New Jersey: Fairleigh Dickinson University Press, 1969.

[1350] _____. "The Soviet View of African Socialism." *AfA* 1968 67: 197-208.

[1351] _____. "The Soviet View of African Socialism in Sub-Saharan Africa, 1955-1964." *DAI* 1967 27: 2573-A.

[1352] _____. "The USSR and Nigeria: The Secession Question." *Miz* 1968 10: 64-70.

[1353] _____. "Why the Soviets Chose Sides (in the Nigerian War)." *AfR* 1968 13: 47-49.

[1354] KLOCHEK, V. "Novye rubezhi vneshnei torgovli SSSR" [New boundaries of the foreign trade of the USSR]. *VT* 1970 (8): 2-7.

[1355] _____. "Vneshniaia torgovlia SSSR za 1970 god" [The foreign trade of the Soviet Union in 1970]. *VT* 1971 (6): 16-21.

[1356] KLOCHKO, MIKHAIL. "The Sino-Soviet Split—The Withdrawal of the Specialists." *IJ* 1971 26: 556-566.

[1357] KNAPP, WILFRID. "The Cold War Revised." *IJ* 1968 23: 344-356.

[1358] KNIAZHINSKII, V. B. *Politicheskaia strategiia Antikommunizma* [The political strategy of anti-Communism]. Moscow: I.M.O., 1969.

[1359] KNOWLE, RUTH SHELDON. "A New Soviet Thrust: The Arab-Israeli Crisis and Two Big Iraq Agreements Help the Russian's Major Oil Putsch in the Middle East." *ME* 1969 9: 5-9.

[1360] KOBAL, DANIEL A. "COMECON as a Political Instrument of Control in Eastern Europe." *MA* 1968 6: 150.

[1361] KOBRIN, M. "Atlanticism Versus Europe." *NT* 1970 (5): 8-10.

[1362] ———. "Mutual Trust is a Great Achievement." *NT* 1971 (44): 5-6.

[1363] KODACHENKO, A. S. "An International Development Strategy for the Third World." *IA(M)* 1969 (3): 48-54.

[1364] KOFTOV, G. "Uchenie V. I. Lenina o gosudarstvenno-monopolis- ticheskom kapitalizme i vneshneekonomicheskie sviazi" [The teaching of V. I. Lenin on state monopoly capitalism and foreign economic ties]. *VT* 1969 (4): 2-7.

[1365] KOH, B. C. "North Korea and the Sino-Soviet Schism." *WPQ* 1969 22: 940-f.

[1366] KOHLER, FOY D. "An American View of Soviet Foreign Policy in the 1970's." *Orb* 1971 15: 72-86.

[1367] ———. *Understanding the Russians: A Citizen's Primer.* New York: Harper and Row, 1970.

[1368] ———, AND MOSE L. HARVEY. "Soviet Science and Technology: Some Implications for U.S. Policy." *Orb* 1969 13: 685-708.

[1369] KOHTANI, ETSUO. "The Present Position of Moscow and Peking in the Communist Bloc and in the Far East." *B,ISUSSR* 1969 16: 11-18.

[1370] ———. "Recent Developments in the Far East and the Reactions of Moscow and Peking." *B,ISUSSR* 1968 15(5): 14-18.

[1371] KOLESNIK, D. N., V. I. KUZNETSOV, AND R. A. TUZMUKHAMEDOV. *Ot dek- reta o mire k deklaratsiia mira* [From the peace decree to the declaration of peace]. Moscow: I.M.O., 1972.

[1372] KOLESNIKOVA, M. I. *Mirnoe sosushchestvovanie i mirovoi revoliutsion- nyi protsess* [Peaceful coexistence and the world revolutionary pro- cess]. Moscow: Moscow University, 1967.

[1373] ———. *Mirnoe sosushchestvovanie i voprosy voiny i mira* [Peaceful coexistence and questions of war and peace]. Moscow: Moscow University, 1968.

[1374] KOL'IAR, K. *Mezhdunarodnye uchrezhdeniia* [International institu- tions]. Moscow: Progress, 1971.

[1375] KOLKO, GABRIEL. *The Politics of War: The World and United States Foreign Policy, 1943-1945.* New York: Random House, 1968.

[1376] KOLKOWICZ, ROMAN. "The Impact of Modern Technology on the Soviet Officer Corps." *Orb* 1967 11: 378-393.

[1377] ———. "Interest Groups in Soviet Politics: The Case of the Military." *CP* 1970 2: 445-472.

[1378] ———. "SALT and the Kremlin: The Policy of Hold-and-Explore." *IP* 1970 3: 33-36.

[1379] ———. *The Soviet Military and the Communist Party.* Princeton, New Jersey: Princeton University Press, 1967.

[1380] ———. "Strategic Parity and Beyond: Soviet Perspectives." *WP* 1971 23: 431-451.

[1381] ———. "The Warsaw Pact: Entangling Alliance." *Sur* 1969 70,71: 86-101.

[1382] ———, MATTHEW P. GALLAGHER, BENJAMIN S. LAMBETH, WALTER C. CLEMENS, JR., AND PETER W. COLM. *The Soviet Union and Arms Control: A Superpower Dilemma.* Baltimore, Maryland: Johns Hopkins Press, 1970.

[1383] ———, ED. *The Warsaw Pact: Report on a Conference on the Warsaw Treaty Organization, Held at the Institute for Defense Analysis, May 17-19, 1967. Research paper P-496.* Arlington, Virginia: Institute for Defense Analysis, International and Social Studies Division, 1969.

[1384] KOLOSKOV, A. G. *Razrabotka V. I. Leninym osnovnykh printsipov vzaimootnoshenii mezhdu Kommunisticheskimi Partiiami* [The elaboration of basic principles of mutual relations among Communist Parties by V. I. Lenin]. Moscow: Mysl', 1970.

[1385] KOLOSKOV, BORIS T. *The Soviet Union and China: Friendship or Alienation?* Moscow: Novosti, 1971.

[1386] ———.*See* 270.

[1387] ———.*See* 271.

[1388] ———.*See* 272.

[1389] KOLOSKOV, I. "Evropeiskaia bezopasnost'; Real'nosti i iliuzii" [European security: realities and illusions]. *MEMO* 1969 (10): 45-55.

[1390] KOLOSOV, IU. *Bor'ba za mirnyi kosmos. Kritika burzhuaznykh teorii kosmicheskogo prava* [The struggle for a peaceful outer space. A critique of bourgeois theories of space law]. Moscow: I.M.O., 1968.

[1391] ———. "Some Urgent Problems of Space Law." *IA(M)* 1970 (9): 24-28.

[1392] ———.*See* 912.

[1393] KOMDEY, KARL-HEINZ. "Problems of Economic Collaboration Between Socialist and Capitalist Industrial Countries—Thoughts on the Discussion." *Co* 1967 4: 15-28.

[1394] *Komintern i Vostok: Bor'ba za Leninskuiu strategiiu i takitiku v natsional'nom dvizhenii* [The Comintern and the East: The struggle for Leninist strategy and tactics in the national movement]. Moscow: Nauka, 1969.

[1395] *Kommunisticheskie i rabochie partii mira. Spravochnik.* [Communist and workers parties of the world. A reference book]. Kiev: Politizdat Ukrainy, 1970.

[1396] *Kommunisticheskii Internatsional* [The Communist International]. Moscow: Politizdat, 1969.

[1397] KOMOCSIN, AOLTAN. "The Class Approach and Internationalism. [The Hungarian Revolution of 1956]." *WMR* 1968 11(10-11): 14-18.

[1398] KOMPANTSEV, I. M. *Pakistan i Sovetskii Soiuz.* [Pakistan and the Soviet Union]. Moscow: Nauka, 1970.

[1399] ———. "The Soviet Union and the Middle East Crisis." *PH* 1970 23: 287-292.

[1400] KONDRASHKIN, O. "Sovetsko-Tseilonskoe sotrudnichestvo" [Soviet-Ceylon cooperation]. *VT* 1968 (3): 39-42.

[1401] *Konferentsiia Evropeiskikh Kommunisticheskikh i Rabochikh Partii po voprosam bezopasnosti v Evrope. Karlovy Vary. 24-26 Aprelia 1967 g* [The conference of the European Communist and Workers Parties on questions of security in Europe. Karlovy Vary. 24-26 April, 1967]. Moscow: Politizdat, 1967.

[1402] KONSTANTINOV, F. "Internationalism and the World Socialist System." *IA(M)* 1968 (7): 3-9.

[1403] KONSTANTINOV, IU. "Investitsionnyi Bank sotsialisticheskikh stran" [The Investment Bank of the socialist countries]. *VT* 1971 (8): 12-16.

[1404] KOPAL, V., I. CSABAFI, AND B. BAKOTIC. "Space Law in the Socialist Countries of Eastern Europe: Czechoslovakia, Hungary and Yugoslavia." *CSISt* 1967 1: 60-78.

[1405] KOPANSKII, IA. M., AND I. I. LEVIT. *Sovetsko-Rumynskie otnosheniia v 1929-1934 gg* [Soviet-Rumanian relations in 1929-1934]. Moscow: Nauka, 1971.

[1406] KORABLYOV, V. "Non-Proliferation and IAEA (International Atomic Energy Agency)." *NT* 1968 (32): 7-9.

[1407] KORBASH, E. P. *Ekonomicheskie "teorii" Maoizma* [Economic "theories" of Maoism]. Moscow: Politizdat, 1971.

[1408] KORBEL, JOSEF. "Soviet-German Relations: The Past and Prospects." *Orb* 1967 10: 1046-1060.

[1409] _____. "West Germany's Ostpolitik: I, Intra-German Relations." *Orb* 1970 13: 1050-1072.

[1410] _____. "West Germany's Ostpolitik: II, a Policy Toward the Soviet Allies." *Orb* 1970 14: 326-348.

[1411] KORBONSKI, ANDRZEJ. "COMECON: The Institutional Structure." In *Regional International Organizations: Structures and Function,* edited by Paul A. Tharp, Jr. New York: St. Martin's; Toronto and London: Macmillan, 1971.

[1412] _____. "East Europe and the United States." *CH* 1969 56: 201-205, 242.

[1413] _____. "Theory and Practice of Regional Integration: The Case of COMECON." *IO* 1970 14: 942-977; Also in *Regional Integration: Theory and Research,* edited by Leon N. Lindberg and Stuart A. Scheingold. Cambridge, Massachusetts: Harvard University Press, 1971.

[1414] _____. "The Warsaw Pact." *IC* 1969 573: 1-73.

[1415] _____. "The Warsaw Uprising Revisited." *Sur* 1970 76: 82-98.

[1416] KOREY, WILLIAM. "The Comintern and the Genealogy of the Brezhnev Doctrine." *PoC* 1969 18(3): 52-58.

[1417] KORHONEN KEIJO. "Disarmament Talks as an Instrument of International Politics." *CaC* 1970 5: 152-167.

[1418] _____.*Finland and the Soviet Union: Essays on Finnish Foreign Policy.* Helsinki: Finnish Political Science Association, 1969.

[1419] KORIONOV, V. G. *Bor'ba protiv imperializma—obshchii dolg Kommunistov* [The struggle against imperialism is the general duty of Communists]. Moscow: Politizdat, 1970.

[1420] KORMNOV, IU. F. *Mezhdunarodnaia spetsializatsiia proizvodstva. Ekonomicheskie problemy na primere sotrudnichestva stran SEV v oblasti mashinostroeniia* [International specialization of production. The economic problems of cooperation of the CMEA countries in the area of machine building]. Moscow: Ekonomika, 1968.

[1421] _____."Nauchno-tekhnicheskaia kooperatsiia stran SEV"[Scientific-technical cooperation of the CMEA countries]. *VE* 1969 (5): 57-68.

[1422] _____.*Spetsializatsiia i kooperiovanie proizvodstva stran-chlenov SEV* [Specialization and production cooperation of the CMEA member countries]. Moscow: Ekonomika, 1972.

[1423] _____, AND B. DIAKIN. "Specialization and Cooperation in Production and Integration of CMEA Countries." *IA(M)* 1971 (8): 11-18.

[1424] KORNEEV, L. "Krakh antikommunisticheskoi 'doktriny'" [The bankruptcy of Anti-Communist "doctrine"]. *AAS* 1969 (12): 16-18.

[1425] KOROTKOVA, E., AND G. RUBINSTEIN. "Torgovlia Sovetskogo Soiuza so stranami Afriki" [The trade of the Soviet Union with the countries of Africa]. *VT* 1967 (12): 13-19.

[1426] KORTUNOV, V. V. *Bitva idei. Ideologicheskaia bor'ba na mezhdunarodnoi arene* [The battle of ideas. The ideological struggle in the international arena]. Moscow: Politizdat, 1969.

[1427] _____. "Lenin i ideologicheskaia bor'ba nashikh dnei" [Lenin and the ideological struggle of our times]. *MEMO* 1969 (10): 3-11.

[1428] _____. "World Politics and Confrontation of Ideas." *IA(M)* 1970 (10): 72-78.

[1429] _____., AND A. F. KUDRIASHEV, EDS. *Spravochnik propagandista-mezhdunarodnika* [Reference book of the international propagandist]. Moscow: Politizdat, 1968, 3rd ed.; 1971, 4th ed.

[1430] KORZHIN, Y. "Important Step Toward Détente." *NT* 1971 (38): 6-7.

[1431] KOSKOV, E., ED. *Leninism and the World Revolutionary Working-Class Movement.* Moscow: Novosti, 1971.

[1432] KOSLENSNIK, A. N., V. I. KUZNETSOV, AND R. A. TUZMUKHAMEDOV. "Deklaratsiia printsipov mirnogo sosushchestvovaniia" [The declaration of the principles of peaceful coexistence]. *SGP* 1971 (6): 66-72.

[1433] *Kosmos i problema vseobshchego mira* [Outer space and the problem of general peace]. Moscow: Nauka, 1968.

[1434] KOS-RABCEWICZ-ZUBKOWSKI, L. *East European Rules on the Validity of International Commercial Arbitration.* Dobbs Ferry, New York: Oceana Publications, 1970.

[1435] KOSTERIN, S., ET AL. *Zastava na Ussuri. Dokumental'naia povest'* [The post on the Ussuri. A documentary narrative]. Moscow: Voenizdat, 1970.

[1436] KOSTIUKHIN, D. "Vozdeistvie nauchno-tekhnicheskogo progressa na sovremennuiu mezhdunarodnuiu torgovliu" [The influence of scientific-technical progress on contemporary international trade]. *VT* 1970 (9): 9-14.

[1437] Kosygin, A. N. *Zaiavlenie pravitel'stva SSSR ob oshovhykh voprosakh vnutrennei i vheshnei politiki* [The statement of the government of the USSR on the basic questions of internal and foreign policy]. Moscow: Novosti, 1967.

[1438] Kotsch, William. "The Tanks of August, 1968." *USNI,P* 1969 95(575): 88-93.

[1439] Kotsev, Venelin. "Battle Against Opportunism for Internationalism." *WMR* 1971 14(8): 65-77.

[1440] _____. "Fighting Anti-Communism Is Our Common Task." *WMR* 1970 13(7): 14-20.

[1441] Kotyk, Vaclov. "Problems of East-West Relations." *JIA* 1968 22: 48-58.

[1442] Kovac, John E. "Iran and the Beginning of the Cold War: A Case Study in the Dynamics of International Politics." *DAI* 1970 31: 2467-A-2468-A.

[1443] Kovach, Robert S., and John T. Farrell. "Foreign Trade of the USSR." In *U.S. Congress, Joint Economic Committee, Economic Performance and the Military Burden in the Soviet Union*, pp. 100-116. Washington, D.C., 1970.

[1444] Kovalev, A. M. *Azbyka diplomatii* [The ABC of diplomacy]. Moscow: I.M.O., 1968.

[1445] _____. "Sovetskii Soiuz i mir v Evrope" [The Soviet Union and peace in Europe]. *Komm* 1967 (4): 93-104.

[1446] _____, ED. *Sovremennaia epokha i mirovoi revoliutsionnyi protsess* [The present epoch and the world revolutionary process]. Moscow: Moscow University, 1970.

[1447] Koval'skii, N. A. *Sotsial'naia deiatel'nost' OON* [The social activities of the U.N.]. Moscow: I.M.O., 1970.

[1448] Kovan, I. "Novye Leninskie dokumenty o vneshneekonomicheskikh otnosheniiakh Sovetskogo gosudarstva" [New Leninist documents on the foreign economic relations of the Soviet state]. *VT* 1970 (10): 2-3.

[1449] _____. "Pravovye voprosy. Nauchno-tekhnicheskogo sotrudnichestva SSSR s sotsialisticheskimi stranami" [Legal questions on scientific-technical cooperation of the USSR with the socialist countries]. *VT* 1971 (8): 7-11.

[1450] _____. "Struktura mezhdunarodnykh nauchno-tekhnicheskikh sviazei SSSR" [The structure of the international scientific-technical ties of the USSR]. *VT* 1971 (10): 20-27.

[1451] KOVNER, MILTON. "Soviet Aid and Trade." *CH* 1967 52: 217-223, 242.

[1452] ———. "Soviet Aid to Developing Countries-A Look at the Record." In *The Soviet Union Under Brezhnev and Kosygin,* pp. 61-74, edited by John W. Strong. New York: Van Nostrand Reinhold, 1971.

[1453] KOVRIG, BENNETT. "Spheres of Influence: A Reassessment." *Sur* 1969 70/71: 102-120.

[1454] KOZHEVNIKOV, F. I., AND I. P. BLISHCHENKO. "Sotsializm i sovremennoe mezhdunarodnoe pravo" [Socialism and contemporary international law]. *SGP* 1970 (4): 88-95.

[1455] ———, AND G. V. SHARMAZANASHVILI. *Mezhdunarodnyi sud OON: Organizatsiia, tseli, praktika* [The international court of the UN: Organization, objectives practice]. Moscow: I.M.O., 1971.

[1456] ———, ED. *Sovetskoe gosudarstvo i mezhdunarodnoe pravo* [The Soviet state and international law]. Moscow: I.M.O., 1967.

[1457] ———, ET AL., EDS. *Kurs mezhdunarodnogo prava* [Text of inter-national law], vol. 4 of 6 vols. Moscow: Nauka, 1968.

[1458] KOZLOV, A., AND B. PYSHKOV. "XXIV S'ezd KPSS i mezhdunarodnoe Kommunisticheskoe dvizhenie" [The 24th Congress of the CPSU and the international Communist movement]. *PS* 1971 (7): 53-61.

[1459] KOZLOV, I. "CMEA Countries' Cooperation in the Development of the Oil and Gas Industry." *IA(M)* 1971 (9): 109-110.

[1460] *KPSS i bratskie partii o proletarskom internatsionalizme* [The CPSU and the fraternal parties on proletarian internationalism]. Moscow: Politizdat, 1971.

[1461] KRAHL, HANS-JURGEN. "Czechoslovakia: The Dialectic of the 'Reforms.'" *NLR* 1969 53: 3-12.

[1462] KRAL, KAREL. "Soviet-Czechoslovak Relations: The Pattern of Domination." *EE* 1969 18(1): 15-21.

[1463] KRAMMER, ARNOLD P. "Russian Counterfeit Dollars: A Case of Early Soviet Espionage." *SIR* 1971 30: 762-773.

[1464] ———. "Soviet Bloc Relations With Israel, 1947-1953." *DAI* 1971 31: 5323-A.

[1465] KRASIN, IU. A. "Dialektika internatsional'nogo i natsional'nogo v revoliutsionnom protsesse" [The dialectic of the international and the national in the revolutionary process]. *MEMO* 1971 (8): 4-18.

[1466] ———. *Lenin, revoluitsiia, sovremennost'* [Lenin, revolution, the present]. Moscow: Nauka, 1967.

[1467] ———. "Leninism i mirovoi revoliutsionnyi protsess" [Leninism and the world revolutionary process]. *MEMO* 1969 (5): 3-14.

[1468] KRASIN, L. B. *Voprosy vneshnei torgovli. Stati i rechi* [Questions of foreign trade. Articles and speeches]. Moscow: I.M.O., 1970.

[1469] KRASNOV, I. M. "Neizvestnye Leninskie dokumenty o Sovetsko-Amerikanskikh otnosheniiakh" [Unknown Lenin documents on Soviet-American relations]. *VI* 1969 (7): 3-8.

[1470] KRAVCHENKO, V. V. *Obshchestvennye organizatsii SSSR na mezhdunarodnom arene* [Social organizations of the USSR in the international arena]. Moscow: I.M.O., 1969.

[1471] KREKER, HANS-JUSTUS. "The Soviet Union and the Mediterranean." *MR* 1970 50: 21-26.

[1472] KREMNEV, V. *O pravom i 'levom' revizionizme* [On right and 'left' revisionism]. Moscow: Politizdat, 1970.

[1473] "Krepit' internatsional'noe edinstvo Kommunistov" [The international unity of Communists grows]. *Komm* 1969 (7): 3-11.

[1474] KRISCH, HENRY. "Soviet Policy in the German Question." *StNCE* 1968-69 2(3): 88-92.

[1475] ———. "Soviet Policy Toward the Warsaw Pact." *StNCE* 1968-69 2(3): 101-111.

[1476] KRISHNAN, NARAIIANA. "Lenin i Indiia" [Lenin and India]. *Komm* 1970 (5): 101-112.

[1477] *Kritika teoreticheskikh kontseptsii Mao Tsee-duna* [Critique of the theoretical conceptions of Mao Tse-tung]. Moscow: Mysl', 1970.

[1478] KRIUKOV, P. "Failure of Bonn's 'New Eastern Policy.'" *IA(M)* 1969 (7): 41-46.

[1479] ———. "The German Question and the Present Situation." *IA(M)* 1967 (2): 11-16.

[1480] ———. "The Soviet Union and Britain." *IA(M)* 1967 (3): 40-43.

[1481] KRONSTEN, JOSEPH A. "East-West Trade: Myth and Matter." *IA(L)* 1967 43: 265-281.

[1482] KROSBY, H. PETER. *Finland, Germany, and the Soviet Union, 1940-1941: The Petsamo Dispute.* Madison: University of Wisconsin Press, 1968.

[1483] KROTKOV, B. *False and True Friends of the Third World.* Moscow: Novosti, 1971.

[1484] KURCZKOWSKI, ADAM. "For a Peaceful Europe." *WMR* 1967 (5): 15-21.

[1485] _____. *Vneshniaia politika Pol'skoi Narodnoi Respubliki* [The foreign policy of the Polish People's Republic]. Moscow: I.M.O., 1968.

[1486] KRUSZEWSKI, Z. ANTHONY. *The Oder-Neisse Boundary and Poland's Modernization.* New York: Praeger, 1971.

[1487] KRUZHIN, PETR. "A New Interpretation of Peaceful Coexistence." *B,ISUSSR* 1970 17: 27-31.

[1488] _____. "The Soviet Fleet in the Mediterranean." *B,ISUSSR* 1969 16(2): 35-41.

[1489] KRYLOV, KONSTANTIN K. "Soviet Military-Economic Complex." *MR* 1971 51(11): 89-97.

[1490] KRYLOV, N. "Sovetsko-Marokkanskaia torgovlia" [Soviet-Moroccan trade]. *VT* 1970 (6): 14-15.

[1491] KUBY, ERICH. *The Russians and Berlin, 1945.* Translated by Arnold J. Pomerans. New York: Hill and Wang, 1968.

[1492] KUDINOV, V. S. *Problemy Evropeiskoi bezopasnosti i bor'ba Sovetskogo Soiuza za obespechenie prochnogo mira v Evrope* [Problems of European security and the struggle of the Soviet Union for the maintenance of a durable peace in Europe]. Moscow: Znanie, 1971.

[1493] KUDRIASHEV, A. F., ED. *Mir sotsializma v tsifrakh i fatakh* [The world of socialism in numbers and facts]. Moscow: Politizdat, published each year.

[1494] _____, ED. *See* 1429.

[1495] KUDRIAVTSEV, V. "Indestructible Friendship (USSR-UAR)." *NT* 1971 (23): 8-10.

[1496] KUKHAREV, N. M. "Ekonomicheskoe i tekhnicheskoe sodeistvie SSSR Kube" [Economic and technical cooperation of the USSR to Cuba]. *VT* 1968 (12): 9-11.

[1497] _____. "SSSR-Kuba: Sotrudnichestvo v oblasti elektroenergetiki" [USSR-Cuba: Cooperation in the area of electro-energy]. *LA* 1971 (3): 93-99.

[1498] KUKLICK, BRUCE. "The Division of Germany and American Policy on the Reparation." *WPQ* 1970 23: 276-293.

[1499] KULAGINA, L. M. *See* 1519.

[1500] KULEBIAKIN, V. "The Moon and International Law." *IA(M)* 1971 (9): 54-57.

[1501] KULSKI, W. W. "The 1969 Moscow Conference of the Communist Parties." *RR* 1969 28: 385-395.

[1502] _____. "Soviet Views of the German Problem." *CSISt* 1969 3: 92-105.

[1503] KUMARAMANGALAM, MOHAN. "Lenin on Peace and Peaceful Co-Existence." *IQ* 1971 27(1): 57-64.

[1504] KUMYKIN, P. N. *50 let Sovetskoi vneshnei torgovli* [50 years of Soviet foreign trade]. Moscow: I.M.O., 1967.

[1505] KUN, JOSEPH C. "North Korea: Between Moscow and Peking." *CQ* 1967 (31): 48-58.

[1506] KUNAEV, D. "V. I. Lenin i natsional'no-osvoboditel'noe dvizhenie" [V. I. Lenin and the national liberation movement]. *Komm* 1969 (17): 50-60.

[1507] KUNZ, W. "Economic Integration-New Stage in CMEA Cooperation." *WMR* 1971 14(5): 64-70.

[1508] KUSAKOV, E. I., ET AL. *Leninizm i mirovoe revoliutsionnoe rabochee dvizhenie* [Leninism and the world revolutionary workers' movement]. Moscow: Politizdat, 1969.

[1509] KUX, ERNST. "Is Russia a Pacific Power?" *PC* 1970 1: 498-510.

[1510] KUZ'MIN, E. *Mirovoe gosudarstvo: Illiuzii ili real'nost? Kritika burzhuaznykh kontseptsii suvereniteta* [A world state: Illusions or reality? A critique of bourgeois conceptions of sovereignty]. Moscow: I.M.O., 1969.

[1511] KUZ'MIN, M. "Leninskie printsipy vneshnei torgovli i razvitie torgovykh sviazei SSSR s zarubezhnymi stranami" [Leninist principles of foreign trade and the development of trade ties of the USSR with foreign countries]. *VT* 1970 (6): 2-7.

[1512] KUZ'MIN, M. S. *Deiatel'nost' partii i Sovetskogo gosudarstva po razvitiiu mezhdunarodnykh nauchnykh i kul'turnykh sviazei SSSR (1917-1932 gg)* [The activity of the party and the Soviet state for the development of international scientific and cultural ties of the USSR (1917-1932)]. Leningrad: Izdatel'stvo Leningradskogo universiteta, 1971.

[1513] KUZNETS, IU. L. *Ot Pirl Kharbora do Potsdama* [From Pearl Harbor to Potsdam]. Moscow: I.M.O., 1970.

[1514] KUZNETSOV, N. "Torgovlia SSSR s Pakistanom" [The trade of the USSR with Pakistan]. *VT* 1968 (11): 17-19.

[1515] _____. "The War Years." *IA(M)* 1970 (2-3): 122-137.

[1516] _____. "The G.D.R. in the Present-Day World." *NT* 1971 (23): 14-15.

[1517] KUZNETSOV, V. I. *See* 1432.

[1518] _____. *See* 1371.

[1519] KUZNETSOVA, N. A., AND L. M. KULAGINA. *Iz istorii Sovetskogo Vostokovedeniia. 1917-1967 gg* [From the history of Soviet Oriental studies. 1917-1967]. Moscow: Nauka, 1970.

[1520] KUZNETSOVA, S. I. "Afrikanskii rabochii klass v osveshchenii Sovetskoi istorigrafii" [The African working class in the interpretation of Soviet historiography]. *VI* 1969 (1): 49-59.

[1521] LABEDZ, LEOPOLD. "Czechoslovakia and After." *Sur* 1968 (69): 7-21.

[1522] _____.*See* 333.

[1523] _____.*See* 918.

[1524] LABIN, SUZANNE, AND DANIEL LYONS. *Fifty Years: The USSR Versus the U.S.A.* New York: Twin Circle Publishing Company, 1968.

[1525] LAFEBER, WALTER. *America, Russia, and the Cold War 1945-1966.* New York: John Wiley, 1967.

[1526] _____, ED. *The Origins of the Cold War.* New York: John Wiley, 1971.

[1527] LAMBETH, BENJAMIN S. "Moscow and the Missile Race." *CH* 1971 60: 215-221.

[1528] _____. "Nuclear Proliferation and Soviet Arms Control Policy." *Orb* 1970 14: 298-325.

[1529] _____.*See* 1382.

[1530] LAMMERS, DONALD N. "The May Crisis of 1938: The Soviet Version Considered." *SAQ* 1970 (Autumn): 480-503.

[1531] LANDA, RONALD D. "Lenin i Arabskii mir." [Lenin and the Arab world]. *AAS* 1969 (5): 2-4.

[1532] _____. "The Triumph and Tragedy of American Containment: Where the Lines of the Cold War Were Drawn in Europe, 1947-1948." *DAI* 1971 32: 2034-A.

[1533] LANDAU, JACOB M. "Russian Journals Dealing With the Middle East." *MESt* 1971 7: 237-240.

[1534] _____. "Soviet Studies on Workers' Movements in the Middle East." *MESt* 1970 6: 346ff.

[1535] LANDIS, LINCOLN. "Petroleum in Soviet Middle East Strategy." *DAI* 1970 30: 4002-A.

[1536] _____. "Soviet Interest in Middle East Oil." *NME* 1969 (3): 16-21.

[1537] LANE, THOMAS A. *The War for the World.* San Diego, California: Viewpoint Books, 1968.

[1538] LAPINA, S. N. *Leninskaia teoriia perekhoda otstalykh stran k sotsializmu* [The Leninist theory of the transition of the backward countries to socialism]. Moscow: Nauka, 1969.

[1539] LAPTEV, V. *See* 1342.

[1540] LAQUEUR, WALTER. "Russia Enters the Middle East." *FA* 1969 47: 296-308.

[1541] ———. *The Struggle for the Middle East: The Soviet Union in the Mediterranean, 1958-1968.* New York: Macmillan, 1969.

[1542] LARSON, THOMAS B. *Disarmament and Soviet Policy, 1964-1968.* Englewood Cliffs, New Jersey: Prentice-Hall, 1969.

[1543] ———. "Soviet Behavior and Intentions: Arms Limitation and Europe." In *The 24th Party Congress and the 9th Five-Year Plan,* pp. 38-42, edited by Norton T. Dodge. Mechanicsville, Maryland: Cremona Foundation, 1971.

[1544] ———. *See* 510.

[1545] LASKY, MELVIN J. *The Hungarian Revolution: A White Book.* Reprint of 1957 ed. Freeport, New York: Books for Libraries, 1970.

[1546] LAVELLE, MICHAEL J. "Soviet Views on American Unemployment, 1953-1963." *Kyk* 1968 21: 313-325.

[1547] LAVRISHCHEV, A. "The Soviet Union and the Developing Countries." *IA(M)* 1968 (1): 59-65.

[1548] LAVROV, K. "Policy of Peace and Resistance to Aggression." *NT* 1971 (17): 4-6.

[1549] ———. "Soviet-French Cooperation." *IA(M)* 1969 (4): 24-30.

[1550] ———. "Top European Priority." *NT* 1970 (29): 4-7.

[1551] "Laws of Development of Socialist World System." *WMR* 1971 14(10): 3-43.

[1552] LAYSON, WALTER W. "The Political and Strategic Aspects of the 1962 Cuban Crisis." *DAI* 1970 31: 814-A-815-A.

[1553] LAZAREV, M. I. "Antikommunizm i mezhdunarodnoe pravo" [Anti-Communism and international law]. *SGP* 1968 (7): 3-12.

[1554] ———. "Mezhdunarodnoe morskoe pravo: Vzgliad v budushchee" [International law of the sea: A look into the future]. *SGP* 1971 (1): 108-115.

[1555] LAZITCH, BRANKO, AND MILORAD M. DRACHKOVITCH. *Lenin and the Comintern.* Stanford: Hoover Institution, 1971.

[1556] LEBEDEV, N. "Proletarian Internationalism and Its Bankrupt Critics." *IA(M)* 1970 (8): 57-64.

[1557] LEBEDEV, V. "V. I. Lenin ob osnovakh mezhdunarodnykh otnoshenii sotsialisticheskogo gosudarstva" [V. I. Lenin on the fundamentals of international relations of the socialist states]. *PS* 1970 (6): 46-52.

[1558] LEE, CHRISTOPHER D. "Russian Trade With Seven Countries of Central Asia and the Middle East, 1945-53." *Miz* 1968 10: 129-140.

[1559] ———. "Soviet and Chinese Interest in Southern Arabia." *Miz* 1971 13: 35-47.

[1560] ———. "The Soviet Contribution to Iran's Fourth Development Plan." *Miz* 1969 11: 237-247.

[1561] LEE, E. PRESTON, AND KARIM A. NASHASHIBI. *Trade Patterns in the Middle East*. Washington, D.C.: American Enterprise Institute for Public Policy Research, 1970.

[1562] LEE, LONG-SEK, AND KI-WAN OH. "The Russian Faction in North Korea." *AsS* 1968 8: 270-288.

[1563] LEE, UNJA. "Chinese-Soviet Relations: 1956-1260: A Study of Inter-Party and Inter-State Relations." *DAI* 1967 28: 753-A.

[1564] LEGVOLD, ROBERT. "European Security Conference." *Sur* 1970 76: 41-52.

[1565] ———. "Moscow's Changing View of Africa's Revolutionary Regimes." *AfR* 1969 14(3-4): 54-58.

[1566] ———. *Soviet Policy in West Africa*. Cambridge, Massachusetts: Harvard University Press, 1970.

[1567] LEIBZON, B. M. "O leninskikh kriteriiakh revoliutsionnosti i formakh revoliutsionnoi bor'by" [On the Leninist criteria of revolutionary character and the forms of the revolutionary struggle]. *Komm* 1968 (8): 38-51.

[1568] ———, ED. *Iz istorii Kominterna. Sbornik* [From the history of the Comintern. A collection]. Moscow: Nauka, 1970.

[1569] LEMIN, I. "Velikaia Oktiabr'skaia sotsialisticheskaia revoliutsiia i mirovaia politika" [The great October socialist revolution and world politics]. *MEMO* 1967 (6): 3-17.

[1570] LENCZOWSKI, GEORGE. *Soviet Advances in the Middle East*. Washington, D.C.: American Enterprise Institute for Public Policy Research, 1971.

[1571] ———. "Soviet Policy in the Middle East." *CH* 1968 55: 268-274, 303-304.

[1572] LENDVAI, PAUL. *Eagles in Cobwebs: Nationalism and Communism in Balkans*. Garden City, New York: Doubleday, 1969.

[1573] _____. "How to Combine Détente With Soviet Hegemony?" *Sur* 1970 77: 75-92.

[1574] _____. "The Possibilities of Social Tensions and Upheavals in Eastern Europe and Their Possible Effects on European Security." *AP* 1970 (71): 23-29.

[1575] LENGYEL, EMIL. *Nationalism—The Last Stage of Communism.* New York: Funk, 1969.

[1576] *Lenin i Pol'sha (problemy, kontakty, otkliki)* [Lenin and Poland (problems, contacts, responses)]. Moscow: Nauka, 1970.

[1577] LENIN, V. I. *Drug narodov Vostoka. Sbornik dokumentov i materialov 1917-1924 gg. vol. 2* [Friend of the peoples of the East. Collection of documents and materials 1917-1924]. Baku: AN Azerb. SSR, 1967.

[1578] _____. *On the National Question and Proletarian Internationalism.* Moscow: Novosti Press, 1969.

[1579] *V. I. Lenin i Sovetskaia vneshniaia politika* [V. I. Lenin and Soviet foreign policy]. Moscow: I.M.O., 1969.

[1580] "Lenin o probuzhdenii narodov Asii i Afriki" [Lenin on the awakening of the peoples of Asia and Africa]. *AAS* 1969 (4): 2-5.

[1581] *Leninism and the Revolutionary Process. (Proceedings of a Conference Held in Prague, November 19-21, 1969).* Prague: Peace and Socialism Publishers, 1970. Russian Edition: *Leninizm i revoliutionnyi protzess* [Leninism and the Revolutionary Process]. Moscow: Izd. Mir i Sotsializm, 1970.

[1582] *Leninist Approach to Unity of the World Communist Movement.* Moscow: Novosti, 1970.

[1583] *Leninizm i edinstvo mezhdunarodnogo Kommunisticheskogo dvizheniia* [Leninism and the unity of the international Communist movement]. Moscow: APN, 1970.

[1584] *Leninizm i mirovoi revoliutsionnyi protsess. Materially Mezhdunarodnoi, Teoreticheskoi Konferentsii, posviashchennoi 100-letiiu so dnia rozhdeniia V. I. Lenina. Moskva, 24-26 Fevr. 1970 g* [Leninism and the world revolutionary process. Materials of the International, Theoretical Conference, devoted to the 100th anniversary of birth of V. I. Lenin. Moscow, 24-26 February, 1970]. Moscow: Politizdat, 1970.

[1585] *Leninizm i sovremennost': Opyt Oktiabria i sovremennyi revoliutsionnyi protsess* [Leninism and the present: The experience of October and the present revolutionary process]. Moscow: I.M.O., 1969.

[1586] "Lenin's Foreign Policy Activity." *IA(M)* 1969 (1): 110-114, (2): 100-103, (3): 112-115, (4): 111-114.

[1587] *Leninskaia politika SSSR v otnoshenii Kitaia* [The Leninist policy of the USSR in relations with China]. Moscow: Nauka, 1968.

[1588] "Leninskaia vneshniaia politika Sovetskogo Soiuza" [The Leninist foreign policy of the Soviet Union]. *Komm* 1970 (14): 3-14.

[1589] *Leninskii analiz imperializma i sovremennyi kapitalizm* [The Leninist analysis of imperialism and contemporary capitalism]. Moscow: Izd. Moskovskogo universiteta, 1969.

[1590] *Leninskoe uchenie ob imperializme i sovremennost'* [The Leninist teaching on imperialism and the present]. Moscow: APN, 1970.

[1591] LENNON, VERNON R. "The Language of the Cold War: A Study of Semantic Evolution." *MA* 1968 6: 150.

[1592] LENSEN, GEORGE ALEXANDER. *Russian Diplomatic and Consular Officials in East Asia: A Handbook of the Representatives of Tsarist Russia and the Provisional Government in China, Japan and Korea From 1858 to 1924 and of Soviet Representatives in Japan From 1925 to 1968. Compiled on the Basis of Russian, Japanese and Chinese Sources With a Historical Introduction.* Tokyo: Sophia University, in cooperation with Tallahassee, Florida: The Diplomatic Press, 1968.

[1593] ———. *The Russo-Chinese War.* Tallahassee, Florida: The Diplomatic Press, 1967.

[1594] LEONHARD, WOLFGANG. *See* 2776.

[1595] LEONIDOV, A. "Lenin and Foreign Policy." *NT* 1969 (1): 3-6, (5): 6-10, (7): 10-13.

[1596] ———. "Lenin and the International Working-Class Movement." *NT* 1969 (17): 3-5, (18): 11-14.

[1597] ———. "Lenin and the United States." *NT* 1969 (3): 4-6.

[1598] ———. "Lenin i nezavisimye gosudarstva Vostoka" [Lenin and the independent states of the East]." *AAS* 1969 (8): 6-9.

[1599] LEONT'EV, L. A. *Leninskaia teoriia imperializma* [The Leninist theory of imperialism]. Moscow: Nauka, 1969.

[1600] ———. "Mezhdunarodnoe znachenie XXIV S'ezda KPSS" [The international meaning of the 24th Congress of the CPSU]. *MEMO* 1971 (5): 4-17.

[1601] ———. "The Way to Victory Over Imperialism." *NT* 1970 (6): 18-21.

[1602] LESECHKO, M. A. "Sotrudnichestvo stran SEV na sovremennom etape" [The cooperation of the countries of CMEA at the present stage]. *Komm* 1971 (4): 82-93.

[1603] _____.*Sovetskii Soiuz v sisteme sotsialisticheskogo razdeleniia truda stran-chlenov SEV* [The Soviet Union in the system of the socialist division of labor of the member countries of CMEA]. Moscow: Ekonomika, 1970.

[1604] _____, ET AL. *Leninism and the Socialist Community.* Moscow: Novosti Press, 1969.

[1605] "Lessons Drawn From the Crisis Development in the Party and Society After the 13th Congress of the Communist Party of Czechoslovakia." *WMR* 1971 (2): 5-54.

[1606] LEVIN, D. B. "Metodologiia Sovetskoi nauki mezhdunarodnogo prava" [The methodology of the Soviet science of international law]. *SGP* 1969 (9): 59-66.

[1607] _____.*Mezhdunarodnoe pravo i sokhranenie mira* [International law and the preservation of peace]. Moscow: I.M.O., 1971.

[1608] LEVIN, VIKTOR. *Kollektivnaia bezopasnost' v Evrope* [Collective security in Europe]. Moscow: Novosti, 1967.

[1609] LEVINE, DAVID C. *The Rift: The Sino-Soviet Conflict.* Jacksonville, Illinois: Harris-Wolfe & Company, 1968.

[1610] LEVIT, I. I. *See* 1405.

[1611] LEVSHIN, F., AND S. MKRTUMOV. "Eksport mashin i oborudovaniia" [The export of machinery and equipment]. *VT* 1967 (7): 10-18.

[1612] LEWIS, BERNARD. "The Great Powers, the Arabs and the Israelis." *FA* 1969 47: 642-652.

[1613] LEWIS, PHILIP C. "Constant Elements of Soviet Inspection Proposals for Disarmament." *MA* 1968 6: 96.

[1614] LI, VL. *Na puti Nekapitalisticheskogo razvitiia* [On the path of non-capitalist development]. Moscow: Znanie, 1967.

[1615] _____. "Sotsializm i natsional'no-osvoboditel'noe dvizhenie" [Socialism and the national-liberation movement]. *PS* 1971 (4): 97-101.

[1616] LIBMAN, G. I. *Sovremennaia epokha i mirovoi revoliutsionnyi protsess* [The contemporary epoch and the world revolutionary process]. Moscow: Vyssh. shkola, 1970.

[1617] LIBRARY AND DOCUMENTATION DEPARTMENT, INSTITUTE FOR INTERNATIONAL POLITICS AND ECONOMICS (PRAGUE). "International Relations —Czechoslovakia." *CSISt,BS* 1968 2(3): 35-41; 1969 3(1): 93-161.

[1618] LICKLIKER, ROY E. "The Missile Gap Controversy." *PSQ* 1970 85: 600-615.

[1619] LIKHACHEV, B. "Leninskaia strategiia revoliutsionnogo edinstva" [The Leninist strategy of revolutionary unity]. *Komm* 1970 (9): 113-120.

[1620] LINDER, I. "Lenin's Foreign Policy Activity (October 1921-March 1922)." *IA(M)* 1969 (12): 46-51.

[1621] LINNES, ERHARD. "Antecedents of the Oder-Niesse Frontier and Present Day Attitudes of the Two Germanies and Poland." *MA* 1968 6: 96.

[1622] LISANN, MAURY. "Moscow and the Chinese Power." *PoC* 1969 18(6): 32-41.

[1623] LISKA, GEORGE. *Alliances and the Third World.* Baltimore, Maryland: Johns Hopkins Press, 1968.

[1624] LITMAN, ALEXEI. *Lenin and Ideological Problems of the National-Liberation Movement.* Moscow: Novosti, 1970.

[1625] LITTELL, ROBERT, ED. *The Czech Black Book. Prepared by the Institute of History of the Czechoslovak Academy of Sciences.* New York: Praeger, 1969.

[1626] LIUBIMOV, N. N., ED. *Mezhdunarodnye ekonomicheskie otnosheniia* [International economic relations]. Moscow: I.M.O., 1969.

[1627] LLOYD, TREVOR. "Czechoslovakia 1968: The Impression of a Geographer." *CSIP* 1968 10: 523-532.

[1628] LODGAARD, SVERRE. *See* 795.

[1629] LOEBL, EUGEN. "Superstalinism: The New Soviet Foreign Policy." *IP* 1969 3(1): 21-24. *MR* 1969 49(12): 77-85.

[1630] LOGORECI, ANTON. "Albania and China: Incongruous Alliance." *CH* 1967 52: 227-231, 245.

[1631] ———. "Albania: The Anabaptists of European Communism." *PoC* 1967 16(3): 22-28.

[1632] LOITER, M. "Voprosy povysheniia effektivnosti kapital'nykh vlozhenii v stranakh-chlenakh SEV" [Questions of raising the effectiveness of capital investments in the member countries of CMEA]. *VE* 1970 (1): 134-139.

[1633] LOKASHIN, L. "Sovetsko-Shveitsarskii torgovye sviazi" [Soviet-Swedish trade ties]. *VT* 1969 (2): 20-23.

[1634] LOMIDZE, G. "Velikaia sila proletarskogo internatsionalizma" [The great strength of proletarian internationalism]. *Komm* 1971 (5): 108-118.

[1635] LOMOV, N. "Historical Significance of the Victory in the Great Patriotic War." *IA(M)* 1970 (6): 3-6.

[1636] LONDON, KURT L. *The Permanent Crisis: Communism in World Politics.* 2d ed. Waltham, Massachusetts: Blaisdell Publishing Company, 1967.

[1637] ———. "The Sino-Soviet Conflict Today." *CH* 1968 55: 159-164, 181.

[1638] ———. "The Soviet Union and the West." *CH* 1969 56: 193-200, 238.

[1639] ———. "The Soviet Union and West Europe." *CH* 1970 59: 199-205.

[1640] ———. "The USSR, East Europe and the Socialist Commonwealth." *CH* 1969 56: 193-199.

[1641] ———. "Vietnam: A Sino-Soviet Dilemma." *RR* 1967 26: 26-37.

[1642] ———, ED. *The Soviet Union: A Half-Century of Communism.* Baltimore, Maryland: Johns Hopkins Press, 1968.

[1643] LONG, FRANKLIN A. "Strategic Balance and the ABM." *BAS* 1968 24(10): 2-5.

[1644] LONGO, LUIGI. "Oktiabr'skaia revoliutsiia i bor'ba za mir" [The October revolution and the struggle for peace]. *Komm* 1967 (17): 35-41.

[1645] LONGRIGG, TONY. "Soviet Science and Foreign Policy." *Sur* 1971 17(4): 30-50.

[1646] LOPUKHOVA, N. "Mezhdunarodnye ekonomicheskie organizatsii stran sotsializma" [International economic organizations of the socialist countries]. *VE* 1969 (12): 118-125.

[1647] LOSHAKOV, M. "SSSR-GDR: Vzaimovygodnoe sotrudnichestvo" [The USSR-GDR: Mutually beneficial cooperation]. *VT* 1969 (10): 10-13.

[1648] LOWENTHAL, RICHARD. "Germany's Role in East-West Relations." *WT* 1967 23: 240-248.

[1649] ———. "Russia and China: Controlled Conflict." *FA* 1971 49: 507-518.

[1650] ———. "The Sparrow in the Cage [Czechoslovakia]." *PoC* 1968 17(6): 2-28.

[1651] ———. "Trends in Soviet Foreign Policy." In *The Soviet Union Under Brezhnev and Kosygin,* pp. 235-248, edited by John W. Strong. New York: Van Nostrand Reinhold, 1971.

[1652] ———, ED. *Issues in the Future of Asia.* New York: Praeger, 1969.

[1653] LUDZ, PETER C. *The German Democratic Republic From the 1960's to the 1970's*. Cambridge, Massachusetts: Center for International Affairs, University, Occasional Paper in International Affairs, (26), 1970.

[1654] LUKAS, RICHARD C. *Eagles East: The Army Air Forces and the Soviet Union, 1941-45*. Tallahasee: Florida State University Press, 1970.

[1655] LUKASZEWSKI, JERZY. "The United States, the West, and the Future of Eastern Europe." *JIA* 1968 22: 16-25.

[1656] ———. "Western Integration and the People's Democracies." *FA* 1968 46: 377-387.

[1657] ———, ED. *The People's Democracies After Prague: Soviet Hegemony, Nationalism, Regional Integration*. Bruges: De Tempel, 1970.

[1658] LUKIN, L. *See* 1248.

[1659] LUKIN, P. I. "Pravo i kosmicheskaia radiosviaz" [Law and space radio communication]. *SGP* 1970 (7): 83-90.

[1660] LUKIN, V. P. " 'Ideologiia razvitiia' i massovoe soznanie v stranakh 'tret'ego mira' " [The "ideology of development" and mass consciousness in the countries of the "third world"]. *VF* 1969 (6): 35-46.

[1661] LUMKOV, N. "Soviet Union's International Cultural Ties." *IA(M)* 1971 (9): 36-41.

[1662] LUND, ERIK. "Khrushchev in Denmark: A Study of the Soviet and East European Press Reactions." *CaC* 1967 (1): 26-35.

[1663] LUNIN, B. *Lenin and the Peoples of the East*. Moscow: Novosti, 1970.

[1664] LUNTS, L. A. *Mezhdunarodnoe chastnoe pravo* [International private law]. Moscow: Iuridicheskaia literatura, 1970.

[1665] LYONS, DANIEL. *See* 1524.

[1666] MACFARLANE, L. J. "Hands Off Russia: British Labor and the Russo-Polish War, 1920." *PP* 1967 38: 126-152.

[1667] MACKINTOSH, MALCOLM. "The Evolution of the Warsaw Pact." *AP* 1969 58.

[1668] ———. *Juggernaut: A History of the Soviet Armed Forces*. New York: Macmillan, 1967.

[1669] ———. "Russia's Defense: A Question of Quality." *IP* 1971 4(2): 14-17.

[1670] ———. "Soviet Foreign Policy." *WT* 1968 24: 145-150.

[1671] ———. "Soviet Policy Towards the Middle East: 1945-1967." *BSJA* 1969 31-36.

[1672] ———. "Soviet Strategic Policy." *WT* 1970 26: 269-276.

[1673] ———. *See* 2776.

[1674] MADDOX, THOMAS ROTH. "American Relations With the Soviet Union, 1933-1941." *DAI* 1970 30: 3888-A.

[1675] MAGGS, PETER B. *See* 196.

[1676] MAHNCKE, DIETER. "The Berlin Agreement: Balance and Prospects." *WT* 1971 27: 511-521.

[1677] "Main Stages in Soviet Foreign Policy." *IA(M)* 1968 (1): 52-56.

[1678] MAISKII, IVAN M. "Diplomats of the Lenin School: Alexandra Kollontai." *NT* 1968 (4): 20-22.

[1679] ———. "Diplomats of the Lenin School: Ambassador Krasin." *NT* 1968 (3): 23-27.

[1680] ———. "Diplomats of the Lenin School: Georgi Chicherin." *NT* 1967 (44): 10-13.

[1681] ———. *Memoirs of a Soviet Ambassador: The War 1939-43.* London: Hutchinson, 1967. New York: Scribner, 1968.

[1682] MAJONICA, ERNST. *East-West Relations: A German View.* New York: Praeger, 1969.

[1683] MAKAROV, V. "Konteinerizatsiia vneshnetorgovykh perevozok stran SEV" [Packaging of foreign trade shipments of the CMEA countries]. *VT* 1970 (12): 13-16.

[1684] MAKSIMOV, I. *Terma "Politika KPSS v oblasti razvitiia mirovogo sotsialisticheskogo khoziaistva"* [The theme "The politics of the CPSU in the area of the development of world socialist economy"]. Minsk: Belarus', 1971.

[1685] MAKSIMOVA, M. "Ekonomicheskaia integratsiia: Nekotorye voprosy metodologii" [Economic integration: Some questions of methodology]. *MEMO* 1969 (5): 15-27.

[1686] MALAKHIN, P. N. "Iz istorii ekonomicheskikh sviazei s SShA" [From the history of economic ties with the USA]. *SShA* 1970 (3): 15-19.

[1687] MALANKE, HANS HEINRICH. "Soviet Doctrine-International Law." *CEJ* 1970 18: 159-167.

[1688] MALASHKO, A. *Voinstvuiushchii natsionalizm—ideologiia i politika imperializma* [Militant nationalism—the ideology and politics of imperialism]. Minsk: Belarus', 1971.

[1689] MALIK, IA. "Dvadtsatipiatiletie OON i mezhdunarodnaia bezopasnost'" [The 25th anniversary of the UN and international security].
Komm 1970 (15): 98-106.

[1690] MALININ, S. A. *Mirnoe ispol'zovanie atomnoi energii (mezhdunarod-
no-pravovye voprosy)* [The peaceful use of atomic energy (international legal questions)]. Moscow: I.M.O., 1971.

[1691] _____. "Pravovaia priroda atomnykh mezhgosudarstvennykh organizatsii" [The legal nature of inter-state atomic organizations]. *SGP*
1970 (9): 66-74.

[1692] MALLIN, JAY, ED. *Strategy for Conquest.* Coral Gables, Florida: University of Miami Press, 1970.

[1693] MALLOW, JAMES M., AND WILLIAM R. CAMPBELL. *Ideology in an Action
Framework: An Approach to Communist Political Behavior.*
Kingston: University of Rhode Island, 1968.

[1694] MANDEL, ERNEST, ED. *Fifty Years of World Revolution (1917-1967).*
New York: Merit, 1968.

[1695] MANESCU, CORNELIU. "Rumania in the Concert of Nations." *IA(L)*
1969 45: 1-14.

[1696] MANFRED, A. Z. *Traditsii druzhby i sotrudnichestva. O Russko-
Frantsuzskikh i Sovetsko-Frantszskikh otnosheniiakh* [Traditions
of friendship and cooperation in Russian-French and Soviet-French
relations]. Moscow: Nauka, 1967.

[1697] _____. "USSR and France in European and World Politics." *IA(M)*
1971 (11): 92-97.

[1698] MANNING, CLARENCE A. "The West and Moscow in 1968." *UQ* 1968
24: 239-246.

[1699] MANRARA, LUIS V. *Betrayal Opened the Door to Russian Missiles in
Red Cuba.* Miami, Florida: The Truth about Cuba Committee,
1968.

[1700] MANSBACH, RICHARD W. "Bilateralism and Multilateralism in the
Soviet Bloc." *IO* 1970 24: 371-380.

[1701] _____. "In Search of a Role: Yugoslavia and Nonalignment." *Orb*
1970 14: 505-509.

[1702] MANZHULO, A. "Rashirenie Obshcheevropeiskogo sotrudnichestva-
velenie vremeni" [The expansion of all-European economic cooperation is a command of the times]. *VT* 1971 (6): 5-8.

[1703] *Maoizm glazami Kommunistov* [Maoism in the eyes of Communists].
Moscow: Progress, 1969.

[1704] MARCHENKO, V. M., AND A. I. SIZONENKO. "SSSR i Latinskaia Amerika v gody Vtoroi Mirovoi Voiny" [The USSR and Latin America in the years of the Second World War]. *LA* 1971 (5): 131-143.

[1705] MARER, PAUL. *See* 316.

[1706] MARGULIES, SYLVIA R. *The Pilgrimage to Russia: The Soviet Union and the Treatment of Foreigners, 1924-1937.* Madison: University of Wisconsin Press, 1968.

[1707] MARION, CAROL J. "Ministers in Moscow [World War II]." *DAI* 1970 31: 2315-A.

[1708] MARKO, JAN. "Czechoslovakia's Foreign Policy: Past and Present." *IA(M)* 1971 (5): 41-51.

[1709] ———. "Twenty-Five Years After Liberation and the Foreign Policy of the Czechoslovak Socialist Republic." *IA(M)* 1970 (6): 23-30.

[1710] MARKS, DONALD M. "The Ussuri River Incident as a Factor in Chinese Foreign Policy." *AUR* 1971 22(4): 53-63.

[1711] MARKS, J. B. "The October Revolution and the National Liberation Movement." *WMR* 1967 (6): 18-23.

[1712] "Marksizm-Leninizm i natsional'noe osvobozhdenie" [Marxism-Leninism and national liberation]. *AAS* 1968 (5): 3-6.

[1713] *Marksizm-Leninizm o proletarskom internatsionalizme. Sbornik* [Marxism-Leninism on proletarian internationalism. A collection]. Moscow: Politizdat, 1969.

[1714] MARSH, WILLIAM W. "East Germany and Africa." *AfR* 1969 14(3-4): 59-64.

[1715] MARTYSHIN, O. V. "Klassy i klassovaia bor'ba v ideologii natsional'noi demokratii" [Classes and class struggle in the ideology of national democracy]. *NAA* 1967 (5): 48-58.

[1716] MARX, KARL, FRIEDRICH ENGELS, AND V. I. LENIN. *O proletarskom internatsionalizme* [On proletarian internationalism]. 2d supplemented ed. Moscow: Politizdat, 1968.

[1717] MARZARI, FRANK. "Western-Soviet Rivalry in Turkey, 1939." *MESt* 1971 7: 63-80, 201-220.

[1718] MASEVICH, ALLA. "Soviet-French Scientific Experiments." *NT* 1971 (2): 18-19.

[1719] MASON, DAVID, AND JESSICA SMITH, EDS. *Lenin's Impact on the United States.* New York: New World Review Publications, 1970.

[1720] MASSON, PHILLIPE, AND J. LABAYLE COUHAT. "The Soviet Presence in the Mediterranean: A Short History." *NWCR* 1971 23(5): 60-66.

[1721] MASTERKOV, L. A., AND I. I. CHEPROV. "Zapreshenie dlia vsekh: O khimicheskom i bakteriologicheskom oruzhii" [Prohibition for all: On chemical and bacteriological weapons]. *SGP* 1969 (7): 60-67.

[1722] MATES, LEO. "Nonalignment and the Great Powers." *FA* 1970 48: 525-537.

[1723] MATVEEV, V. "European Security and NATO." *IA(M)* 1970 (2-3): 88-92.

[1724] _____. "Lessons of History and European Security." *IA(M)* 1970 (6): 9-14.

[1725] MATZNER, EGON. *Trade Between East and West: The Case of Austria.* Stockholm: Almqvist and Wiksell, 1970.

[1726] MAX, ALPHONSE E. "Soviet Interest in the South Atlantic Ocean." *MR* 1968 48(10): 92-96.

[1727] MAXWELL, NEVILLE. "Russia and China: The Irrepressible Conflict." *PC* 1970 (1): 551-563.

[1728] MAY, ALBERT E. "The Soviet Merchant Marine." *NWCR* 1971 23(10): 45-50.

[1729] MAY, BENJAMIN M., JR. "Themes of Soviet War Propaganda, 1941-45." *DAI* 1971 31: 4233-A.

[1730] MAYER, PETER. *Cohesion and Conflict in International Communism: A Study of Marxist-Leninist Concepts and Their Application.* The Hague: Martinus Nijhoff, 1968.

[1731] _____. "Why the Ussuri?" *MR* 1970 50: 22-32.

[1732] _____. *Why the Ussuri? Reflections of the Latest Sino-Soviet Fracas.* Waltham, Massachusetts: Westinghouse Electric Corporation Advanced Studies Group, ASG-Monographs, 1, 1969.

[1733] MAZANOV, G. G. "Integrational Tasks of International Socialist Credit." *IA(M)* 1970 (12): 36-43.

[1734] _____. *Mezhdunarodnye raschety stran—chlenov SEV* [The international accounts of the member countries of CMEA]. Moscow: Finansy, 1969.

[1735] McCAUSLIN, HELEN. "International Relations—Yugoslavia." *CSISt,BS* 1968 2(2): 70-72.

[1736] McFARLANE, B. J. "The Politics of Economic Reform in Eastern Europe, 1965-1969." *AuO* 1970 24: 164-177.

[1737] McGOVERN, RAYMOND L. "Moscow and Hanoi." *PoC* 1967 16(3): 64-71.

[1738] McGwire, Michael. "The Background to Soviet Naval Developments." *WT* 1971 27: 93-103.

[1739] McLane, Charles B. "Foreign Aid in Soviet Third World Policies." *Miz* 1969 11: 210-250.

[1740] _____. "Russia and the Third World." *StSU* 1967 6(3): 73-90.

[1741] _____. "The Russians and Vietnam: Strategies of Indirection." *IJ* 1968 24: 47-64.

[1742] McLellan, David S. "The Changing Nature of Soviet and American Relations With Western Europe." *A,AAPSS* 1967 (372): 16-32.

[1743] McMillan, Carl. "Some Recent Developments in Soviet Foreign Trade Theory." *CSIP* 1970 12: 243-272.

[1744] McNeal, Robert H., ed. *International Relations Among Communists.* Englewood Cliffs, New Jersey: Prentice-Hall, 1967.

[1745] McNeill, William Hardy. *America, Britain and Russia—Their Cooperation and Conflict 1941-1946.* Reprint of 1953 edition. London, New York and Toronto: Johnson Reprint Corporation, 1971.

[1746] McSherry, James E. *Khrushchev and Kennedy in Retrospect.* Palo Alto, California: Open-Door Press, 1971.

[1747] _____. *Stalin, Hitler, and Europe. Vol. I: The Origins of World War II, 1933-1939.* Cleveland, Ohio: World, 1968.

[1748] _____. *Stalin, Hitler, and Europe. Vol. II: The Imbalance of Power, 1939-1941.* New York: World Publishing Company, 1970.

[1749] Mehnert, Klaus. *See* 333.

[1750] _____. *See* 2777.

[1751] Meissner, Boris. "The Breznev Doctrine." *EEM* 1970 (2): 1-79.

[1752] _____. "Soviet Concepts of Peace and Security: The Limits of Coexistence." *ModA* 1968 12: 232-246. *ACQ* 1968 6: 413-424.

[1753] Mekler, G. K. "O nekotorykh voprosakh Sovetsko-Iapanskikh ekonomicheskikh otnoshenii" [On some questions of Soviet-Japanese economic relations]. *NAA* 1968 (1): 117-120.

[1754] Mellor, R. E. H. *COMECON: Challenge to the West.* New York: Van Nostrand Reinhold, 1971.

[1755] Mel'nikov, D. "Germanskaia natsiia i sud'by Evropy" [The German nation and the fate of Europe]. *MEMO* 1968 (11): 39-50.

[1756] _____. "Sovetsko-Zapadnogermanskii dogovor i razmezhevanie politicheskikh sil v FRG" [The Soviet-West German agreement and demarcation of political forces in the FRG]. *MEMO* 1970 (12): 15-24.

[1757]   MENGES, CONSTANTINE C. "Resistance in Czechoslovakia—An Underground in the Open." *T-A* 1968 6(2): 36-41.

[1758]   MENSHIKOV, V. "Soviet-Cyprus Friendship." *NT* 1971 (22): 14-15.

[1759]   MERLIN, SAMUEL, ED. *The Big Powers and the Present Crisis in the Middle East.* Rutherford, New Jersey: Fairleigh Dickinson University Press, 1968.

[1760]   MERTENS, RENÉ. "The Soviet Fleet in Arab Politics." *NME* November 1969 (14): 21-25.

[1761]   MERZYN, GERHARD. "The Soviet Union and the Eastern Policy of the Federal German Republic." *ACQ* 1969 7: 196-202.

[1762]   METROWICH, F. R. *Africa and Communism: A Study of Successes, Setbacks, and Stooge-States.* Johannesburg-Pretoria: Voortrekkerpers, 1967.

[1763]   MEYERDORFF, BARON ALEXANDER. "My Cousin, Foreign Commissar Chicherin." *RR* 1971 30: 173-178.

[1764]   "Mezhdunarodnaia Konferentsiia Marksistov k 50-letiiu vykhoda v svet knigi V. I. Lenina 'Imperializm, kak Vysshaia Stadiia Kapitalizma' "[The International Conference of Marxists in commemoration of the publication of V. I. Lenin's "Imperialism, the Highest Stage of Capitalism"]. *MEMO* 1967 (6): 58-106; 1967 (7): 68-90; 1967 (8): 54-87.

[1765]   *Mezhdunarodnaia pravosub"ektivnost'* [International legal personality]. Moscow: Iuridicheskaia literatura, 1971.

[1766]   *Mezhdunarodnoe Kommunisticheskoe i rabochee dvizhenie. Spravochnik-ezhegodnik* [The international Communist and workers' movement. Annual reference book]. Moscow: Politizdat, published annually.

[1767]   *Mezhdunarodnoe obozrenie. (Sbornik statei)* [International review: A collection of articles]. Tbilisi: Sabchota Sakartvelo, 1967.

[1768]   *Mezhdunarodnye organizatsii sotsialisticheskikh stran* [International organizations of the socialist countries]. Moscow: I.M.O., 1971.

[1769]   *Mezhdunarodnye sviazi stran tsental'noi vostochnoi i iugovostochnoi Evropy i Slaviano-Germanskie otnosheniia* [International ties of the countries of central, east, and southeast Europe and Slavic-German relations]. Moscow: Nauka, 1968.

[1770]   *Mezhdunarodnyi ezhegodnik. Politika i ekonomika* [International annual. Politics and economics]. Moscow: Politizdat, published annually.

[1771] MICHAEL, FRANZ. "Moscow and the Current Chinese Crisis." *CH* 1967 52: 141-147, 175.

[1772] ———. "Struggle for Power." *PoC* 1967 16(3): 12-21.

[1773] ———. "Twenty Years of Sino-Soviet Relations." *CH* 1969 57: 150-155.

[1774] MICHAL, JAN M. "Czechoslovakia's Foreign Trade." *SIR* 1968 27: 212-229.

[1775] "The Middle East: Soviet Anxieties." *Miz* 1967 9: 145-153.

[1776] "Middle East: The Soviet Stance." *Miz* 1968 10: 141-150.

[1777] "Middle East: The Soviet-UAR Posture." *Miz* 1970 12: 1-6.

[1778] MIECZOWSKI, Z. "The Soviet Far East: Problem Region of the USSR." *PA* 1968 41: 214-229.

[1779] MIELI, RENATO. *See* 918.

[1780] MIKHAILOV, E. "Politika SSSR—proletarskii internatsionalizm v deistvii" [The politics of the USSR—proletarian internationalism in action]. *MEMO* 1968 (6): 144-152.

[1781] MIKHAILOV, IA., A. MIRONOV, AND B. ZANERIN. *K sobytiiam v Kitae* [The events in China]. Moscow: Politizdat, 1967.

[1782] MIKHAILOV, M. *Mezhdunarodnyi dnevnik* [International diary]. Moscow: Izvestiia, 1968.

[1783] MIKHAILOV, V. "Sovetsko-Frantsuskie torgovo-ekonomicheskie otnosheniia" [Soviet-French economic-trade relations]. *VT* 1968 (11): 12-15.

[1784] MIKHEEV, IU., AND V. ZELENTSOV. *On the Side of a Just Cause: Soviet Assistance to the Heroic Vietnamese People.* Moscow: Progress, 1970.

[1785] MIKHEEVA, G. *See* 3233.

[1786] MIKLEIKOVSKII, A. "Lenin's Theory of Imperialism and New Phenomena in Capitalist Economy." *WMR* 1970 13(6): 28-34.

[1787] ———. "Leninskii ekonomicheskii analiz imperializma i kapitalizm nashikh dnei" [The Leninist economic analysis of imperialism and capitalism of our days]. *MEMO* 1970 (4): 18-30.

[1788] MIKOYAN, SERGO. "NATO, the Soviet Union and European Security." *Orb* 1969 13: 59-67 *ACQ* 1969 7: 342-350.

[1789] MIKSCHE, FERDINAND O. "Soviet Influence in the Mediterranean." *MR* 1971 51(9): 62-65.

[1790] ———. "Soviet Policy and Détente." *MR* 1969 49(10): 77-81.

110

[1791] ———. "The Soviet Union as a Mediterranean Power." *MR* 1968 48(7): 32-36.

[1792] MIKUL'SKII, K. I. "Aktual'nye problemy balansa trudovykh resursov v stranakh-chlenakh SEV" [Actual problems of the balance of labor resources in the member countries of CMEA]. *VE* 1969 (7): 131-140.

[1793] ———. "Economic Effectiveness in the CMEA Countries." *IA(M)* 1969 (3): 59-64.

[1794] ———. "Intensifikatsiia proizvodstva i ekonomicheskaia integratsiia stran SEV" [Intensification of production and economic integration of the CMEA countries]. *VE* 1971 (3): 94-105.

[1795] ———.*Leninskoe uchenie o mirovom khoziaistve i sovremennost'* [The Leninist teaching on world economy and the present]. Moscow: I.M.O., 1970.

[1796] ———.*Natsional'nye resursy i mezhdunarodnoe sotrudnichestvo* [National resources and international cooperation]. Moscow: I.M.O., 1967.

[1797] ———. "New Scientific and Technological Horizons in the CMEA Countries." *IA(M)* 1970 (6): 38-43.

[1798] ———. "Trends in World Economic Development." *IA(M)* 1971 (4): 9-17.

[1799] ———.*Trudovye resursy Evropeiskikh stran sotsializma* [Labor resources of the European socialist countries]. Moscow: Statistika, 1969.

[1800] MILBANK, DAVID L. "Yugoslav Policy Toward Algeria in Perspective." *SAIS* 1967 12(1): 4-14.

[1801] MILENKOVITCH, MICHAEL M. "Soviet-Yugoslav Relations and the Brezhnev Doctrine." *StNCE* 1968-69 2(3): 112-121.

[1802] MILLAR, T. B. "Soviet Policies South and East of Suez." *FA* 1970 49: 70-80.

[1803] ———.*Soviet Policies in the Indian Ocean Area.* Canberra: Australian National University, Strategic and Defense Studies Centre, 1970.

[1804] MILLIKAN, GORDON. "Soviet and Comintern Policy Toward Germany, 1928-1933: A Case Study of Strategy and Tactics." *DAI* 1971 32: 363-A.

[1805] MILLS, J. RUSSELL, JR. *See* 1210.

[1806] MILSOM, JOHN. *Russian Tanks, 1900-1970: The Complete Illustrated History of Soviet Armoured Theory and Design.* Harrisburg, Pennsylvania: Stackpole Books, 1971.

[1807] MINISTERSTVO INOSTRANNYKH DEL SSSR. *Dokumenty vneshnei politiki SSSR* [Documents of the foreign policy of the USSR], vols. 12-16, covering 1929-1933. Moscow: Politizdat, 1967-1970.

[1808] MINISTERSTVO VNESHNEI TORGOVLI SSSR. *Vneshniaia torgovlia SSSR. Statisticheskii obzor* [Foreign trade of the USSR. Statistical survey]. Moscow: I.M.O., published annually.

[1809] MIRONOV, A. *See* 1781.

[1810] MIRONOV, N. V. *Pravovoe regulirovnaie vneshnikh snoshenii SSSR* [The legal regulation of the foreign dealings of the USSR]. Moscow: I.M.O., 1971.

[1811] _____.*Sovetskoe zakonodatel'stvo i mezhdunarodnoe pravo* [Soviet legislation and international law]. Moscow: I.M.O., 1968.

[1812] MIROSHNICHENKO, A. "Mezhdunarodnoe razdelenie truda v mashinos-troenii stran-chlenov SEV" [The international division of labor in the engineering industry of the member countries of CMEA]. *VE* 1970 (7): 106-111.

[1813] MIROSHNICHENKO, B. P. "The International Significance of Soviet Planning Experience." *IA(M)* 1967 (9): 10-16.

[1814] _____.*See* 3023.

[1815] *Mirovaia sotsialisticheskaia sistema i Antikommunizm* [The World socialist system and Anti-Communism]. Moscow: Nauka, 1967.

[1816] *Mirovoi sotsializm i razvivaiushchiesia strany (ekonomicheskie otno-sheniia sotsialisticheskikh stran Evropy s razvivaiushchimisia stranami)* [The World socialist system and the developing countries (economic relations of the socialist countries of Europe with the developing countries]. Moscow: Mysl', 1968.

[1817] MIRSKII, GEORGII. "Soviet View on the Future of the Suez Canal." *NME* January 1969 (4): 16-18.

[1818] MITCHELL, DONALD W. "The Soviet Naval Challenge." *Orb* 1970 14: 129-153.

[1819] MITIN, M. B., ED. *Leninizm i bor'ba protiv burzhuaznoi ideologii i An-tikommunizma na sovremennom etape* [Leninism and the struggle against bourgeois ideology and anti-Communism at the present stage]. Moscow: Nauka, 1970.

[1820] MKHITARIAN, S. "Lenin i osvobozhdenie V'etnama" [Lenin and the liberation of Vietnam]. *AAS* 1970 (8): 6-7.

[1821] MKRTUMOV, S. *See* 1611.

[1822] MLADENOV, V. "Ekonomicheskoe sotrudnichestvo s Sovetskim Soiuzom—vazhnyi faktor sotsialisticheskogo razvitiia Bolgarii" [Economic cooperation with the Soviet Union is an important factor in the socialist development of Bulgaria]. *VT* 1969 (8): 8-13.

[1823] MODELSKI, GEORGE. "Communism and the Globalization of Politics." *IStQ* 1968 12: 380-393.

[1824] MODESTOV, V. "Albania in Peking's Plans." *NT* 1970 (14): 25-26.

[1825] MODIGLIANI, ANDRÉ. *See* 801.

[1826] ———.*See* 802.

[1827] MODRZHINSKAIA, E. "Lenin's Theory and Modern International Relations." *IA(M)* 1970 (1): 56-62.

[1828] MODZHORIAN, L. A. "Sub"ekty mezhdunarodno-pravovoi otvetstvennosti" [Subjects of international legal responsibility]. *SGP* 1969 (12): 122-125.

[1829] MOKHANTI, D. CH. "Lenin i razvitie natsional'no-osvoboditel'nogo dvizheniia v Indii" [Lenin and the development of the national liberation movement in India]. *PS* 1970 (3): 77-84.

[1830] MOLCHANOV, E. L. *Komintern: U istokov politiki edinogo proletarskogo fronta* [The Comintern: The sources of a policy of a common proletarian front]. Moscow: Mysl', 1969.

[1831] MOLCHANOV, IU. "Major Milestone in Uniting the Anti-Imperialist Forces." *IA(M)* 1970 (7): 3-8.

[1832] ———. "24th Congress of the CPSU: The International Position of the USSR and CPSU Foreign Policy Today." *IA(M)* 1971 (9): 68-75.

[1833] MONKS, ALFRED L. "Soviet Military Doctrine: 1964 to Armed Forces Day 1969." *DAI* 1970 31: 1349-A.

[1834] MONTIAS, JOHN MICHAEL. "Obstacles to the Economic Integration of Eastern Europe." *StCC* 1969 2: 38-60.

[1835] ———.*See* 333.

[1836] MORDVINOV, V. "Sotrudnichestvo SSSR so stranami Arabskogo Vostoka" [The cooperation of the USSR with the countries of the Arab East]. *VT* 1970 (3): 22-26.

[1837] MORGAN, CARLYLE. "NATO: A New Desire to Exist [After Czechoslovakia]." *ACQ* 1969 7: 55-58.

[1838] MORGENTHAU, HANS J. "Changes and Chances in American-Soviet Relations." *FA* 1971 49: 429-441.

[1839] ———.*See* 805.

[1840] MORISON, DAVID L. "Africa and Asia: Some Trends in Soviet Thinking." *Miz* 1968 10: 167-184.

[1841] ———. "Africa of Moscow and Peking." *AfA* 1967 66: 343-347.

[1842] ———. "From Feudal to Bourgeois: The Soviet View of Iran Today." *Miz* 1969 11: 248-251.

[1843] ———. "The Middle East: The Soviet Entanglement." *Miz* 1969 11: 165-173.

[1844] ———. "Moscow and the Problems of Third World Communists: The Lessons of Sudan." *Miz* 1971 13: 111-125.

[1845] ———. "Recent Soviet Interest in Population Problems of the Developing Countries." *Miz* 1967 9: 181-196.

[1846] ———. "Russia, Israel and the Arabs." *Miz* 1967 9: 91-107.

[1847] ———. "Soviet Influence: Prospects for 1967." *Miz* 1967 9: 31-37.

[1848] ———. "Soviet Interest in Middle East Oil." *Miz* 1968 10: 79-85.

[1849] ———. "Soviet Interest in Middle East Oil." *Miz* 1971 13: 30-34.

[1850] ———. "Soviet Views on African Law." *Miz* 1968 10: 23-28.

[1851] ———. "Tropical Africa: The New Soviet Outlook." *Miz* 1971 13: 48-57.

[1852] ———. "The USSR and the War in Nigeria." *Miz* 1969 11: 31-39.

[1853] ———. "USSR and Third World I: Ideal and Reality." *Miz* 1970 12: 7-25.

[1854] ———. "USSR and Third World II: Questions of Foreign Policy." *Miz* 1970 12: 69-79.

[1855] ———. "USSR and Third World III: Questions of Economic Development." *Miz* 1970 12: 124-152.

[1856] ———, AND W. E. R. "After Mali." *Miz* 1969 11: 205-210.

[1857] ———, AND W. E. R. "Soviet Comment on Iran's Land Reform." *Miz* 1969 11: 252-254.

[1858] MOROKHOV, I. D., AND V. M. SHMELER. "Magate: Dogovor o nerasprostraniem iadernogo oruzhiia" [IAEA: Agreement on the non-proliferation of nuclear weapons]. *SGP* 1971 (5): 59-62.

[1859] MOROZOV, G. I. "Mezhdunarodnye nepravitel'stvennye organizatsii i pravo" [International non-governmental organizations and law]. *SGP* 1968 (4): 57-67.

[1860] ———. *Mezhdunarodnye organizatsii. Nekotorye vorposy teorii* [International organizations: Some questions of theory]. Moscow: Mysl', 1969.

[1861] ———. "OON v sovremennom mire" [The UN in the present world]. *MEMO* 1970 (9): 19-30.

[1862] ———, AND V. SHKUNAEV. *UNO: 25 Years.* Moscow: Novosti, 1970.

[1863] ———, ED. *OON. Itogi, tendentsii, perspektivy. (k 25-letiiu OON)* [The UN: Results, tendencies, prospects (in commemoration of 25 years of the UN)]. Moscow: I.M.O., 1970.

[1864] MOROZOV, L. F. *Ot kooperatsii burzhuaznoi k kooperatsii sotsialisticheskoi* [From bourgeois cooperation to socialist cooperation]. Moscow: Mysl', 1968.

[1865] MORRIS, BERNARD S. *See* 2777.

[1866] MORRIS, JERRY J. "The Developing Image of the Soviet Union: A Case Study of Soviet Participation in UNESCO, 1946 to 1957." *MA* 1968 6: 97.

[1867] MORRIS, MILTON D. "The Development Process in Soviet Perspective —The Non-Capitalist Path in Tropical Africa." *DAI* 1971 31: 6690-A.

[1868] MORSE, WILLIAM P. "Leonid Borisovich Krasin: Soviet Diplomat, 1918-1926." *DAI* 1971 32: 3219-A.

[1869] MORTIMER, REX. *See* 2777.

[1870] "The Moscow Meeting and Fundamental Problems of International Relations (Discussion Sponsored by the Editorial Board of International Affairs)." *IA(M)* 1969 (9): 50-60; 1969 (10): 40-53.

[1871] MOSELEY, GEORGE. *A Sino-Soviet Cultural Frontier: The Ili Kazakh Autonomous Chou.* Cambridge, Massachusetts: East Asian Research Center, Harvard University, 1967.

[1872] MOSELY, PHILIP E. "Eastern Europe in World Politics: Where De-Stalinization Has Led." *ModA* 1969 11: 119-130.

[1873] ———. "The Kremlin and the Third World." *FA* 1967 46: 64-77.

[1874] ———. "Soviet Search for Security." *APS,P* 1969 29: 216-227.

[1875] ———. "The United States and East-West Détente: The Range of Choice." *JIA* 1968 22: 5-15.

[1876] ———, ED. *New Trends in Kremlin Policy, Special Report, Series 9.* Washington, D.C.: Center for Strategic Studies, Georgetown University, 1970.

[1877] MOSKVICHEV, L. "Teoriia 'deideologizatsii': Istoki i sotsial'naia suschnost'," [The theory of "deideologization": Results and social essence]. *MEMO* 1968 (12): 3-15.

[1878] MOVCHAN, A. P. *Kodifikatsiia i progressivnoe razvitie mezhdunarod-nogo prava* [The codification and progressive development of international law]. Moscow: Iurid. lit, 1972.

[1879] MSHVENIERADZE, V. L. *Antikommunizm—politika i ideologiia imperializma* [Anti-Communism—the politics and ideology of imperialism]. Moscow: Politizdat, 1971.

[1880] MUDZHIRI, A. N. *Razvitie natsional'no-osvoboditel'nogo dvizheniia i raspad kolonial'noi sistemy na sovremennom etape* [The development of the national liberation movement and the collapse of the colonial system at the present stage]. Tbilisi: Sabchota Sakartvelo, 1967.

[1881] MUELLER, ERNST F. "Attitudes Toward Westbound Refugees in the East German Press." *JCR* 1971 14(3).

[1882] MUELLER, GORDON HERBERT. "The Road to Rapallo: Germany's Relations With Russia, 1919-1922." *DAI* 1971 31: 5991-A.

[1883] MUHLEN, NORBERT. "Germany's New Ostpolitik: An American Dilemma." *Int* 1970 3: 4-10.

[1884] MUHRI, FRANZ. "The Importance of International Communist Party Contacts." *WMR* 1971 14(8): 39-46.

[1885] MUKERJEE, HIREU. "Lenin and India." *NT* 1969 (51): 6-9.

[1886] MÜLLER, KURT. *The Foreign Aid Programs of the Soviet Bloc and Communist China*. New York: Walker, 1967.

[1887] MUNK, FRANK. "Communist Heresies: Hopes and Hazards." *WPQ* 1969 22: 921-925.

[1888] MUNTIAN, M. A. *Bor'ba Sovetskogo Soiuza za priem v OON Bolgarii, Vengrii i Rumynii (1945-1955 gg)* [The struggle of the Soviet Union for the entrance into the UN of Bulgaria, Hungary and Rumania (1945-1955)]. Kishinev: Shtiintsa, 1972.

[1889] _____.*Ocherk vneshnei politiki Rumynskoi Narodnoi Respubliki 1948-1955 gg* [A sketch of the foreign policy of the Rumanian People's Republic, 1948-1955]. Kishinev: AN MSSR Inst istorii, 1971.

[1890] MURBY, ROBERT N. "Canadian Economic Commission to Siberia, 1918-1919." *CSIP* 1969 11: 374-393.

[1891] MURETOVA, K. "Sovetsko-Rumynskie torgovye sviazi" [Soviet-Rumanian trade ties]. *VT* 1969 (8): 14-17.

[1892] MURPHY, FRANK M. "Sea Power and the Satellites." *USNI,P* 1969 96(11): 75-83.

[1893] ———. "The Soviet Navy in the Mediterranean." *USNI,P* 1967 93: 38-44.

[1894] MUSTAFA, ZUBEIDA. "The Sino-Soviet Border Problem." *PH* 1969 22(4).

[1895] ———. "USSR and Indian Action in East Pakistan." *PH* 1971 24(3): 60-74.

[1896] MUTAGIROV, D. Z. *Strategiia i taktika mezhdunarodnogo Kommunisti-cheskogo dvizheniia* [The strategy and tactics of the international Communist movement]. Leningrad: Leningrad University, 1969.

[1897] MZHAVANADZE, V. "KPSS—partiia internatsionalistov-Lenintsev" [The CPSU is the party of Leninist internationalists]. *Komm* 1970 (2): 12-23.

[1898] *Na novom puti. Natsional'no-osvoboditel'noe dvizhenie v Asii i Afrike* [On a new path. The national liberation movement in Asia and Africa]. Moscow: Nauka, 1968.

[1899] NADEZHDIN, A. "Peking Against the Socialist Community." *NT* 1971 (33): 18-20.

[1900] NADEZHDIN, Iu. "Torgovlia SSSR s Afganistanom" [The trade of the USSR with Afghanistan]. *VT* 1969 (9): 18-19.

[1901] NAGORSKI, ZYGMUNT, JR. "Soviet International Propaganda: Its Role, Effectiveness, and Future." *A,AAPSS* 1971 398: 130-139.

[1902] NAIK, J. A. "Indo-Soviet Relations: No Deal for Delhi." *FEER* 1969 64: 572-573.

[1903] ———. *Soviet Policy Towards India: From Stalin to Brezhnev.* Delhi: Vikas Publications, 1970.

[1904] NALIN, Y. "Anti-Communism, Atlantic Variant." *IA(M)* 1970 (7): 49-54.

[1905] NARAIN, VIRENDRA. "Kashmir and Major Powers: Study of Motives in Retrospect." *PSR* 1969 8: 418-449.

[1906] NASHASHIBI, KARIM A. *See* 1561.

[1907] NASSAR, FUAD. "Lenin i osvoboditel'naia bor'ba Arabskikh narodov" [Lenin and the liberation struggle of the Arab peoples]. *Komm* 1970 (5): 113-119.

[1908] *Natsionalisticheskaia politika gruppy Mao-Tsze-Duna i SShA* [The nationalist policy of the Mao Tse-tung group and the USA]. Moscow: Nauka, 1968.

[1909] *Nauchno-tekhnicheskoe sotrudnichestvo sotsialisticheskikh stran. Sbornik mezhdunarodnykh dokumentov i materialov* [Scientific-technical cooperation of the socialist countries. Collection of international documents and materials]. Moscow: Politizdat, 1971.

[1910] NAUMOV, P. "International Security—The Focal Issue." *NT* 1970 (41): 4-5.

[1911] ———. "U.N. Anniversary Session." *NT* 1970 (43): 4-5.

[1912] ———. "U.N. Significant Problems." *NT* 1970 (44): 4-5.

[1913] NAZARKIN, K. "International Bank for Economic Cooperation and the CMEA Countries." *IA(M)* 1971 (7): 46-50.

[1914] NEAL, FRED WARNER. "Coexistence After Czechoslovakia: On What Basis Can the United States and the Soviet Union Coexist in the Wake of the Russian's Invasion of Czechoslovakia?" *W/PR* 1969 9: 3-6.

[1915] NEDOREZOV, A. "The October Revolution in Russia and the Establishment of Czechoslovakia." *IA(M)* 1968 (12): 67-73.

[1916] "Nekotorye tendentsii v mirovoi torgovle" [Some tendencies in world trade]. *MEMO* 1970 (8): 150-157.

[1917] NEKRASOV, A. IA. "O vneshneekonomicheskoi politike gruppy Mao Tsee-duna." [On the foreign economic policy of the Mao Tse-tung group]. *Komm* 1968 (12): 102-112.

[1918] ———. "Second UN Development Decade." *IA(M)* 1971 (2): 36-40.

[1919] ———.*SSSR i razvivaiushchiesia strany v OON* [The USSR and the developing countries in the UN]. Moscow: I.M.O., 1970.

[1920] NEMES, D. "Leninism and Development of the Socialist World System." *WMR* 1970 13(1): 15-23.

[1921] "Neodolimaia tendentsiia k edinstvu" [The invincible tendency to unity]. *Komm* 1968 (9): 3-9.

[1922] NESTEROV, M. V. "East-West Trade." *NT* 1968 (28): 16-17.

[1923] NEUBERGER, EGON. *See* 317.

[1924] NEUMANN, WILLIAM L. *After Victory: Churchill, Roosevelt, Stalin, and the Making of the Peace.* New York: Harper and Row, 1967.

[1925] NEVERDINOV, A., AND L. SEVERIANIN. *Sovetskii Soiuz i Evropeiskaia bezopasnost'* [The Soviet Union and European security]. Moscow: I.M.O., 1971.

[1926] "New Stage in Preparation for All-European Conference." *IA(M)* 1970 (9): 3-6.

[1927] "New Stage in USSR-GDR Cooperation." *NT* 1970 (34): 6-7.

[1928] *New Trends in Kremlin Policy.* Washington, D.C.: Center for Strategic and International Studies, Georgetown University, Special Report Series, no. 11, 1970.

[1929] NEWLIN, STEPHEN ROBERT. "The Functions of Conflict and the International Communist System." *DAI* 1970 31: 449-A.

[1930] NEWTH, J. A. *See* 1955.

[1931] NEWTON, WILLIAM M. "Soviet Arms and Weaknesses." *ACQ* 1968 6: 321-330.

[1932] NIEHBUHR, REINHOLD. "The Social Myths in the 'Cold War.' " *JIA* 1967 21: 40-56.

[1933] NIELSEN, WALDEMAR A. *The Great Powers and Africa.* New York: Praeger, 1969.

[1934] NIEMEYER, GERHART. *Deceitful Peace: A New Look at the Soviet Threat.* New Rochelle, New York: Arlington House, 1971.

[1935] NIKHOVICH, E. S. *Ekonomicheskoe sotrudnichestvo i manevry antikommunistov* [Economic cooperation and the maneuver of the anti-Communists]. Moscow: I.M.O., 1969.

[1936] NIKIFOROV, V. N. *Sovetskie istoriki o problemakh Kitaia* [Soviet historians on the problems of China]. Moscow: Nauka, 1970.

[1937] NIKITIN, Y. "Goodneighbourly and Equal Cooperation." *IA(M)* 1970 (7): 65-67.

[1938] NIKOLAEV, A. "Strany sotsializma i borb'a za Evropeiskuiu bezopasnost'" [The socialist countries and the struggle for European security]. *PS* 1971 (8): 67-75.

[1939] NIKOLAEV, G. "Soviet-Turkish Relations." *IA(M)* 1968 (11): 37-40.

[1940] NIKOLAEV, K. "Ekonomicheskoe sotrudnichestvo SSSR i KNDR" [The economic cooperation of the USSR and North Korea]. *VT* 1970 (10): 10-12.

[1941] NIKOLAEV, N. "Non-Proliferation and Peace." *NT* 1968 (8): 19-20.

[1942] NIKOLAEV, V. "Ideologicheskaia bor'ba i obshchestvennoe mnenie" [The ideological struggle and social opinion]. *Komm* 1970 (2): 107-115.

[1943] NIKOLAEVA, A. V. *Ekonomicheskoe sotrudnichestvo GDR i SSSR* [The economic cooperation of the GDR and the USSR]. Moscow: Nauka, 1968.

[1944] NIKOL'SKII, N. M. *Nauchno-tekhnicheskaia revoliutsiia i mezhdunarodnye otnosheniia* [The scientific-technical revolution and international relations]. Moscow: I.M.O., 1970.

[1945] Nikonov, A. "Sovremennaia revoliutsiia v voennom dele i nauka o mezhdunarodnykh otnosheniiakh" [The contemporary revolution in military affairs and the science of international relations]. *MEMO* 1969 (2): 3-14.

[1946] Nishakov, M. *See* 23.

[1947] Niunka, Vladas. *Vatikan i Anti-kommunizm* [The Vatican and Anti-Communism]. Vil'nus: Mintis, 1970.

[1948] Norden, Albert. "Lenin and Germany." *NT* 1970 (15): 9-11.

[1949] Norlund, I. "Preventing Imperialist Aggression: Opportunities and Tasks." *WMR* 1967 (9): 3-8.

[1950] Northedge, F. S., ed. *The Foreign Policies of the Powers.* New York: Praeger, 1969.

[1951] Norton, John H. "Russia, China, and Insurgency." *NWCR* 1970 23(2): 53-68.

[1952] Nosov, F. V. *Lenin o mire i 'revoliutsionnoi voine'* [Lenin on peace and "revolutionary war"]. Moscow: Lenizdat, 1968.

[1953] Novak, Bogdan C. *Trieste 1941-1954: The Ethnic, Political and Ideological Struggle.* Chicago: Chicago University Press, 1970.

[1954] Nove, Alec. "Soviet Defense Spending." *Surv* 1971 13: 328-332.

[1955] _____, and J. A. Newth. *The Soviet Middle East: A Communist Model for Development.* New York: Praeger, 1967.

[1956] _____. *See* 2777.

[1957] Novikov, N. "The Decisive Force in the Anti-Imperialistic Struggle." *IA(M)* 1970 (12): 24-30.

[1958] _____. *See* 978.

[1959] Novoseltsev, E. "Bonn's 'Eastern Policy' and European Security." *IA(M)* 1968 (7): 27-33.

[1960] _____. "Europe Twenty-Five Years Later." *IA(M)* 1970 (7): 15-22.

[1961] _____. "Leninist Foreign Policy and the Revolutionary Renewal of the World." *IA(M)* 1971 (5): 9-18.

[1962] _____, and N. Khomutov. "Soviet Relations With Leading Capitalist Countries." *IA(M)* 1968 (3): 68-74.

[1963] Novosel'tseva, A. A. *Vliianie dvukh sistem na ekonomiku razvivaiushchikhsia stran* [The influence of the two systems on the economy of the developing countries]. Moscow: Izdatel'stvo Moskovskogo Universiteta, 1969.

[1964] Novy, Vilem. "Czechoslovakia After the Plenum." *NT* 1971 (5): 4-6.

[1965] NUKHOVICH, E. S. *Ekonomicheskoe sotrudnichestvo i manevry Antikommunistov* [Economic cooperation and the maneuvers of the Anti-Communists]. Moscow: I.M.O., 1969.

[1966] NYERGES, JANOS. "Problems of Trade Between Countries Having Different Systems." *Co* 1971 8: 65-72.

[1967] ———. "Some Thoughts on East-West Trade." *Co* 1967 4: 129-132.

[1968] *O edinstve mezhdunarodnogo Kommunisticheskogo dvizheniia* [On the unity of the international Communist movement]. Moscow: Progress, 1967.

[1969] "O politicheskom kurse Mao Tsee-duna na mezhdunarodnoi arene" [On the political course of Mao Tse-tung in the international arena]. *Komm* 1968 (8): 95-108.

[1970] "Ob aktual'nykh problemakh mezhdunarodnogo polozheniia i bor'be KPSS za splochennost' mirovogo Kommunisticheskogo dvizheniia. Postanovlenie plenuma TSK KPSS, priniatoe 10 Aprelia 1968 goda" [On the actual problems of the international situation and the struggle of the CPSU for the solidarity of the world Communist movement. Resolution of the plenum of the CC, CPSU, passed 10 April, 1968]. *Komm* 1968 (6): 3-5.

[1971] "Ob itogakh mezhdunarodnogo Soveshchaniia Kommunisticheskikh i Rabochikh Partii. Postanovlenie plenuma Tsentral'nogo Kimiteta KPSS, priniatoe 26 Iiunia 1969 goda" [On the results of the Conference of Communist and Workers' Parties. Resolution of the plenum of the Central Committee of the CPSU, passed 26 June, 1969]. *Komm* 1969 (10): 3-7.

[1972] O'BALLANCE, EDGAR. "Sino-Soviet Influence on the War in Vietnam." *CR* 1967 210: 176-187.

[1973] "Ob"em vneshnei torgovli SSSR" [The rise of the foreign trade of the USSR]. *VT* 1970 (6): 53-55.

[1974] OBMINSKII, E. E. *Vneshnee ekonomicheskie sviazi razvivaiushchikhsia stran* [The foreign economic ties of the developing countries]. Moscow: I.M.O., 1970.

[1975] OCHIR, E. "50 let druzhestvennykh Mongolo-Sovetskikh ekonomicheskikh otnoshenii" [Fifty years of fraternal Mongolian-Soviet economic relations]. *VT* 1971 (7): 2-8.

[1976] OCHSNER, M. A. "Chinese Communist Attitudes Toward the Soviet Union, 1949-1965: A Constant Analysis of Official Documents." *DAI* 1969 29: 4080-A.

[1977] "The October Revolution and Proletarian Internationalism." *WMR* 1967 (5): 3-11.

[1978] "The October Revolution and the World Socialist System. Conference Held in Moscow, September 5-7, 1967, Sponsored by the Institute of Economics of the World Socialist System of the USSR Academy of Sciences and the Secretariat of the Council for Mutual Economic Assistance." *IA(M)* 1967 (11): 96-106; 1967 (12): 77-84.

[1979] ODUM, BENJAMIN CHINAKA. "Soviet Relations With Sub-Saharan Africa: 1957-1967." *DAI* 1971 31: 5495-A-5496-A.

[1980] OH, KI-WAN. *See* 1562.

[1981] OKAMOTO, THUMPEI. "The Oligarchic Control of Foreign Policy." *DAI* 1970 30: 4517-A-4518-A.

[1982] *Oktiabr'skaia Revoliutsiia i mirovoi revoliutsionnyi protsess. Osnov-nye itogi mezhdunarodnogo revoliutsionnogo dvizheniia za 50 let* [The October Revolution and the world revolutionary process. Basic results of the international revolutionary movement in 50 years]. Moscow: Politizdat, 1967.

[1983] *Oktiabr'skaia Revoliutsiia i natsional'no-osvoboditel'naia bor'ba narodov Blizhnego Vostoka* [The October Revolution and the national liberation struggle of the peoples of the Near East]. Tbilisi: Metsniereba, 1967.

[1984] *Oktiabr'skaia Revoliutsiia i proletarskii internatsionalizm* [The October Revolution and proletarian internationalism]. Moscow: Nauka, 1970.

[1985] OLEINIK, I. P. *Mirovoe sotsialisticheskoe khoziaistvo* [World socialist economy]. Moscow: I.M.O., 1969.

[1986] ———. "Nekotorye teoreticheskie problemy razvitiia dvukh mirovykh sistem" [Some theoretical problems of the development of the two world systems]. *VE* 1969 (3): 15-26.

[1987] OL'SEVICH, IU. IA. *See* 3217.

[1988] ———. *See* 3223.

[1989] ———. *See* 3224.

[1990] OLSIENKIEWICZ, HENRYK. "Czechoslovakia's Economic Dilemma Under Soviet Tutelage." *B,ISUSSR* 1969 16(3): 3-25.

[1991] ———. "The Role of 'Convergence' in the Ideological Conflict Between East and West." *B,ISUSSR* 1970 17: 7-22.

[1992] OLSZOWSKI, STEFAN. "The Polish United Workers' Party and World Problems." *WMR* 1969 12(2): 22-29.

[1993] *OON i mezhdunarodnoe ekonomicheskoe sotrudnichestvo* [The UN and international economic cooperation]. Moscow: Mysl', 1970.

122

[1994] OREN, NISSAN. "Popular Front in the Balkans: Bulgaria." *JCH* 1970 3(5): 69-82.

[1995] ORGANIS'IAN, IU. "Marksizm-Leninizm o sootnoshenii natsional'nogo i international'nogo" [Marxism-Leninism on the relationship of the national and the international]. *PS* 1970 (5): 74-81.

[1996] ORLEANS, LEO A. "The Fallacy of Sino-American Enmity: The View From Moscow." *WA* 1971 134: 261-266.

[1997] ORLIK, I. I. *Imperialisticheskie derzhavi i Vostochnaia Evropa (1945-1965)* [The imperialist powers and East Europe (1945-1965)]. Moscow: Nauka, 1968.

[1998] _____, AND V. RAZMEROV. "European Security and Relations Between the Two Systems." *IA(M)* 1967 (5): 3-8.

[1999] ORLOV, I. *See* 3040.

[2000] ORLOVSKII, A. V. *Otvetstvennost' gosudarstv za agressiiu* [The responsibility of states for aggression]. Minsk: Nauka i tekhnika, 1969.

[2001] ORNATSKII, IA. I. "United Nations: Two Lines of Economic Development and Cooperation." *IA(M)* 1971 (11): 50-55.

[2002] OSAKWE, CHRIS. "Contemporary Soviet Doctrine on the Juridical Nature of Universal International Organizations." *AJIL* 1971 65(3): 502-521.

[2003] _____. "Izmenenie uchreditel'nykh aktov mezhdunarodnykh organizatsii" [The change of constitutive acts of international organizations]. *SGP* 1970 (7): 112-117.

[2004] OSERS, EWALD. "The Liberation of Prague." *Sur* 1970 76: 99-111.

[2005] OSIPOV, N. "Soviet Natural Gas for France." *NT* 1971 (34): 5-6.

[2006] OS'MOVA, M. N. *Khoziaistvennye reformy i mezhdunarodnoe sotsialisticheskoe razdelenie truda* [Economic reforms and the international socialist division of labor]. Moscow: Izdatel'stvo Moskovskogo universiteta, 1969.

[2007] *Osnovnye etapy razvitiia mirovogo revoliutsionnogo protsessa posle Oktiabria* [Basic stages of development of the world revolution process after October]. Moscow: Mysl', 1968.

[2008] OSTROVSKII, IA. *OON i prava cheloveka* [The UN and the rights of man]. Moscow: I.M.O., 1968.

[2009] _____. *See* 413.

[2010] OSWALD, J. GREGORY. "The Development of Soviet Studies on Latin America." *B,ISUSSR* 1968 15(3).

[2011] _____, AND ANTHONY J. STROVER, EDS. *The Soviet Union and Latin America.* New York: Praeger, 1971.

[2012] OTEGVEYE, T. "For a United Front of All Anti-Imperialist and Antifeudal Forces." *IA(M)* 1970 (1): 27-33.

[2013] _____. "Leninism and African Revolution." *WMR* 1970 13(8): 78-83.

[2014] OVERGAARD, WILLARD MICHELE. "Legal Norms and Normative Bases for the Progressive Development of International Law, as Defined in Soviet Treaty Relations, 1945-1964." *DAI* 1970 31: 449-A.

[2015] OWEN, GAIL L. "Dollar Diplomacy in Default: The Economics of Russian-American Relations." *HJ* 1970 13: 251-272.

[2016] _____. "The Metro-Vickers Crisis: Anglo-Soviet Relations Between Trade Agreements, 1932-1934." *SlEER* 1971 49: 92-112.

[2017] OWEN, HENRY. "Durable Dangers in Central Europe." *Int* 1970 13: 24-26.

[2018] PACHKAEVA, M. "Osnova uspeshnoi torgovli s razvivaiushchimisia stranami" [The basis of successful trade with developing countries]. *VT* 1968 (7): 24-27.

[2019] PAGE, STANLEY N. *Lenin and World Revolution.* Gloucester, Massachusetts: P. Smith, 1968.

[2020] PAGE, STEPHEN. "Moscow and the Persian Gulf Countries, 1967-1970." *Miz* 1971 13: 72-88.

[2021] _____. *The USSR and Arabia.* London: Central Asian Research Center, 1971.

[2022] PALAYNES, HARRY A. *Soviet Strategy in the Underdeveloped Areas.* Chicago: Adams Press, 1968.

[2023] PALETSKIS, IUSTUS. "Lenin and the National Question." *NT* 1970 (15): 6-8.

[2024] _____. "V. I. Lenin i velikoe sodruzhdestvo natsii" [V. I. Lenin and the great concord of nations]. *SGP* 1970 (4): 11-18.

[2025] PALMER, MICHAEL. "The Prospects for a European Security Conference." *ACQ* 1971 9: 293-300.

[2026] _____, AND DAVID THOMAS. "Arms Control and the Mediterranean." *WT* 1971 27: 495.

[2027] PANCHENKO, V. "Economic Ties With Northern Europe." *NT* 1971 (39): 22-23.

[2028] PANKRASHOVA, M., AND V. SIPOLS. *Why War Was Not Prevented: A Documentary Review of the Soviet-British-French Talks in Moscow, 1939.* Moscow: Novosti, 1970.

[2029] PAONE, ROCCO M. "The Soviet Threat in the Indian Ocean." *MR* 1970 50: 48-55.

[2030] PAPACHRISTOU, JUDITH R. "American-Soviet Relations and United States Policy in the Pacific, 1933-1941." *DAI* 1968 29: 856-A.

[2031] PAPAIOANNOU, E. "Lenin and Some Problems of National Liberation Movement." *WMR* 1970 13(4): 26-32.

[2032] PAROMONOV, V. B. *V. I. Lenin ob Amerikanskom imperializme* [V. I. Lenin on American imperialism]. Moscow: Voenizdat, 1969.

[2033] PARRISH, MICHAEL. *The 1968 Czechoslovak Crisis: A Bibliography, 1968-1970.* Santa Barbara, California: Clio Press, American Bibliographical Center, 1971.

[2034] _____. *The Soviet Armed Forces. Books in English 1950-1967.* Stanford: Hoover Institution, 1970.

[2035] PARRY, ALBERT. "Soviet Aid to Vietnam." *MR* 1967 47(6): 13-22. *Surv* 1967 9: 76-82.

[2036] PARTIGUL, S. "Voprosy torgovli v tekushchei piatiletke" [Questions of trade in the current five-year plan]. *VE* 1967 (2): 12-23.

[2037] PASTUSHENKO, M. "Mezhdunarodnyi pushnoi rynok" [The international fur trade]. *VT* 1970 (9): 36-41.

[2038] PASTUSIAK, LONGIN. "A Marxist Approach to the Study of International Relations." *EEQ* 1970 3: 285-293.

[2039] PATAI, RAPHAEL, ED. *Israel Between East and West.* Westport, Connecticut: Greenwood Publishing Corporation, 1971.

[2040] PATERSON, THOMAS G., ED. *Cold War Critics: Alternatives to American Foreign Policy in the Truman Years.* Chicago: Quadrangle Books, 1971.

[2041] _____, ED. *The Origins of the Cold War.* Lexington, Massachusetts: D. C. Heath, 1970.

[2042] PATOLICHEV, NIKOLAI. "25 let Sovetskoi vneshnei torgovli" [25 years of Soviet foreign trade]. *VT* 1968 (4): 4-14.

[2043] _____. *Sovetskaia vneshniaia torgovlia: proshloe, nastoiashchee i budushchee* [Soviet foreign trade: Past, present, and future]. Moscow: Novosti, 1967.

[2044] _____. "Soviet Foreign Trade." *NT* 1970 (15): 18-19.

[2045] _____. "Soviet Foreign Trade." *NT* 1970 (50): 20-22.

[2046] _____. "Soviet Foreign Trade Minister on the U.N. Trade and Development Conference." *NT* 1968 (15): 6-9.

[2047] _____. "Soviet-Japanese Trade." *NT* 1971 (42): 20-21.

[2048] _____. "Voploshchenie Leninskikh printsipov vo vneshnei torgovle Sovetskogo Soiuza" [The embodiment of Leninist principles in the foreign trade of the Soviet Union]. *VT* 1970 (4): 4-17.

[2049] PAUL, DAVID W. "Soviet Foreign Policy and the Invasion of Czechoslovakia: A Theory and a Case Study." *IStQ* 1971 15: 159-202.

[2050] PAVLOV, A. "Na Osnove sotsialisticheskogo internatsionalizma" [On the basis of socialist internationalism]. *VT* 1970 (9): 6-8.

[2051] PAVLOV, B. "UN Jubilee." *IA(M)* 1970 (10): 86-89.

[2052] _____. *See* 928.

[2053] PAVLOV, K. "Sino-Russian Territorial Controversies: Past and Present." *B,ISUSSR* 1969 16(5): 36-40.

[2054] PAVLOV, K. A. *See* 3058.

[2055] PAVLOV, O. "Indissoluable Alliance of Two Fraternal Peoples (Czechoslovakia and USSR)." *IA(M)* 1969 (12): 52-55.

[2056] _____. "Proletarian Internationalism and Defence of Socialist Gains." *IA(M)* 1968 (10): 11-16.

[2057] PAVLOV, V. "Ties of Fraternity and Friendship (the 50th Anniversary of the Rumanian Communist Party)." *IA(M)* 1971 (6): 37-42.

[2058] PAVLOVSKII, V. "Soviet-Indian Cooperation." *IA(M)* 1970 (1): 46-49.

[2059] PAVPEROV, V. "Sovetsko-Bolgarskoe ekonomicheskoe sotrudnichestvo" [Soviet-Bulgarian economic cooperation]. *VT* 1969 (9): 13-16.

[2060] PCHELINTSEV, S. "Printsipy ustava OON v svete Leninskikh polozhenii o mezhdunarodnoi organizatsii" [The principles of the UN charter in the light of the Leninist position on international organization]. *SGP* 1971 (2): 44-52.

[2061] PEGOV, NIKOLAI M. "Lenin on Peace and Peaceful Coexistence." *IQ* 1971 27(1): 65ff.

[2062] PEKSHEV, V. "The Leninist Principles of External Economic Relations." *NT* 1970 (14): 18-21.

[2063] PENDRILL, C. GRANT, JR. " 'Bipartisanship' in Soviet Foreign Policy-Making." In *The Conduct of Soviet Foreign Policy,* pp. 61-75, edited by Erik P. Hoffmann and Frederic J. Fleron, Jr. Chicago: Aldine-Atherton, 1971.

[2064] ———. "Foreign Policy and Political Factions in the USSR, 1952-1956: The Post-Stalin Power Struggle and the Developing Nations." *DAI* 1969 30: 2595-A.

[2065] PENNAR, JAAN. "The Arabs, Marxism and Moscow: A Historical Survey." *MEJ* 1968 22: 433-447.

[2066] ———. "The Soviet Road to Damascus." *Miz* 1967 9: 23-30.

[2067] PERETZ, DON. "Détente or Entente in Great Power Diplomacy [In the Middle East]." *NME* May 1969 (8): 16-21.

[2068] PERLO, VICTOR. "The Impact of October on the Capitalist World." *NT* 1967 (46-47): 9-12.

[2069] PERRAULT, GILLES. *The Red Orchestra.* New York: Simon and Schuster, 1969.

[2070] *Perspektivnoe planirovanie v stranakh-chlenakh SEV* [Prospective planning in the member countries of CMEA]. Moscow: Ekonomika, 1970.

[2071] PERTOT, V. "Yugoslavia's Economic Relations With Eastern European Countries." *Co* 1967 4(1): 7-13.

[2072] PETERS, I. A. *SSSR, Chekhoslovakiia i Evropeiskaia politika nakanune Miuchena* [The USSR, Czechoslovakia and European politics on the eve of Munich]. Kiev: Naukova Dumka, 1971.

[2073] PETERS, JOHN GEOFFREY. "Yugoslav Foreign Policy Toward the Nonaligned Countries." *DAI* 1970 31: 3004-A.

[2074] PETERSON, SOPHIA. "Conflict, Communism, and Mutual Threat in Soviet-American and Sino-Soviet Relations: A Statistical Examination of Inter-Relationships." *DAI* 1970 30: 5051-A.

[2075] ———. *The Nuclear Test Ban Treaty and Its Effect on International Tension.* Los Angeles: Security Studies Project, University of California, 1967.

[2076] PETROV, A. I., ED. *Perspektivnoe planirovanie v stranakh-chlenakh SEV* [Prospective planning of the member-countries of CMEA]. Moscow: Ekonomika, 1970.

[2077] PETROV, B. "Space Exploration: Progress and Trends." *WMR* 1971 14(4): 82-87.

[2078] PETROV, F. P. *Mezhdunarodnoe nauchno-tekhnicheskoe sotrudnichestvo: Tseli i perspektivy* [International scientific-technical cooperation: Goals and prospects]. Moscow: I.M.O., 1971.

[2079] ———. "Razvitie druzhestvennykh otnoshenii mezhdu Bolgariei i Chekhoslovakiei" [The development of fraternal relations between Bulgaria and Czechoslovakia]. *VI* 1967 (3): 42-52.

127

[2080] PETROV, M. "An Important Aspect of Disarmament." *IA(M)* 1970 (2-3): 53-56.

[2081] ———. "Non-Nuclear Zones—A Pressing Demand." *IA(M)* 1967 (6): 12-16.

[2082] ———. "The Urgent Need to Prohibit Chemical and Bacteriological Warfare." *IA(M)* 1969 (8): 40-43.

[2083] PETROV, V. "Deiatel'nost' mezhdunarodnogo torgovogo tsentra" [The activity of the international trade center]. *VT* 1970 (12): 48-51.

[2084] PAVLOV, VLADIMIR. "Eastern Europe, a Battleground." *Orb* 1971 15: 697-706.

[2085] ———. "The Nazi-Soviet Pact: A Missing Page in Soviet Historiography." *PoC* 1968 17(1): 42-51.

[2086] ———. "Soviet Foreign Policy and the Collapse of Communist Unity." *ModA* 1971 15: 338-349.

[2087] PETROVICH, MICHAEL B. "United States Policy in East Europe." *CH* 1967 52: 193-199, 243-244.

[2088] PETRUSHEV, A. "Ekonomicheskoe sotrudnichestvo SSSR s sotsialisticheskimi stranami" [Economic cooperation of the USSR with the socialist countries]. *VT* 1967 (6): 3-9.

[2089] ———. "Krepnut Sovetsko-Arabskie ekonomicheskie otnosheniia" [Soviet-Arab economic relations are growing]. *VT* 1971 (7): 9-14.

[2090] ———. "Sovetskii Soiuz razvivaiushchimsia stranam" [The Soviet Union and the developing countries]. *VT* 1967 (9): 3-9.

[2091] ———. "Vneshneekonomicheskoe sotrudnichestvo SSSR v 1968 godu" [Foreign economic cooperation of the USSR in 1968]. *VT* 1969 (5): 16-24.

[2092] PFALTZGRAFF, ROBERT L., JR. "The Czechoslovak Crisis and the Future of the Atlantic Alliance." *Orb* 1969 13: 210-222.

[2093] ———. *See* 1321.

[2094] PHARAND, D. "Soviet Union Warns United States Against Use of Northeast Passage." *AJIL* 1968 62: 927-935.

[2095] *50 let bor'by SSSR za razoruzhenie. Sbornik dokumentov i materialov* [50 years of struggle of the USSR for disarmament. Collection of documents and materials]. Moscow: Nauka, 1967.

[2096] PICHUGIN, B. "East-West Economic Relations." *IA(M)* 1970 (11): 40-47.

[2097] PICK, O. "Soviet Alliance Policies in Retrospect." *IJ* 1967 22: 576-592.

[2098] PIERRE, ANDREW J. "The Bonn-Moscow Treaty of 1970: Milestone or Mirage." *RR* 1971 30: 17-26.

[2099] ———. "Implications of the Western Response After Czechoslovakia." *ACQ* 1969 7: 59-75.

[2100] ———. "Political-Military Power: America Down, Russia Up." *FP* 1971 1(4): 163-187.

[2101] ———. "Reconciliation in Europe." *Int* 1970 8: 16-20.

[2102] PIMENOV, P. "The Soviet Trade Unions' International Ties." *NT* 1971 (28): 13-15.

[2103] PINDER, JOHN. "An Ostpolitik for the European Community." *Sur* 1971 17(3): 157-179.

[2104] PINKHENSON, D. M. *SSSR v mezhdunarodnom razdelenii truda* [The USSR in international division of labor]. Leningrad: Znanie, 1967.

[2105] PIOTROW, F. JACKSON. "Collaboration and Convergence: Some Recent Books on Communism, Russia, and Eastern Europe." *WA* 1971 133: 304-314.

[2106] PIPES, RICHARD E. "Background and Prospects [Soviet Foreign Policy]." *Sur* 1971 17(4): 1-9.

[2107] ———. "Russian Policy in the Middle East." *BSJA* 1968 (2).

[2108] ———. "Russia's Mission, America's Destiny: The Premises of U.S. and Soviet Foreign Policy." *Enc* 1970 35(4): 3-11.

[2109] ———. "Russia's Politics: Fatigue for the Elite." *IP* 1971 4(2): 5-8.

[2110] PIRADOV, A. S. "Organizatsiia Ob"edinennykh Natsii, 1945-1970 gg" [The United Nations, 1945-1970]. *SGP* 1970 (10): 78-83.

[2111] ———, AND V. RYBAKOV. "First Space Treaty." *IA(M)* 1967 (3): 21-26.

[2112] ———.*See* 233.

[2113] PIROZHKOVA, VERA. "The Recent Events in Czechoslovakia and the Fundamentals of Soviet Foreign Policy." *B,ISUSSR* 1968 15(10): 5-13.

[2114] PISAR, SAMUEL. *Coexistence and Commerce: Guidelines for Transactions Between East and West.* New York: McGraw Hill, 1970.

[2115] PISKULOV, IU. "Aktual'nye zadachi Sovetsko-Finliandskogo ekonomicheskogo sotrudnichestva" [Actual tasks of Soviet-Finnish economic cooperation]. *VT* 1971 (2): 5-10.

[2116] PISZCZKOWSKI, T. "The German Problem." *PG* 1967 11(39-40): 21-39.

[2117] PIZINGER, DONALD D. "Present Soviet Policy in Latin America." *NWCR* 1969 21(8): 99-114.

[2118] PLATTE, WILLIAM A. "Peking, Moscow, and the SALT Talks." *NWCR* 1970 22(9): 93-111.

[2119] PLETNEV, E. "Leninskoe uchenie o monopolisticheskom kapitalizme i sovremennye imperialisticheskie protivorechiia" [The Leninist teaching on monopoly capitalism and present imperialist contradictions]. *Komm* 1969 (16): 22-34.

[2120] PLETNEVA, E. P., ED. *Diplomatiia i mirovoe khoziaistvo* [Diplomacy and world economy]. Moscow: I.M.O., 1967.

[2121] PLISCHKE, ELMER. "Eisenhower's 'Correspondence Diplomacy' With the Kremlin—Case Study in Summit Diplomatics." *JP* 1968 30: 137-159.

[2122] PLOSS, SIDNEY, I. "A Cautious Verdict in Moscow: The Twenty-Fourth Party Congress." *Orb* 1971 15: 561-575.

[2123] ———. "Studying the Domestic Determinants of Soviet Foreign Policy." *CSISt* 1967 1: 44-59.

[2124] POCHKAEVA, M. "Mezhgosudarstvennye ekonomicheskie otnosheniia i mezhdunarodnoe pravo" [Inter-state economic relations and international law]. *VT* 1970 (4): 51-56.

[2125] "Pod znamenem proletarskogo internatsionalizma" [Under the banner of proletarian internationalism]. *Komm* 1968 (18): 3-7.

[2126] "Pod znamenem proletarskogo internatsionalizma" [Under the banner of proletarian internationalism]. *MEMO* 1969 (7): 3-14.

[2127] *Pod znamenem proletarskogo internatsionalizma. Deiatel'nost' Rumynskikh internatsionalistov na territorii strany Sovetov 1917-1920 gg* [Under the banner of proletarian internationalism. Activity of Rumanian internationalists on territory of Soviet Russia, 1917-1920]. Moscow: Nauka, 1970.

[2128] POLACH, JAROSLAV G. "Nuclear Power in Eastern Europe." *EE* 17(5): 3-12.

[2129] "Poland: Law on Contiguous Fishery Zone." *ILM* 1970 9: 776-777.

[2130] "Poland-Union of Soviet Socialist Republics: Treaty on the Course of the Boundary of the Continental Shelf." *ILM* 1970 9: 697-698.

[2131] POLIANOV, N. "Europe: Peace Zone or Hotbed of War?" *IA(M)* 1969 (5): 3-9.

[2132] ———. "Evropa: Voennoe protivostoianie i bezopasnost'" [Europe: Military opposition and security]. *MEMO* 1967 (9): 42-53.

[2133] POLIANSKII, V. *Proletarian Internationalism: Guideline of the Communists.* Moscow: Novosti, 1970.

[2134] _____.*See* 48.

[2135] _____, ED. *Proletarskii internatsionalizm na sovremennom etape. Sbornik statei* [Proletarian internationalism at the present stage. Collection of articles]. Moscow: Novosti, 1971.

[2136] POLIENKO, A. "Torgovye otnosheniia so stranami SEV uspeshno razvivaiutsia" [Trade relations with the countries of CMEA successfully grow]. *VT* 1971 (6): 22-25.

[2137] POLISENSKY, JOSEF V. *Canada and Czechoslovakia.* Translated by Jessie Kocmannova. Prague: Orbis, 1967.

[2138] "Politika gruppy Mao Tsee-duna na mezhdunarodnoi arene" [The politics of the Mao Tse-tung group in the international arena]. *Komm* 1969 (5): 104-116.

[2139] "Politika mira i druzhby mezhdu narodami" [The politics of peace and friendship between peoples]. *Komm* 1969 (11): 17-22.

[2140] PONOMAREV, B. "Aktual'nye problemy teorii mirovogo revoliutsionnogo protessa" [Actual problems of the theory of the world revolutionary process]. *Komm* 1971 (15): 37-71.

[2141] _____.*Mezhdunarodnoe revoliutsionnoe dvizhenie rabochego klassa* [The international revolutionary process of the working class]. Moscow: Progress, 1967.

[2142] _____. "Under Banner of Marxism-Leninism and Proletarian Internationalism." *WMR* 1971 14(6): 3-19.

[2143] _____, A. GROMYKO, AND V. KHVOSTOV, EDS. *Istoriia vneshnei politiki SSSR.* Moscow: Nauka, 1967, 1971. 2 vols. Vol. 1 appeared in English as *History of Soviet Foreign Policy, 1917-1945.* Moscow: Progress, 1969.

[2144] POPISAKOV, G. *Ekonomicheskie otnosheniia mezhdu Bolgariei i SSSR.* [The economic relations between Bulgaria and the USSR]. Moscow: Progress, 1969.

[2145] POPOV, B. "Sovetsko-Angliiskie torgovye otnosheniia" [Soviet-English trade relations]. *VT* 1969 (1): 18-23.

[2146] POPOV, I. V. *Osnovnye napravleniia tekhnicheskogo progressa v stranakh SEV* [Basic trends of technical progress in the CMEA countries]. Moscow: Mysl', 1969.

[2147] POPOV, K. I. "Leninskii printsip monopolii vneshnei torgovli i ego osuchchestvlenie v stranakh sotzializma" [The Leninist principle of the monopoly of foreign trade and its realization in the socialist countries]. *VT* 1969 (3): 81-92.

[2148] ————.*Razvitie ekonomicheskikh sviazei stran sotsializma* [The development of economic ties of the socialist countries]. Moscow: Mysl', 1968.

[2149] ————. "Zapadnoevropeiskaia integratsiia i mezhdunarodnoe sotrudnichestvo" [West European integration and international cooperation]. *VE* 1971 (1): 98-108.

[2150] POPOV, MILORAD. *See* 2689.

[2151] POPOV, N. N. *Po puti sovershenstvovaniia primenenie novoi sistemy planirovaniia i rukovodstva vo vneshnei torgovle i v promyshlennosti GDR* [On the path of perfection: The application of a new system of planning and leadership in the foreign trade and in the production of the GDR]. Moscow: I.M.O., 1967.

[2152] POPOV, V. "Lenin and Soviet Diplomacy." *NT* 1970 (30): 18-20.

[2153] ————. "Leninist Foreign Policy." *NT* 1971 (13): 6-9.

[2154] POPOVA, E. I. "1920-1922: Amerikantsy i Sovetskaia Rosiia" [1920-1922: Americans and Soviet Russia]. *SShA* 1970 (11): 56-62.

[2155] POPPINO, ROLLIE E. "The Early Cold War Period." *CH* 1969 56: 340-345.

[2156] PORSHNEV, B. *Leninist Theory of Revolution and Social Psychology.* Moscow: Novosti, 1970.

[2157] PORSHOLT, LARS. "New Developments in Hungarian Foreign Trade Regulations." *InP* 1970 (1): 74-88.

[2158] POSPELOV, P. N., ET AL., EDS. *Velikaia otechestvennaia voina Sovetskogo Soiuza. 1941-1945. Kratkaia istoriia* [The great patriotic war of the Soviet Union, 1941-1945. Short history]. Moscow: Voenizdat, 1970.

[2159] POSSONY, STEFAN T. "The USSR: Beyond Its Zenith?" *Orb* 1971 15: 87-103.

[2160] POTICHNYJ, PETER J. *See* 1039.

[2161] POUNDS, NORMAN J. G. "Fissures in the Eastern European Bloc." *A,AAPSS* 1967 (372): 40-58.

[2162] POWER, PAUL F. "The Peoples' Solidarity Movement: Evolution and Continuity." *Miz* 1967 9: 10-22.

[2163] POWERS, DAVID R. "Five Issues of Politico-Military Strategy: A Content Analysis of Sino-Soviet Documents 1960-1963." *DAI* 1971 32: 1600-A.

[2164] POWERS, RICHARD J. "Containment: From Greece to Vietnam and Back?" *WPQ* 1969 22: 846-861.

[2165] POZDNIAKOV, V. S. *Gosudarstvennaia monopoliia vneshnei torgovli v SSSR* [The state monopoly of foreign trade in the USSR]. Moscow: I.M.O., 1969.

[2166] ———. "V. I. Lenin i monopoliia vneshnei torgovli" [V. I. Lenin and the monopoly of foreign trade]. *VT* 1970 (3): 6-10.

[2167] ———. "Pravovoe regulirovanie sotrudnichestva stran SEV" [The legal regulation of cooperation of the CMEA countries]. *VT* 1971 (1): 53-54.

[2168] POZNANSKI, V. J. "Brandt's Ostpolitik." *PG* 1970 14(1-2): 3-7.

[2169] PRATT, LAWRENCE. "North Vietnam and Sino-Soviet Tension." *BH* 1967 26(6).

[2170] "Pravo v ideologicheskoi borb'e sovremennosti" [Law in the ideological struggle of the present]. *SGP* 1971 (10): 10-19.

[2171] PRAZSKY, JAN. "The Communists and European Security." *WMR* 1967 10(6): 11-17.

[2172] ———. "Europe: Peace or Conflict." *WMR* 1971 14(7): 147-153.

[2173] ———. "Peace Offensive." *WMR* 1971 14(11): 62-68.

[2174] ———. "'Superpowers': A False Concept." *WMR* 1971 14(9): 128-134.

[2175] "Press Conference at the Soviet Foreign Ministry." *NT* 1970 (4): 16-17.

[2176] PRICE, THOMAS. "An Element of International Image Construction: A Twenty-Year Printed Media Image of the Soviet Union, 1947-1967." *DAI* 1970 31: 4869-A.

[2177] PRIFTI, PETER R. "Albania Gets the Jitters." *EE* 1969 18(1): 9-13.

[2178] PRINCE, HOWARD T. "SALT, National Security, and International Politics." *JICSt* 1971 4(1): 14-27.

[2179] *Principles of Lenin's Foreign Policy.* Moscow: Novosti Press, 1969.

[2180] PRITZEL, KONSTANTIN. "Twenty Years of COMECON." *CEJ* 1969 17: 251-255.

[2181] PRIVALOV, V. V. *Obrazovanie Kommunisticheskogo Internatsionala Moledezhi* [The formation of the Communist Youth International]. Leningrad: UN-TA, 1968.

[2182] *Problemy mezhdunarodnogo sotsialisticheskogo razdeleniia truda*
[Problems of international socialist division of labor]. Leningrad:
Nauka, 1967.

[2183] *Problemy razvitiia mirovogo revoliutsionnogo protsessa* [Problems of
the development of the world revolutionary process]. Moscow: Izdatel'stvo Moskovskogo universiteta, 1970.

[2184] *Problemy sovershenstvovaniia vneshneekonomicheskikh sviazei sotsialisticheskikh stran* [Problems of the perfection of foreign economic ties of the socialist countries]. Moscow: Izdatel'stvo
Moskovskogo universiteta, 1969.

[2185] "Problemy teorii mezhdunarodnykh otnoshenii"[Problems of the theory of international relations]. *MEMO* 1969 (9): 88-106, (11): 78-
99.

[2186] *Problemy voiny i mira. Kritika sovremennykh burzhuaznykh sotsial'-
no-filosofskikh kontseptsii* [Problems of war and peace. Critique of
contemporary bourgeois social-philosophical conceptions]. Moscow: Mysl', 1967.

[2187] "Programma bor'by za uprochenie mira" [The program of the struggle
for the consolidation of peace]. *Komm* 1967 (8): 3-8.

[2188] "Programme of Struggle for Peace and International Security." *IA(M)*
1971 (6): 3-7.

[2189] PROKHOROV, G. "Optimizatsiia vneshnikh ekonomicheskikh sviazei
sotsialisticheskikh stran" [The optimization of foreign economic
ties of the socialist states]. *VE* 1969 (11): 117-126.

[2190] ———. "Ties Born of the October Revolution. *IA(M)* 1967 (10):
21-26.

[2191] ———. "V. I. Lenin i novyi tip mezhdunarodnykh ekonomicheskikh
otnoshenii" [V. I. Lenin and the new type of international economic
relations]. *VE* 1970 (7): 15-22.

[2192] PROKOPENKO, N. I. *Mezhdunarodnoe revoliutsionnoe dvizhenie rabochego klassa* [International revolutionary movement of the working
class]. Moscow: Moscow University, 1967.

[2193] PROKOP'EV, I. "Sovetsko-Shvedskaia torgovlia." [Soviet-Swedish
trade]. *VT* 1968 (9): 6-9.

[2194] ———. "Vazhnyi etap torgovykh otnoshenii SSSR i Finlandii" [Im-
portant stage of the trade relations of the USSR and Finland]. *VT*
1970 (1): 11-15.

[2195] PROKOP'EV, N. "Problems of War and Peace in Our Age." *IA(M)*
1967 (12): 57-62.

[2196] "Proletarskii internatsionalizm—znamiakh mezhdunarodnogo Kommunisticheskogo dvizheniia" [Proletarian internationalism—the banner of the international Communist movement]. *Komm* 1968 (12): 24-30.

[2197] "Protiv imperializma za sotsial'nyi progress" [Against imperialism, for social progress]. *AAS* 1971 (2): 2-3.

[2198] PROTOPOPOV, A. S. *Liga Natsii, OON i Sovetskii Soiuz* [The League of Nations, the UN, and the Soviet Union]. Moscow: Mysl', 1968.

[2199] _____. *Sovetskii Soiuz i Suetskii krizis 1956 goda (Iiul'-Noiabr')* [The Soviet Union and the Suez crisis of 1956 (July-November)]. Moscow: Nauka, 1969.

[2200] PROVAZNIK, JAN. "The Politics of Retrenchment." *PoC* 1969 18(4-5): 2-16.

[2201] PRYBYLA, JAN S. "Albania's Economic Vassalage." *EE* 1967 16(1): 9-14.

[2202] _____. "The China Trade." *EE* 1967 16(3): 15-20.

[2203] _____. "Recent Trends in Sino-Soviet Economic Relations." *B,ISUSSR* 1967 14(5): 11-21.

[2204] _____. "The Soviet View of Mao's Cultural Revolution." *VQR* 1968 44: 385-398.

[2205] _____. *See* 2469.

[2206] _____, ED. *Communism and Nationalism.* University Park: Center for Continuing Liberal Education and Slavic and Soviet Area Center, Pennsylvania State University, 1969.

[2207] _____, ED. *Communism at the Crossroads.* University Park: Center for Continuing Liberal Education and Slavic and Soviet Area Center, Pennsylvania State University, 1968.

[2208] PSOMIADES, HARRY J. "Soviet-American Rivalry in the Mediterranean and Beyond." *StNCE* 1968-69 2(4): 228-233.

[2209] PTICHKIN, N. "Bratskoe sodruzhestvo stran SEV—podtverzhdenie zhiznennosti Leninskikh idei" [Fraternal collaboration of the CMEA countries—confirmation of the vitality of Leninist ideas]. *VT* 1970 (4): 25-31.

[2210] _____. "Kurs na dal'neishee razvitie sotsialisticheskoi ekonomicheskoi integratsii" [The course toward the further development of socialist economic integration]. *VT* 1971 (10): 2-11.

[2211] _____. "Mezhdunarodnyi institut ekonomicheskikh problem mirovoi sotsialisticheskoi sistemy" [The international institute of the economic problems of the world socialist system]. *VT* 1971 (5): 3-15.

[2212] ———. "Novyi tip mezhdunarodnykh ekonomicheskikh otnoshenii" [A new type of international economic relations]. *VT* 1967 (10): 3-9.

[2213] PUIIA, F. *Edinstvo i diskussiia v mezhdunarodnom Kommunisticheskom dvizhenii* [Unity and debate in the international Communist movement]. Moscow: I.M.O., 1970.

[2214] ———. *Problemy mirnogo sosushchestovaniia* [The problems of peaceful coexistence]. Moscow: I.M.O., 1969.

[2215] PUSHMIN, E. A. *Posrednichestvo v mezhdunarodnom prave* [Contradictions in international law]. Moscow: I.M.O., 1970.

[2216] PYSHKOV, B. *See* 1458.

[2217] QUARONI, PIETRO. "Divided Europe: The Situation Today." *B,ISUSSR* 1971 18(7): 14-32.

[2218] QUESTED, J. "Russian Interest in Southeast Asia: Outlines and Sources, 1803-1970." *JSEASt* 1971 1(1): 48-60.

[2219] QUESTER, GEORGE H. "Missiles in Cuba, 1970." *FA* 1971 49: 493-506.

[2220] ———. *Nuclear Diplomacy: The First Twenty-Five Years*. New York: Dunellen Publishing Company, 1971.

[2221] QUIGLEY, JOHN B., JR. "Soviet Conflict Rules: Merchant Shipping Code of 1968." *AJIL* 1969 63: 529-535.

[2222] ———. *See* 361.

[2223] QURESKI, KHALIDA. "Pakistan's Relations With Yugoslavia." *PH* 1970 23: 149-163.

[2224] RA'ANAN, URI. "Chinese Factionalism and Sino-Soviet Relations." *CH* 1970 59: 134-141.

[2225] ———. "Soviet Global Policy and the Middle East." *Mid* 1969 15: 3-13.

[2226] ———. "Soviet Global Policy and the Middle East." *NWCR* 1971 24(1): 19-29.

[2227] ———. *The USSR Arms the Third World: Case Studies in Soviet Foreign Policy*. Cambridge: Massachusetts Institute of Technology Press, 1969.

[2228] RABINOWITCH, EUGENE. "The Sakharov Manifesto: Progress, Peaceful Coexistence, Intellectual Freedom." *BAS* 1968 24(9): 2-7.

[2229] *Rabochii klass v bor'be protiv imperializma, za revoliutsionnoe obnovlenie mira* [The working class in the struggle against imperialism, for the revolutionary renovation of the world]. Moscow: Nauka, 1968.

[2230] RACZ, BARNABAS. "Political Changes in Hungary After the Soviet Invasion of Czechoslovakia." *SIR* 1970 29: 633-650.

[2231] RADULESCU, G. "Rumania in Economic and Technical Cooperation." *WMR* 1970 13(11): 56-62.

[2232] RADVANYI, JANOS. "The Hungarian Revolution and the Hundred Flowers Campaign." *CQ* 1970 43: 121-129.

[2233] _____.*Hungary and the Superpowers.* Stanford: Hoover Institution Press, 1971.

[2234] RAJASEKHARIAH, A. M. "Soviet Foreign Policy Towards China: An Assessment." *ModR* 1968 124: 383-389, 434-438.

[2235] RAKHIMOV, T. *Natsionalizm i shovinizm—osnova politiki gruppy Mao Tsee-duna* [Nationalism and chauvinism—the foundation of the politics of the Mao Tse-tung group]. Moscow: Mysl', 1968.

[2236] RAKHMANINOV, IU. "Alternative to a Divided Europe." *IA(M)* 1967 (4): 41-47.

[2237] _____. "For European Security." *IA(M)* 1967 (11): 81-87.

[2238] _____. "Soviet-French Cooperation in Western Europe." *IA(M)* 1968 (9): 37-43.

[2239] _____. "Soviet-French Relations and European Security." *IA(M)* 1970 (11): 33-39.

[2240] RAM, RAGHU NATH. "The Soviet Attitude Towards Colonialism with Special Reference to India." *IJPS* 1968 29: 114-126.

[2241] RAMUNDO, B. A. *Peaceful Coexistence: International Law in the Building of Communism.* Baltimore, Maryland: Johns Hopkins Press, 1967.

[2242] RANGER, ROBERT. "Nato's Reaction to Czechoslovakia: The Strategy of Ambiguous Response." *WT* 1969 25: 19-25.

[2244] RANSOM, C. F. G. "The Future of EEC-COMECON Relations." *WT* 1971 27: 438-447.

[2244] _____. "Obstacles to the Liberalization of Relations Between E.E.C. and COMECON." *StCC* 1969 2(3-4): 61-78.

[2245] RAPOPORT, ANATOL. *The Big Two: Perceptions of Soviet-American Relations Since World War II.* New York: Pegasus, 1970.

[2246] *Rasprostranenie Marksizma-Leninizma v stranakh Vostoka. Sbornik statei* [The diffusion of Marxism-Leninism in the countries of the East. A collection of articles]. Moscow: Nauka, 1970.

[2247] *Rastsvet sotsialisticheskikh natsii i ikh sblizhenie* [The growth of the socialist nations and their drawing together]. Tashkent: FAN, 1967.

[2248] RAU, ERWIN M. "Russia and the Baltic Sea, 1920-1970." *NWCR* 1970 23(1): 23-30.

[2249] RAUCH, ELMER. "Treaty Between the Federal Republic of Germany and the Union of Soviet Socialist Republics of August 12, 1970: A Textual Analysis." *NYUJIL* 1971 4(1).

[2250] RAY, HEMEN. "Changing Soviet Views on Mahatma Gandhi." *JASt* 1969 29(1): 85-106.

[2251] ———. "Soviet Diplomacy in Asia." *PoC* 1970 19: 46-49.

[2252] RAYNER, WILLIAM. "The USSR and Zambia." *Miz* 1969 11: 265-270.

[2253] RAZMEROV, V. "Loyalty to Proletarian Internationalism—Fundamental Condition for Success of All Revolutionary Forces." *IA(M)* 1970 (4): 51-58.

[2254] ———, AND D. G. TOMASHEVSKII. "The Soviet State's Struggle against Imperialist Aggression." *IA(M)* 1967 (1): 54-60.

[2255] ———. *See* 1998.

[2256] "Recent Developments in Trade Between Eastern and Western European Countries." *EBE* 1967 19(1): 38-55.

[2257] "Recent Soviet Books on Africa, the Middle East and Asia." *Miz* 1969 11: 325-333.

[2258] "Recent Soviet Books on Africa, the Middle East and Asia." *Miz* 1971 13: 126-137.

[2259] REES, DAVID. *The Age of Containment: The Cold War 1945-1965.* London: Macmillan; New York: St. Martin's, 1967.

[2260] REINTANZ, G. "International Relations—German Democratic Republic." *CSISt,BS* 1968 2(3): 42, 2(4): 130-131, 3(3): 61, 3(4): 36, 4(2): 137; 1971 5(4): 69.

[2261] REISKY DE DUBNIC, VLADIMIR. "The 'China Peril' Theme in Soviet Global Strategy." *B,ISUSSR* 1971 18(6): 3-19.

[2262] ———. "Germany and China: The Intermediate Zone Theory and the Moscow Treaty." *AsQ* 1971 (4): 343-358.

[2263] *Religiia v planakh Antikommunizma* [Religion in the plans of anti-Communism]. Moscow: Mysl', 1970.

[2264] REMINGTON, ROBIN ALISON. "Czechoslovakia and the Warsaw Pact." *EEQ* 1970 3: 315-336.

[2265] ———. "Moscow, Peking and Black American Revolution." *Sur* 1970 74-75: 237-252.

138

[2266] _____.Revolutionary Role of the Afro-American: An Analysis of Sino-Soviet Polemics on the Historical Importance of the American Negro. Cambridge: Massachusetts Institute of Technology, Center for International Studies, 1968.

[2267] _____. The Warsaw Pact: Case Studies in Communist Conflict Resolution. Cambridge: Massachusetts Institute of Technology Press, 1971.

[2268] _____, ED. Winter in Prague: Documents on Czechoslovak: Communism in Crisis. Cambridge: Massachusetts Institute of Technology Press, 1969.

[2269] REPIN, A. "The Soviet Union and the U.A.R." NT 1968 (27): 4-5.

[2270] "A Research Note on Industrial Cooperation as a Factor in East-West European Trade." EBE 1970 21(1): 67-88.

[2271] Resursy i mezhdunarodnoe sotrudnichestvo [Resources and international cooperation]. Moscow: I.M.O., 1968.

[2272] REUTOV, G. N. Bor'ba SSSR protiv imperialisticheskoi agressii, za polnuiu likvidatsiiu kolonializma [The struggle of the USSR against imperialist aggression, for the full liquidation of colonialism]. Leningrad: Un-t, 1967.

[2273] REZNIKOV, A. "Bor'ba V. I. Lenina protiv sektanskikh izvrashchenii v natsional'no-kolonial'nom voprose" [The struggle of V. I. Lenin against sectarian perversion in the national-colonial question]. Komm 1968 (5): 36-47.

[2274] _____. "V. I. Lenin o natsional'no-osvoboditel'nom dvizhenii" [Lenin on the national-liberation movement]. Komm 1967 (7): 91-102.

[2275] RHEE, TONG-CHIN. "Japan and the Soviet Union." WAI 1970 133: 240-257.

[2276] _____. "Sino-Soviet Military Conflict and the Global Balance of Power." WT 1970 26: 29-37.

[2277] RIABUSHKIN, T. B., ED. Ekonomika evropeiskikh stran-chlenov SEV [The economy of the member-countries of CMEA]. Moscow: Nauka, 1968.

[2278] _____, ED. Mirovaia sotsialisticheskaia sistema. Nekotorye problemy razvitiia na sovremennom etape [The world socialist system. Some problems of development at the present stage]. Moscow: Nauka, 1971.

[2279] RICHARDS, GUY. "The Persian Gulf's Strait of Ormuz: A New Area of U.S.-Soviet Conflict?" EE 1971 20(1): 8-15.

[2280] _____. "The Soviet Naval Strategy." EE 1971 20(3): 2-11.

[2281] RICHARDSON, ELLIOT L. "U.S.-Soviet Relations in an Era of Negotiation." *Department of State Bulletin.* 1969 61(December 22): 584-588.

[2282] RICHARDSON, JAMES. "Germany's Eastern Policy: Problems and Prospects." *WT* 1968 24: 375-396.

[2283] RICKOFF, HAROLD VON. *See* 309.

[2284] RINCHIN, LODONGIYN. "Mongolian-Soviet Friendship." *NT* 1971 (3): 4.

[2285] RISTE, OLAV. "Free Ports in North Norway: A Contribution to the Study of FDR's Wartime Policy Towards the USSR." *JCH* 1970 5: 77-96.

[2286] RITSCH, FREDERICK F. "East-West Polarization and the Contemporary World." *IIP* 1968 33: 193-200.

[2287] ROBERTS, ADAM. *See* 3137.

[2288] ROBERTS, CHALMERS M. *The Nuclear Years: The Arms Race and Arms Control 1945-1970.* New York: Praeger, 1970.

[2289] ROBERTS, FRANK. "The German-Soviet Treaty and Its Effects on European and Atlantic Policies: A British View." *ACQ* 1971 9: 184-195.

[2290] ROBERTS, HENRY L. *Eastern Europe: Politics, Revolution and Diplomacy.* New York: Knopf, 1970.

[2291] ROBERTS, JACK L. "The Growing Soviet Naval Presence in the Caribbean: Its Politico-Military Impact upon the United States." *NWCR* 1971 23(10): 31-41.

[2292] DEROBIEN, LOUIS. *The Diary of a Diplomat in Russia, 1917-1918.* Translated by Camilla Sykes. London: Michael Joseph, 1969.

[2993] ROBINSON, THOMAS W. *The Border Negotiations and the Future of Sino-Soviet-American Relations.* Santa Monica, California: RAND Corporation, 1971.

[2294] ――――. "Games Theory and Politics: Recent Soviet Views." *StST* 1970 10: 291-315.

[2295] ――――. "A National Interest Analysis of Sino-Soviet Relations." *IStQ* 1967 11: 135-175.

[2296] ――――. *The Sino-Soviet Border Dispute: Background, Development, and the March 1969 Clashes.* Santa Monica, California: The RAND Corporation, 1970.

[2297] ――――. "Systems Theory and the Communist System." *IS* 1969 13: 398-420.

[2298] ROBINSON, WILLIAM F. "Czechoslovakia and Its Allies: January-June 1968." *StCC* 1968 1: 141-170.

[2299] RODES, ROBERT M. "Soviet Attitudes Toward the Independence Movements in South and Southeast Asia, 1945-1952." *DAI* 1969 30: 1221-A.

[2300] ROGERS, ROBERT B. "Trends in Soviet Naval Strategy." *NWCR* 1969 21(6): 30-42.

[2301] ROHLEDER, CLAUS. "USSR's Partner, Rumania." *CEJ* 1969 17: 287-291.

[2302] ROKITKO, A. I. *Na osnove ravnopraviia i vzaimnoi vygody. Ekonomicheskaia pomoshch' SSSR razvivaiushchimsia stranam* [On the basis of equality and mutual benefit. Economic assistance of the USSR to the developing countries]. Kiev: Znanie, 1967.

[2303] ROLEY, PAUL L. "In Search of Accomodation: Anglo-Soviet Relations, 1919-1921." *DAI* 1967 27: 3821-A.

[2304] ROMANCE, FRANCIS J. "Sino-Soviet Relations Towards the Mongolian People's Republic, 1945-1965: A Study of the Political and Economic Factors Involved." *DAI* 1967 28: 756-A.

[2305] ROMANOV, IU. "Vneshtorgovaia statistika v stranakh SEV" [Foreign trade statistics in the CMEA countries]. *VT* 1969 (9): 46-48.

[2306] RONIANOV, IU. "Ekonomicheskoe sotrudnichestvo Marokko so stranami sotsializma" [Economic cooperation of Morocco with the socialist countries]. *VT* 1968 (11): 34-35.

[2307] RONNEBERGER, FRANZ. *Southeast Europe in Contemporary International Politics*. Kansas City, Missouri: Park College, East Europe Monographs, 1969.

[2308] ROSS, THOMAS B. *See* 3141.

[2309] ROSSER, RICHARD F. *An Introduction to Soviet Foreign Policy*. Englewood Cliffs, New Jersey: Prentice-Hall, 1969.

[2310] ROSTOW, WALT W., AND WILLIAM E. GRIFFITH. *East-West Relations: Is Détente Possible?* Washington, D.C.: American Enterprise Institute, 1970.

[2311] _____.*See* 919.

[2312] ROTH, HERBERT. "Moscow, Peking and N.Z. Communists." *Pol* 1969 4: 168-185.

[2313] ROTHERMUND, DIETMAR. "India and the Soviet Union." *A,AAPSS* 1969 386: 78-88.

[2314] ROTHSCHILD, JOSEPH. "The Soviet Union and Czechoslovakia." In *Conflict in World Politics,* pp. 115-138, edited by Steven L. Spiegel and Kenneth N. Waltz. Cambridge, Massachusetts: Winthrop, 1971.

[2315] ROTHSTEIN, ROBERT L. "The ABM, Proliferation and International Stability." *FA* 1968 46: 487-502.

[2316] ROUCEK, JOSEPH S. *Central-Eastern Europe: Crucible of World Wars.* Reprinted from 1946 edition. Westport, Connecticut: Greenwood Press, 1970.

[2317] ———. "Growing Soviet Threat to the Mediterranean World." *UQ* 1969 25: 54-66.

[2318] ———. "Racial Elements in the Sino-Russian Dispute." *CR* February 1967 210: 77-84.

[2319] ROZALIEV, Y. *See* 1282.

[2320] ROZENBERG, M. G. "Unifikatsiia norm o vneshnetorgovoi postavke stran-chlenov SEV" [Unification of norms concerning the foreign trade deliveries of the member countries of CMEA]. *SGP* 1969 (7): 51-59.

[2321] ———. *See* 341.

[2322] ———. *See* 342.

[2323] RUBANIK, K. P. *Mezhdunarodnopravovye problemy IUNESKO* [The international legal problems of UNESCO]. Moscow: I.M.O., 1969.

[2324] ———. "Universal'nost' mezhdunarodnykh organizatsii i priem GDR v IUNESKO" [Universality of international organizations and the admission of the GDR into UNESCO]. *SGP* 1971 (5): 53-58.

[2325] RUBINSHTEIN, M. "International Scientific Cooperation." *NT* 1969 (19-20): 34-37.

[2326] ———. "Mezhdunarodnoe znachenie nauchnotekhnicheskogo progressa SSSR" [The international meaning of the scientific-technical progress of the USSR]. *MEMO* 1967 (8): 3-15.

[2327] RUBINSTEIN, ALVIN Z. "Balkan Kaleidoscope." *CH* 1967 52: 220-226, 244-245.

[2328] ———. "Reforms, Nonalignment, and Pluralism (Yugoslavia)." *PoC* 1968 12(2): 31-40.

[2329] ———. "Soviet Policy Toward the Third World in the 1970's." *Orb* 1971 15: 104-117.

[2330] ———. "Tito's Acentric Communism and the Sino-Soviet Rivalry in the Third World." *Orb* 1968 12: 685-705.

[2331] ———. *Yugoslavia and the Nonaligned World.* Princeton, New Jersey: Princeton University Press, 1970.

[2332] ———. "Yugoslavia's Foreign Policy Since the June War." *CSISt* 1969 3: 528-543.

[2333] ———. "Yugoslavia's Non-Aligned Role in Africa." *AfR* 1970 15(8): 14-17.

[2334] ———, AND GEORGE GINSBURGS, EDS. *Soviet and American Policies in the United Nations: A Twenty-Five-Year Perspective.* New York: New York University Press, 1971.

[2335] ———. *See* 199.

[2336] RUBINSTEIN, G. "Aspects of Soviet-African Economic Relations." *JMAS* 1970 8: 389-404.

[2337] ———. *See* 1425.

[2338] RUINA, J. P. "Nuclear Arms Race: Diagnosis and Treatment." *BAS* 1968 24(8): 19-22.

[2339] RUPEN, ROBERT A., AND ROBERT FARRELL, EDS. *Vietnam and the Sino-Soviet Dispute.* New York: Praeger, 1967.

[2340] RUSH, MYRON, ED. *The International Situation and Soviet Foreign Policy: Key Reports by Soviet Leaders From the Revolution to the Present.* Columbus, Ohio: Charles E. Merrill, 1970.

[2341] RUSIN, E. I. *Razvitie i ukreplenie Sovetsko-Vengerskogo ekonomicheskogo sotrudnichestva. 1945-1969 gg* [The development and strengthening of Soviet-Hungarian economic cooperation, 1945-1969]. L'vov: Izd. L'vovskogo Un-ta, 1970.

[2342] RUSNAK, ANDREW JOHN. "Poland and the Molotov-Ribbentrop Pact: A Study of Selected Slavic-American Editorial Opinion, Mid-March Through September, 1939." *DAI* 1971 31: 5996-A.

[2343] RUSSELL, CHARLES A., AND ROBERT E. HILDNER. "The Role of Communist Ideology in Insurgency." *AUR* 1971 22(1): 42-48.

[2344] "Russian Play for 'Status Quo' and Captive Nations." *UQ* 1970 26: 117-123.

[2345] *Russko-Frantsuzkie sviazi. Sbornik* [Russian-French ties. A Collection]. Moscow: Nauka, 1968.

[2346] RUTGAIZER, V. "CMEA: New Horizons." *NT* 1970 (21): 20-21.

[2347] RYBAKOV, IU. M. "Mezhdunarodno-pravovoe sotrudnichestvo v kosmose" [International legal cooperation in space]. *SGP* 1970 (2): 40-47.

[2348] RYBAKOV, V. *See* 2111.

[2349] RYDER, AMBROSE. *The Science of Coexistence.* New York: Philosophical Library, 1968.

[2350] RYDER, VINCENT. "East West." *CR* 1971 219(1269): 169-172.

[2351] RYIIA, FRID'ESH. *Problemy mirnogo sosushchestvovaniia* [Problems of peaceful coexistence]. Moscow: I.M.O., 1969.

[2352] RYMALOV, V. "Uchenie Lenina ob imperializme i kapitalisticheskoe mirovoe khoziaistvo" [The teaching of Lenin on imperialism and the capitalist world economy]. *VE* 1970 (2): 16-28.

[2353] RZHEVSKY, V. "European Security and the Stability of Frontiers." *IA(M)* 1970 (5): 80-84.

[2354] SAAKOV, RAFAEL'. *"Put', otkrytyi dlia vsekh. Istoriia razvitiia kul'turnykh sviazei mezhdu Sovetskim Soiuzom i zarubezhnymi stranami"* [The path open to all. History of the development of cultural relations between the Soviet Union and foreign countries]. Moscow: Novosti, 1967.

[2355] SABLE, MARTIN H., AND M. WAYNE DENNIS. *Communism in Latin America: An International Bibliography; 1900-1945, 1960-1967.* Los Angeles: Latin American Center, University of California, 1968.

[2356] SAFRON, NODAV, AND YAIR EVRON. "From Involvement to Intervention—The Soviet Union in Egypt." *NME* 1970 (June): 14-17.

[2357] SAGATELIAN, M. "Cold War Winds Again?" *NT* 1970 (43): 14-15.

[2358] SAGER, PETER. *Moscow's Hand in India: An Analysis of Soviet Propaganda.* Berne: Swiss Eastern Institute, 1966; Bombay: Lalvani Publishers, 1967.

[2359] SAIANOV, O. "Europe and the USSR-FRG Treaty." *IA(M)* 1971 (8): 44-47.

[2360] SALISBURY, HARRISON E. "The Asian Traingle-China, Russia, America." *PC* 1971 2: 445-454.

[2361] ———. "Russia vs. China: Global Conflict?" *AR* 1967 27: 425-439.

[2362] ———. *War Between Russia and China.* New York: Norton, 1969.

[2363] SALLOCH, ROGER. "International Communism: A Survey." *Sur* 1969 70/71: 32-35.

[2364] ———. "International Communism: Budapest to Moscow." *Sur* 1968 (68): 44-55.

[2365] SALYCHEV, S. "Revoliutsionnoe dvizhenie nashikh dnei" [The revolutionary movement of our days]. *MEMO* 1971 (4): 27-40.

[2366] SAMARTSEV, N. T. *Mezhdunarodnoe pravo v dokumentakh. Sbornik vashneishikh mezhdunarodno-pravovykh aktov* [International law in documents. A collection of the most important international legal acts]. Moscow: I.M.O., 1969.

[2367] SANAKOEV, SH. P. "At the Jubilee UN General Assembly." *IA(M)* 1970 (12): 30-35.

[2368] ———. "Formation and Development of Socialist International Relations." *IA(M)* 1967 (10): 3-11.

[2369] ———. *Mirovaia sotsialisticheskaia sistema* [The world socialist system]. Moscow: I.M.O., 1968.

[2370] ———. "The Problems of International Security at the UN Anniversary Session." *IA(M)* 1971 (1): 15-21, 27.

[2371] ———. "Proletarian Internationalism: Theory and Practice." *IA(M)* 1969 (4): 9-15.

[2372] ———. "Socialist Foreign Policy and Human Progress." *IA(M)* 1970 (5): 21-28.

[2373] ———. "Socialist Foreign Policy and the Community of Fraternal Countries." *IA(M)* 1968 (10): 71-81.

[2374] ———. "Socialist Foreign Policy: Coordination and Effectiveness." *IA(M)* 1971 (6): 8-15.

[2375] ———. *Teoriia i praktika sotsialisticheskikh mezhdunarodnykh otnoshenii* [The theory and practice of socialist international relations]. Moscow: Politizdat, 1970.

[2376] ———. "U.N. General Assembly: Fact and Fiction." *IA(M)* 1968 (12): 18-23.

[2377] ———, AND N. I. KAPCHENKO. "Triumph of the Principles of Proletarian Internationalism." *IA(M)* 1969 (8): 32-39.

[2378] ———, ET AL., EDS. *Tegeran-Ialta-Potsdam. Sbornik dokumentov* [Teheran-Yalta-Potsdam: Collection of documents]. Moscow: I.M.O., 1970.

[2379] SAN'KO, A. "Primenenie vooruzhennykh sil ot imeni OON" [The use of military forces in the name of the UN]. *SGP* 1968 (1): 90-95.

[2380] SANNESS, J. "Eastern Europe—Integration, Hegemony, Empire." *CaC* 1967 (1): 47-53.

[2381] SAPRYKOV, V. "Velikaia Oktiabr'skaia sotsialisticheskaia revoliutsiia i ee mezhdunarodnoe znachenie" [The great October socialist revolution and its international meaning]. *PS* 1970 (8): 74-81.

[2382] SARAN, VIMIA. *Sino-Soviet Schism: A Bibliography 1954-1964*. Amsterdam: Erasmus, 1970.

[2383] SAVENKO, IU. "Problemy toplovno-energeticheskogo balansa v stranakh-chlenov SEV" [Problems of the fuel-energy balance in the member countries of CMEA]. *VE* 1969 (7): 120-130.

[2384] _____.*See* 43.

[2385] SAVINOV, V., AND V. SIMCHERA. "The CMEA Countries' Five-Year Plans." *NT* 1971 (46): 18-19.

[2386] SAVOST'IANOV, V. "Faktory razvitiia vneshnei torgovli" [Factors of the development of foreign trade]. *VT* 1970 (10): 46-49.

[2387] SAWCZUK, KONSTANTYN. "The Ukraine in the United Nations Organization: A Study in Soviet Foreign Policy." *DAI* 1970 31: 1738-A.

[2388] *Sbornik deistvuiushchikh dogovorov, soglashenii i konventsii, zakliuchennykh SSSR s inostrannymi gosudarstvami. 21. Ianvar' 1959-31 Dek. 1960 gg* [A collection of treaties, agreements and conventions in force, entered into by the USSR with foreign states. 21 January 1959-31 December 1960]. Moscow: Politizdat, 1967.

[2389] *Sbornik normativnykh materialov po voprosam vneshnei torgovli* [A collection of normative materials on the questions of foreign trade]. Moscow: I.M.O., 1970.

[2390] SCANLAN, JAMES P. "Disarmament and the USSR." *MR* 1970 50: 29-42.

[2391] _____. "Does Soviet Policy Offer Genuine Possibilities for International Disarmament?" In *Soviet Strategy for the 70's, 3rd. Annual Soviet Affair Symposium, 4-6 June 1969*, pp. 87-95. Garmisch, Germany: U.S. Army Institute for Advanced Russian and East European Studies, 1969.

[2392] SCHAEFER, HENRY. "East Europe's New Look at the Common Market." *EE* 1971 20(3): 12 17.

[2393] SCHAPIRO, LEONARD. "The Border Issue. China and the Soviet Union: Communists in Collision." *StCC* 1969 2(3-4): 121-130.

[2394] SCHARNDORF, WERNER. "East European Countries in the Forefront of Soviet Aid to the 'Third World.' " *B,ISUSSR* 1971 18(2): 28-31.

[2395] SCHEELS, WALTER. *See* 291.

[2396] SCHLEIFSTEIN, JOSEF. "Anti-Communism and Anti-Sovietism." *NT* 1971 (20): 26-28.

[2397] SCHLESINGER, ARTHUR, JR. "Origins of the Cold War." *FA* 1967 46: 22-52.

[2398] ———.*See* 805.

[2399] SCHLESINGER, RUDOLPH. "Competitive Co-Existence vs. Escalation: Trends and Theories." *Co* 1968 5: 49-62.

[2400] ———. "Is the Cold War Inherently Necessary?" *Co* 1967 4: 29-36.

[2401] SCHMIDT, HELMUT. "The Consequences of the Brezhnev Doctrine." *ACQ* 1969 7: 184-195.

[2402] SCHMITT, HANS A. "Two Germanies: A Nation Without a State." *CH* 1969 56: 224-229, 244.

[2403] SCHNEIDER, MARK B. "Strategic Arms Limitation." *MR* 1970 50: 20-28.

[2404] SCHÖPFLIN, GEORGE. "Rumania and the Middle East Crisis." *WT* 23: 315-316.

[2405] ———. "The Soviet Attitude [Toward European Integration]." *Surv* 1970 12: 410-414.

[2406] ———, ED. *The Soviet Union and Eastern Europe: A Handbook.* London: Anthony Blond, 1970.

[2407] SCHRATZ, PAUL R. "Red Star Over the Southern Sea [Indian Ocean]" *USNI,P* 1970 96(6): 22-31.

[2408] SCHUMACHER, ANN. "Joint Business Ventures of Yugoslav Enterprises and Foreign Firms." *JICSt* 1970 2(2): 50-65.

[2409] SCHUMAN, FREDERICK L. *The Cold War: Retrospect and Prospect?* 2d ed. Baton Rouge: Louisiana State University Press, 1967.

[2410] ———. "The USSR in World Affairs: An Historic Survey of Soviet Foreign Policy." In *The USSR after 50 Years: Promise and Reality,* edited by Samuel Hendel and Randolph L. Braham. New York: Knopf, 1967.

[2411] SCHWARTZ, HARRY. *Prague's 200 Days: The Struggle for Democracy in Czechoslovakia.* New York: Praeger, 1968.

[2412] SCHWARTZ, LEONARD E. "Manned Orbiting Laboratory for War or Peace." *IA* 1967 43: 51-64.

[2413] ———. "Perspective on Pugwash." *IA* 1967 43: 498-515.

[2414] SCHWARTZ, MORTON. The Cuban Missile Venture. In *Cases in Comparative Politics,* pp. 268-301, edited by James B. Cristoph and Bernard E. Brown. Boston: Little, Brown, 1969.

[2415] _____. The "Motive Forces" of Soviet Foreign Policy: A Reappraisal. Denver: University of Denver (for the Social Science Foundation and Graduate School of International Studies), 1971.

[2416] SCOTT, HARRIET FAST. See 1322.

[2417] SCOTT, J. "Dialogue in Moscow." *RR* 1969 28: 1-10.

[2418] SCOTT, ROBERT. "China, Russia and the United States. A British View." *FA* 1970 48: 334-343.

[2419] SEABURY, PAUL. *The Rise and Decline of the Cold War*. New York: Basic Books, 1967.

[2420] _____, AND BRIAN THOMAS. "Cold War Origins." *JCH* 1968 3: 169-198.

[2421] SEARLES, ERNEST. "Peaceful Coexistence: A Fundamental Doctrine of the Soviet Union." *DAI* 1971 31: 6691-A.

[2422] SEATON, ALBERT. *The Russo-German War, 1941-45*. New York: Praeger, 1971.

[2423] SEBO, PAUL G. "Prelude to Polycentrism: The Maturation of Three East European Communist Parties." *MA* 1967 5(3): 26.

[2424] SEDOV, L., AND V. BARANOV. "Sovety po eksportu v deistvii" [Export councils in action]. *VT* 1968 (7): 2-6.

[2425] SEIFUL'MULIUKOV, A. "Sovetsko-Siriiskie torgovye sviazi" [Soviety-Syrian trade ties]. *VT* 1969 (9): 23.

[2426] SELEZNEV, L. D. *Natsional'noosvoboditel'nye revoliutsii sovremennoi epokhi* [The national liberation movement of the present epoch]. Leningrad: Izd-vo Leningrad Un-ta, 1972.

[2427] SELIANINOV, O. "The International and the National in the Policy of the Socialist States." *IA(M)* 1970 (8): 14-19.

[2428] _____. "Internationalism of Soviet Foreign Policy." *IA(M)* 1971 (7): 11-16.

[2429] _____. "Proletarian Internationalism and the Socialist State." *IA(M)* 1969 (11): 10-14.

[2430] SELLEKAERTS, WILLY. "The Effects of the E.E.C. on East-West Trade." *DAI* 1971 32: 2864-A.

[2431] SELTON, ROBERT W. "Sino-Soviet Conflict in the Developing Areas." *MR* 1967 47(1): 42-50.

[2432] SEMENOV, IU. See 1150.

[2433] SEMENOV, V. "The Leninist Principles of Soviet Diplomacy." *IA(M)* 1969 (4): 3-8.

[2434] SEMIN, N. S. "CMEA and Africa." *NT* 1968 (23): 23-24.

[2435] ———. "Ravnopravnoe i vzaimovygodnoe sotrudnichestvo" [Equality and mutually beneficial cooperation]. *Komm* 1968 (14): 70-79.

[2436] ———. "SSSR i ChSSR: Ekonomicheskoe sotrudnichestvo" [The USSR and the CzSSR: Economic cooperation]. *Komm* 1969 (12): 60-64.

[2437] ———.*See* 952.

[2438] SEMIRIAGA, M. I. *Sovetskie liudi v Evropeiskom soprotivlenii (Vtoraia Mirovaia Voina v issledovaniiakh, vospominaniiakh i dokumentakh)* [The Soviet peoples in the European resistance (the Second World War in papers, memoirs and documents)]. Moscow: Nauka, 1970.

[2439] SEMONOVA, L. "Technological Progress and the Socialist Countries." *IA(M)* 1968 (6): 29-33.

[2440] SEN GUPTA, BHABANI. "The Fulcrum of Asia." *DAI* 1971 32: 3401-A.

[2441] ———. *The Fulcrum of Asia: A Study of the Relations Among China, India, Pakistan and the USSR.* New York: Pegasus, 1969.

[2442] ———. "Moscow, Peking, and the Indian Scene After Nehru." *Orb* 1968 12: 534-562.

[2443] SENIN, M. V. "CMEA Economic Study Centre." *NT* 1971 (47): 20-21.

[2444] ———.*Nemtsy i Evropa* [The Germans and Europe]. Moscow: I.M.O., 1968.

[2445] ———.*Razvitie mezhdunarodnykh ekonomicheskikh sviazei* [The development of international economic ties]. Moscow: Mysl', 1968.

[2446] ———.*Sotsialisticheskaia integratsiia* [Socialist integration]. Moscow: I.M.O., 1969.

[2447] SERGEEV, A. *See* 3204.

[2448] SERGEEV, N. "CMEA Countries and the Arab World." *IA(M)* 1969 (5): 83-87.

[2449] SERGEEV, V. "Cooperation With Developing Nations." *NT* 1967 (7): 4-6.

[2450] ———. "Economic Cooperation With India." *NT* 1970 (9): 23-25.

[2451] ———. "The Soviet Union and the Developing Countries." *NT* 1971 (3): 18-20.

[2452] ———. "The Soviet Union and the Developing Countries." *IA(M)* 1971 (5): 25-31.

[2453] ———. "Technical Aid to Developing Countries." *NT* 1970 (32): 16-17.

[2454] SERGEEV, V. P. *Problemy ekonomicheskogo sblizheniia stran sotsializma* [Problems of economic collaboration of the socialist countries]. Moscow: Nauka, 1969.

[2455] ———. "Sotsialisticheskaia ingetratsiia i pokazateli razdeleniia truda" [Socialist integration and indices of the division of labor]. *VT* 1970 (3): 28-33.

[2456] ———. *See* 1266.

[2457] SEROV, D. "SSSR na mezhdunarodnykh iarmarkakh 1968 goda" [The USSR in the international fairs of 1968]. *VT* 1969 (7): 40-41.

[2458] SETH, RONALD. *The Executioners: The Story of SMERSH*. Englewood Cliffs, New Jersey: Prentice-Hall, 1968.

[2459] SETH, S. P. "Russia's Role in Indo-Pak Politics." *AsS* 1969 9: 614-624.

[2460] SETON-WATSON, HUGH. "Czechoslovakia—1938-1948 and 1968." *GO* 1969 4: 163-168.

[2461] ———. "Russia Over Central Europe." *Int* 1969 3(2): 11-13.

[2462] ———. *See* 2777.

[2463] SEVERIANIN, L. *See* 1925.

[2464] SEVOST'IANOV, G. N. "Istoriia mezhdunarodnogo rabochego i natsional'no-osvoboditel'nogo dvizheniia" [The history of the international workers' and national-liberation movement]. *VI* 1967 (9): 171-175.

[2465] SEVOST'IANOV, IU. "Leninist Scientific Foresight in Foreign Policy." *IA(M)* 1971 (10): 60-67.

[2466] SHABAEV, B. "Oktiabr' i rabochii Vostok" [October and the laboring East]. *AAS* 1967 (5): 2-7.

[2467] SHABSHINA, F. I. *See* 1310.

[2468] SHAFFER, HARRY G., ED. *The Communist World: Marxist and Non-Marxist Views*. New York: Appleton-Century-Crofts, 1967.

[2469] ———, AND JAN S. PRYBYLA, EDS. *From Underdevelopment to Affluence: Western, Soviet, and Chinese Views*. New York: Appleton-Century-Crofts, 1968.

[2470] SHAKHOV, V. "European Security System: Soviet Effort." *IA(M)* 1971 (5): 32-37.

[2471] ———. "How to Solve Europe's Vital Problems." *IA(M)* 1970 (1): 11-15.

[2472] SHAMRAI, IU. F. "Problemy sovershenstvovaniia ekonomicheskogo sotrudnichestva sotsialisticheskikh i razvivaiushikhsia stran" [The problems of perfecting economic cooperation of the socialist and the developing countries]. *NAA* 1968 (4): 3-15.

[2473] ————. "Tseny na spetsializirovannuiu produktsiiu v torgovle mezhdu stranami-chlenami SEV" [Costs of specialized production in the trade between the member countries of CMEA]. *VE* 1970 (8): 88-96.

[2474] SHARKOV, A. "SSSR i Iaponiia: Ekonomicheskie otnosheniia" [The USSR and Japan: Economic relations]. *MEMO* 1967 (8): 28-40.

[2475] SHARMAZANASHVILI, G. V. *See* 1455.

[2476] SHARP, SAMUEL L. "The USSR and the West." In *The Soviet Union Under Brezhnev and Kosygin,* pp. 249-263, edited by John W. Strong. New York: Van Nostrand Reinhold, 1971.

[2477] SHASPOSHNIKOV, V. "European Security and Public Opinion." *NT* 1971 (42): 6-7.

[2478] SHASTITKO, P. M. "V. I. Lenin i Indiiskie revoliutsionery" [V. I. Lenin and the Indian revolutionaries]. *NAA* 1969 (4): 39-46.

[2479] SHATALOV, I. "The Leninist Foreign Policy and the National Liberation Movement." *IA(M)* 1969 (1): 70-76.

[2480] SHATROV, V., AND N. IUR'EV. "All-European Conference." *IA(M)* 1969 (12): 3-6.

[2481] ————. "Key Problem Today (European Security Conference)." *IA(M)* 1970 (4): 59-62.

[2482] SHCHEGOLEV, B. N. "Real'nost' Sovetsko-Argentinskoi torgovli" [The reality of Soviet-Argentine trade]. *LA* 1970 (3): 69-81.

[2483] SHCHETININ, V. D., ED. *Ekonomicheskoe planirovanie i diplomatiia* [Economic planning and diplomacy]. Moscow: I.M.O., 1967; rev. ed., 1970.

[2484] SHEEHAN, EDWARD R. F. "The United States, the Soviet Union and Strategic Consideration in the Middle East." *NWCR* 1971 23(10): 22-30.

[2485] SHEEHY, ANN. "Soviet Views on Sinkiang." *Miz* 1969 11: 271-283.

[2486] SHEFIAKOV, F. N., ED. *Razvitie ekonomicheskogo sotrudnichestva sotsialisticheskikh stran* [The development of economic cooperation of the socialist countries]. Moscow: Mysl', 1969.

[2487] SHEIDIN, L. "Programma bor'by za mir i mezhdunarodnoe sotrudnichestvo" [The program of struggle for peace and international cooperation]. *Komm* 1971 (9): 86-99.

[2488] SHELDON, CHARLES S., II. "An American 'Sputnik' for the Russians?" *BAS* 1969 25(7): 23-27.

[2489] ———.*Review of the Soviet Space Program.* New York: McGraw Hill, 1968.

[2490] SHELEPIN, V. "Socialist Integration." *NT* 1969 (46): 9-11.

[2491] ———. "The Socialist World and the Developing Countries." *NT* 1970 (9): 20-23.

[2492] SHELTON, WILLIAM. *Soviet Space Exploration: The First Decade.* New York: Washington Square Press, 1968.

[2493] ———. "The United States and the Soviet Union—Fourteen Years in Space." *RR* 1971 30: 322-334.

[2494] SHENAEV, V. "V. I. Lenin o Germanskom imperializme i sovremennyi imperializm FRG" [V. I. Lenin on German imperialism and the contemporary imperialism of the FRG]. *MEMO* 1968 (12): 16-30.

[2495] SHEREMET'EV, I. K. "Leninskoe uchenie ob imperializme i Latinskaia Amerika" [The Leninist teaching on imperialism in Latin America]. *LA* 1970 (1): 7-19.

[2496] SHERSHNEV, E. S. "K voprosu o Sovetsko-Amerikanskoi torgovle" [The question of Soviet-American trade]. *SShA* 1970 (2): 19-28.

[2497] SHESTOV, V. "The Main Disarmament Problem." *IA(M)* 1970 (10): 35-38.

[2498] ———. "Major Success for the Cause of Peace (the Non-Proliferation Treaty)." *IA(M)* 1968 (8): 3-9.

[2499] ———. "Morskie glubiny i mirovaia politika" [The maritime depths and world politics]. *MEMO* 1970 (3): 73-75.

[2500] ———. "Soviet Programme of Nuclear Disarmament." *IA(M)* 1971 (9): 78-82.

[2501] ———.*See* 47.

[2502] SHEVCHENKO, A. "Disarmament: A Problem That Can Be Solved." *IA(M)* 1971 (5): 66-72.

[2503] ———. "Some Lessons of the Disarmament Struggle." *IA(M)* 1971 (3): 29-36.

[2504] ———. "United Nations: Arena of Struggle for World Peace." *IA(M)* 1970 (11): 65-71.

[2505] SHILLINGLAW, THOMAS L. "The Soviet Union and International Satellite Telecommunications." *SJISt* 1970 5: 199-226.

[2506] SHINTIAPIN, IU. P. *Razvitie irritatsii v stranakh-chlenakh SEV i ee ekonomicheskoe znachenie* [The development of irritants in the CMEA member countries and their economic meaning]. Moscow: 1971.

[2507] ———.*See* 337.

[2508] SHIRIAEV, IU. "Novyi etap ekonomicheskoi integratsii sotsialisticheskikh stran" [A new stage in economic integration of the socialist countries]. *MEMO* 1971 (9): 3-12.

[2509] ———. "Problemy i perspektivy ekonomicheskogo sotrudnichestva stran-chlenov SEV" [Problems and prospects of economic cooperation of the member countries of CMEA]. *VE* 1971 (4): 102-109.

[2510] ———. "Sovershenstvovanie proizvodstvennogo sotrudnichestva stran SEV" [The perfection of production cooperation in the CMEA countries]. *VE* 1969 (11): 109-116.

[2511] ———.*See* 182.

[2512] SHIRIAEV, N. "Razvitie ekonomicheskikh otnoshenii Sovetskogo Souiza s Iaponiei" [The development of economic relations of the Soviet Union with Japan]. *VT* 1971 (10): 15-19.

[2513] ———. "USSR Trade With CMEA Countries in the Ninth Five-Year Plan." *IA(M)* 1971 (10): 113-114.

[2514] SHIRINIA, K. K., ED. *V. I. Lenin i Kommunisticheskii internatsional* [V. I. Lenin and the Communist international]. Moscow: IPL, 1970.

[2515] SHIRK, PAUL R. "Thai-Soviet Relations." *AsS* 1969 9: 682-693.

[2516] ———. "Warsaw Treaty Organization." *MR* 1969 49(5): 28-37.

[2517] SHISHKOV, IU. "All-European Cooperation: Economic Aspects." *NT* 1970 (33): 23-25.

[2518] ———. "Integration: Two Approaches (CMEA)." *NT* 1971 (41): 18-21.

[2519] ———. "Two Integration Tendencies in Opposition." *NT* 1969 (50): 11-12.

[2520] SHITOV, N. "K. Marks i F. Engel's o proletarskom internatsionalizme" [K. Marx and F. Engels on proletarian internationalism]. *Komm* 1968 (7): 32-43.

[2521] SHKOLENKO, Y. "Cooperation in Space." *NT* 1971 (6): 23-24.

[2522] SHKUNAEV, V. G. *Mezhdunarodnaia Organizatsiia Truda vchera i segodnia* [The International Labor Organization yesterday and today]. Moscow: I.M.O., 1968.

[2523] ———.*See* 1862.

[2524] SHMELEV, V. M. *See* 1858.

[2525] SHONFIELD, A. "Changing Commercial Policies in the Soviet Bloc." *IA(L)* 1968 44: 1-13.

[2526] SHUB, ANATOLE. *An Empire Loses Hope: Communist Europe in the 1960's.* New York: Norton, 1970.

[2527] ———. "Lesson of Czechoslovakia." *FA* 1969 47: 266-280.

[2528] ———. *The New Russian Tragedy.* New York: W. W. Norton, 1970.

[2529] SHUGAEV, E. "Krepnut sviazi SSSR i GDR" [Ties of the USSR and the GDR are growing]. *VT* 1970 (2): 16-17.

[2530] SHU-KAI, CHOW. "Significance of the Rift Between the Chinese Communist Regime and the Soviet Union." *A,AAPSS* 1967 (372): 64-71.

[2531] SHUL'GOVSKII, A. F. "Latinskaia Amerika i opyt Respublik Sovetskogo Vostoka" [Latin America and the experience of the Republics of the Soviet East]. *LA* 1970 (3): 82-88.

[2532] ———. "Proletarskaia revoliutsiia v Rossii i antiimperialisticheskoe dvizhenie v Latinskoi Amerike" [The proletarian movement in Russia and the anti-imperialist movement in Latin America]. *VI* 1967 (11): 92-106.

[2533] SHUL'MAN, A. "Koordinizatsiia planov ekonomicheskogo razvitiia stran SEV" [The coordination of economic development plans of the CMEA countries]. *VT* 1969 (9): 30-35.

[2534] ———. "Koordinatsiia planov stran SEV: Itogi i perspektivy" [The coordination of the plans of the CMEA countries: Results and prospects]. *VT* 1971 (4): 8-14.

[2535] SHULMAN, MARSHALL D. "'Europe' Versus 'Détente?'" *FA* 1967 45: 389-402.

[2536] ———. "A European Security Conference." *Surv* 1969 11: 373-381.

[2537] ———. "Recent Soviet Foreign Policy: Some Patterns in Retrospect." *JIA* 1968 22: 26-47.

[2538] ———. "Soviet Proposals For a European Security Conference." *StNCE* 1968-69 2(3): 67-80.

[2539] ———. "What Does Security Mean Today?" *FA* 1971 49: 607-618.

[2540] SHUMEIKO, G. "A Quarter-Century of the WFTU." *NT* 1970 (40): 8-9.

[2541] SHURSHALOV, V. M. *Mezhdunarodnye pravootnosheniia* [International legal relations]. Moscow: I.M.O., 1971.

[2542] Shvedkov, Y. "West European Political Forces and European Security." *IA(M)* 1968 (3): 8-13.

[2543] Shwandran, Benjamin. "Soviet Posture in the Middle East." *CH* 1967 52: 331-336, 368-369.

[2544] ———. "The Soviet Role in the Middle East Crisis." *CH* 1971 40: 1-6.

[2545] ———. "The Soviet Union in the Middle East." *CH* 1967 52: 72-77.

[2546] Shweitzer, Karmi. "Soviet Policy Towards Israel, 1946-1956." *Miz* 1969 11: 18-30, 174-181.

[2547] Sibirtsev, Iu. "Prospects for German Rapprochement?" *IA(M)* 1969 (3): 38-42.

[2548] Sick, Gary G. "Russia and the West in the Mediterranean: Perspectives for the 1970's." *NWCR* 1970 22(10): 48-69.

[2549] ———. "The USSR and the Suez Canal Closure." *Miz* 1970 12: 91-99.

[2550] Sidzikauskas, Vociovas. "Thirty Years of Infamy: Soviet-Nazi Secret Deals of 1939." *BR* 1969 (October): 2-10.

[2551] Siegel, Richard L. "Chinese Efforts to Influence Soviet Policy Towards India." *IQ* (July-September): 1968.

[2552] ———. *Evaluating the Results of Foreign Policy: Soviet and American Efforts in India.* Denver, Colorado: Social Science Foundation and Graduate School of International Studies; Monographs Series in World Affairs 6(4), 1969.

[2553] ———. "Soviet Policy Towards India, 1956-1964: Causes and Effects of Sino-Soviet Divergence." *DAI* 1968 28: 5129-A.

[2554] Sik, Ota. "Prague's Spring: Roots and Reasons, the Economic Impact of Stalinism." *PoC* 1971 20(3): 1-10.

[2555] Siljegovic, Bosko. "Can Communist Countries Coexist?" *EE* 1969 18(5): 26-28.

[2556] Silverlight, J. *The Victor's Dilemma: Allied Intervention in the Russian Civil War.* London: Barrie and Jenkins; New York: Weybright and Talley, 1970.

[2557] Silverman, Jerry M. "Indonesianizing Marxism-Leninism: The Development and Consequences of Communist Polycentrism (1919-1966)." *DAI* 1968 29: 308-A.

[2558] Simai, Mihaly. *See* 2983.

[2559] Simchera, V. *See* 2385.

[2560] Simon, Sheldon W. "The Kashmir Dispute in Sino-Soviet Perspective." *AsS* 1967 7: 176-187.

[2561] SIMONIIA, N. "Avantiuristicheskaia liniia Pekina v natsional'no-osvoboditel'nom dvizhenii" [The adventurist line of Peking in the national liberation movement]. *Komm* 1969 (12): 86-97.

[2562] _____.*Peking and the National Liberation Struggle.* Moscow: Novosti, 1970.

[2563] _____. "Revoliutsionnaia demokratiia i nekapitalisticheskii put'" [Revolutionary democracy and the non-capitalist path]. *AAS* 1967 (9): 2-4.

[2564] _____. "Za aktivizatsiiu antiimperialisticheskoi bor'by" [For the activization of the anti-imperialist struggle]. *AAS* 1971 (10): 2-4.

[2565] SIMUNEK, O. "Czechoslovakia in the CMEA System." *IA(M)* 1968 (3): 22-26.

[2566] SINGER, HERMAN. "The Integration of COMECON: Where to Begin." *EE* 1969 18(10): 31-33.

[2567] SINGER, JEROME E. *See* 658.

[2568] SINGH, K. R. "The Soviet-UAR Relations." *IQ* 1969 25: 139-152.

[2569] "The Sino-Soviet Border Dispute." *MR* 1970 50: 77-83.

[2570] *The Sino-Soviet Dispute.* Keesing's Research Report no. 3. New York: Scribner's, 1969.

[2571] SIPOLS, V. *See* 2028.

[2572] SIRC, LJUBO. *Economic Revolution in Eastern Europe.* London & Harlow: Longmans, 1969.

[2573] SIUKIIANINEN, I. I. "V. I. Lenin i Finlandiia" [V. I. Lenin and Finland]. *NNI* 1969 (5): 3-11.

[2574] SIZONENKO, A. I. "God 1970: Itogi i perspektivy Sovetsko-Latino-Amerikanskikh otnoshenii" [1970: Present and prospects of Soviet-Latin American relations]. *LA* 1971 (1): 89-110.

[2575] _____. "Leninskie vneshnepoliticheskie printsipy v otnosheniiakh SSSR s Kapitalisticheskimi stranami Latinskoi Ameriki" [Leninist foreign policy principles in the relations of the USSR with the capitalist countries of Latin America]. *LA* 1970 (2): 125-141.

[2576] _____.*Ocherki istorii Sovetsko-Latinoamerikanskikh otnoshenii* [Sketches of history: Soviet-Latin American relations]. Moscow: Nauka, 1971.

[2577] _____.*See* 1704.

[2578] SKACHKOV, S. "Ekonomicheskoe i tekhnicheskoe sotrudnichestvo SSSR s zarubezhnymi stranami" [Economic and technical cooperation of the USSR with foreign countries]. *VT* 1967 (11): 15-24.

[2579] ———. "Sodeistvie SSSR ekonomicheskomu i tekhnicheskomu razvitiiu zarubezhnykh stran" [The assistance of the USSR to the economic and technical development of foreign countries]. *VT* 1970 (4): 18-24.

[2580] SKITT, JOHN. *See* 635.

[2581] SLADKOVSKII, M. I. "Some Lessons of the Second World War in the Far East." *IA(M)* 1970 (10): 39-43.

[2582] ———, ED. *Antimarksistskaia sushchnost' vzgliadov i politiki Mao Tsze-duna* [The anti-Marxist essence of the views and policy of Mao Tse-tung]. Moscow: Politizdat, 1969.

[2583] ———, ED. *Leninskaia politika SSSR v otnoshenii Kitaia* [The Leninist policy of the USSR in relations with China]. Moscow: Nauka, 1968.

[2584] *Leninskaia Partii—partiia proletarskogo internatsionalizma* [The Leninist Party—the party of proletarian internationalism]. Moscow: IPL, 1970.

[2585] SLOCOMBE, WALTER. "The Political Implications of Strategic Parity." *AP* 1971 77: 1-32.

[2586] SLON, EUGENE. "American Students' Views on U.S.-Soviet Relationship." *UQ* 1970 26: 304-311.

[2587] SLUSSER, ROBERT M. *See* 671.

[2588] SMART, IAN. "The Strategic Arms Limitation." *WT* 1970 26: 296-304.

[2589] SMART, TERRY L. "The French Intervention in the Ukraine, 1918-1919." *DAI* 1969 30: 259-A.

[2590] SMIRNOV, B. *Znat' drug druga. (Kul'turnye sviazi SSSR s zarubezhnymi stranami)* [Know one another. (The cultural ties of the USSR with foreign countries)]. Moscow: Novosti, 1967.

[2591] SMIRNOV, N. "An Important Factor of Peace and Security (Soviet-Indian Treaty)." *IA(M)* 1971 (11): 89-91.

[2592] SMIRNOV, V. "Sotrudnichestvo SSSR s Arabskimi stranami" [The cooperation of the USSR with the Arab countries]. *VT* 1968 (1): 10-16.

[2593] SMITH, ASA P. "Eastern Europe and GATT: A Case Study of Accomodation in Economic Relations." *Columbia Essays in International Affairs The Dean's Papers, 4 (1968)*. New York, 1969.

[2594] SMITH, BRUCE L. R. "The Non-Proliferation Treaty and East-West Détente." *JIA* 1968 22: 89-106.

[2595] SMITH, CANFIELD F. "The Rocky Road to Communist Unity." *EE* 1969 18(2): 3-9.

[2596] SMITH, DON D. "Some Effects of Radio Moscow's North American Broadcasts." *POQ* 1970 34: 539-551.

[2597] SMITH, FREDERIC N. "The American Role in the Repatriation of Certain Soviet Citizens, Forcible and Otherwise, to the USSR Following World War II." *DAI* 1971 31: 3486-A.

[2598] SMITH, FREDERICK WALTON. "Soviet-East Europe Relations, 1956-1958." *DAI* 1969 29: 9778-A.

[2599] SMITH, JEAN EDWARD. "The German Democratic Republic and the West." *YR* 1969 58: 372-387.

[2600] ———. "The United States, German Unity, and the Deutsche Demokratische Republik." *QQ* 1967 74: 21-35.

[2601] SMITH, JESSICA. *See* 1719.

[2602] SMITH, ROBERT A. "Mongolia: In the Soviet Camp." *AsS* 1970 10: 25-29.

[2603] SMOLANSKY, OLES M. "Moscow and the Cuban Missile Crisis: Reflections on Khrushchev's Brinkmanship." *IIP* 1968 33: 509-526.

[2604] ———. "Moscow and the Persian Gulf: An Analysis of Soviet Ambitions and Potential." *Orb* 1970 14(14): 92-108.

[2605] ———. "Moscow and the Problems of National Socialism: An Ideological Approach." *CSISt* 1967 1: 196-211.

[2606] SMOLIANSKII, V. "Ekonomicheskie sviazi sotsialisticheskikh stran i ideologi Antikommunizma" [The economic ties of the socialist countries and the ideologues of anti-Communism]. *VE* 1967 (1): 81-90.

[2607] SNECHKUS, A. "Natsional'naia i internatsional'naia otvetstvennost' Kommunistov" [The national and the international responsibility of Communists]. *Komm* 1970 (6): 58-69.

[2608] SNEDJAREK, ANTONIN. "Soviet Policy in Perspective." *IP* 1971 4(1): 17-20.

[2609] SNEH, MOSHE. "The Soviet-Egyptian 'Solution' to the Israel Problem." *IP* 1969 7(1-2): 24-28.

[2610] SNIGIREV, V. "Sovetsko-Avstriiskaia torgovlia: Ee perspektivy" [Soviet-Austrian trade and its prospects]. *VT* 1968 (8): 6-11.

[2611] ———. "Sovetsko-Avstriiskaia torgovlia razvivaetsia" [Soviet-Austrian trade is developing]. *VT* 1970 (12): 7-9.

[2612] ———. "Torgovlia SSSR s Bel'giei" [The trade of the USSR with Belgium]. *VT* 1969 (2): 24-26.

[2613] Sobolev, A. I. "Mirovoi revoliutsionnyi protsess i Kommunisticheskoe dvizhenie" [The world revolutionary process and the Communist movement]. *NNI* 1969 (6): 3-16.

[2614] "Socialism's Place in History, Stages and Criteria of its Development." *WMR* 1970 13(12): 46-75.

[2615] *Socialist Community. Problems of Development.* Moscow: Novosti, 1970.

[2616] Socianu, Horia. "The Foreign Policies of Rumania in the Thirties and Sixties." *DAI* 1971 32: 2774-A.

[2617] Sodaro, Michael J. "France, Russia, and the European Defense Community." *WA* 1970 133: 29-46.

[2618] Sofinskii, N. "Plodotvornoe sotrudnichestvo: O pomoshchi SSSR osvobodivshimsia stranam v podgotovke spetsialistov" [Fruitful cooperation: On the aid of the USSR to the developing countries in the preparation of specialists]. *Komm* 1970 (15): 107-113.

[2619] Sokolov, A. I. *Problemy sovershenstvovaniia ekonomicheskogo sotsializma* [Problems of perfecting the economic cooperation of the socialist countries]. Moscow: Znanie, 1967.

[2620] ———. "Razrabotka metodologicheskikh problem ekonomicheskogo sotrudnichestva stran-chlenov SEV" [The resolution of methodological problems of cooperation of the member countries of CMEA]. *VE* 1967 (1): 99-105.

[2621] ———. "Socialist Countries: Highroad of Economic Development." *IA(M)* 1971 (6): 16-23.

[2622] ———. *Mirnoe khoziaistvo i revoliutsionnyi protsess* [The world economy and the revolutionary process]. Moscow: I.M.O., 1971.

[2623] ———. "Novye iavleniia v mirovoi ekonomike i revoliutsionnyi protsess" [New occurrences in the world economy and the revolutionary process]. *Komm* 1970 (3): 92-105.

[2624] Sokolovskii, Marshal V. D., ed. *Voennaia strategiia* [Military strategy]. Moscow: Voenizdat, 1968.

[2625] Solodovnikov, V. G. "Leninizm i osvobozhdaiushchaiasia Afrika" [Leninism and liberated Africa]. *MEMO* 1970 (4): 67-78.

[2626] ———. *Nekotorye voprosy teorii i praktiki nekapitalisticheskogo puti reavitiia* [Some questions on the theory and practice of the noncapitalist path of development]. Moscow: Nauka, 1971.

[2627] ———. "Zadachi Sovetskoi Afrikanistiki" [The tasks of Soviet African studies]. *NAA* 1968 (3): 3-13.

[2628] "Some Features of Present-Day International Relations, Seminar Held in Moscow on June 11, 1968 Under the Sponsorship of the Editorial Board of International Affairs." *IA(M)* 1968 (7): 55-67.

[2629] SOMMER, THEODOR. "Bonn's New Ostpolitik." *JISt* 1968 22: 59-78.

[2630] ———. "Détente and Security: The Options." *AP* 1970 (70): 10-16.

[2631] ———. "Détente and Security: The Options." *ACQ* 1971 9(1): 34-49.

[2632] SONTAG, J. P. "International Communism and Soviet Foreign Policy." *RP* 1970 32: 78-90.

[2633] ———. "Moscow and the Search for Unity." *PoC* 1969 18(1): 44-49.

[2634] SORENSEN, THEODORE C. "Why We Should Trade With the Soviets." *FA* 1968 46: 575-583.

[2635] SORENSON, JAY B. "Communism: Asian Defense Soviet Style." *FEER* 1969 65: 84-85.

[2636] ———. "Indonesia: Moscow's Djarkarta Dilemma." *FEER* 1969 64: 613-615.

[2637] ———. "The Russians Are Coming: Soviet Trade in Asia." *FEER* 1968 60: 302-303.

[2638] ———. "That Certain Smile: Japan—Soviet Union." *FEER* 1969 66: 230-232.

[2639] SOROKIN, G. M. "Lenin i ekonomicheskie problemy mirovoi sotsialisticheskoi sistemy" [Lenin and the economic problems of the world socialist system]. *VE* 1969 (6): 3-15.

[2640] ———. "Mezhdunarodnoe razdelenie truda—vazhnyi faktor ekonomicheskogo rosta" [The international division of labor—an important factor of economic growth]. *VE* 1970 (2): 108-119.

[2641] ———. *Mirovaia sistema sotsialisma—voploshchenie idei Marksizma-Leninizma* [The world socialist system—the realization of the ideas of Marxism-Leninism]. Moscow: Znanie, 1968.

[2642] ———. "Oktiabr'skaia revoliutsiia i mirovaia sistema sotsializma" [The October revolution and the world socialist system]. *VE* 1967 (4): 3-15.

[2643] ———. *Problemy ekonomicheskoi integratsii stran-chlenov SEV* [Problems of the economic integration of the member countries of CMEA]. Moscow: Ekonomika, 1970.

[2644] SOSNA, S. A. *See* 653.

[2645] *Sotrudnichestvo sotsialisticheskikh stran* [The cooperation of the socialist countries]. Leningrad: Voen. akad., 1970.

[2646] *Sotsializm i mezhdunarodnye otnosheniia* [Socialism and international relations]. Moscow: Nauka, 1969.

[2647] "Sotsial'nye sily i perspektivy 'tret'ego mira' "[Social forces and prospects in the "third world"]. Discussion in connection with the publication of V. L. Tiagunenko, ed., Klassy i klassovaia bor'ba v razvivaiushchikhsia stranakh, Moscow: Mysl', 1967,3 vols. *MEMO* 1968 (5): 90-104.

[2648] *Sotsiologicheskie problemy mezhdunarodnykh otnoshenii* [Sociological problems of international relations]. Moscow: Nauka, 1970.

[2649] SOVETOV, A. "The Present Stage in the Struggle Between Socialism and Imperialism." *IA(M)* 1968 (11): 3-9.

[2650] ———. "World Socialist System: Key Problems of Development and Consolidation." *IA(M)* 1971 (10): 47-54.

[2651] *Sovetskii ezhegodnik mezhdunarodnogo prava* [Soviet yearbook of international law]. Moscow: Nauka, published annually.

[2652] *Sovetskii Soiuz i organizatsiia Ob"edinnykh Natsii, 1961-1965 gg* [The Soviet Union and the United Nations, 1961-1965]. Moscow: Nauka, 1968.

[2653] *Sovetsko-Bolgarskie otnosheniia, 1944-1948 gg. Dokumenty i materialy* [Soviet-Bulgarian relations, 1944-1948: Documents and materials]. Moscow: Politizdat, 1969.

[2654] *Sovetsko-Kitaiskie otnosheniia. 1917-1967 gg* [Soviet-Chinese relations, 1917-1967]. Moscow: Nauka, 1967.

[2655] *Sovetsko-Vengerskie otnosheniia. 1945-1968. Dokumenty i materialy* [Soviet-Hungarian relations, 1945-1968. Documents and materials]. Moscow: Politizdat, 1969.

[2656] "Sovetskoi vneshnoi torgovle-50 let" [Fifty years of Soviet foreign trade]. *VT* 1968 (4): 2-61.

[2657] "Soviet-American Relations and World Order: Arms Limitations and Policy." *AP* 1970 (65).

[2658] "Soviet-American Relations and World Order: The Two and the Many." *AP* 1970 (66).

[2659] "Soviet Bilateral Development Assistance: The Legal Form and Structure." *CJTL* 1968 7: 48-89.

[2660] "The Soviet Military Presence in the UAR." In *Strategic Survey 1970,* pp. 46-50. London: Institute for Strategic Studies, 1971.

[2661] *The Soviet Military Technological Challenge.* Washington, D.C.: Center for Strategic Studies, Georgetown University, 1967.

[2662] "The Soviet Navy." *MR* 1969 49(4): 10-17.

[2663] *Soviet Sea Power. Special Report Series no. 10.* Washington, D.C.: Center for Strategic Studies, Georgetown University, 1969.

[2664] "The Soviet-UAR and Soviet-Indian Treaties: A Comparison." *Surv* 1971 13: 349-353.

[2665] "The Soviet Union and Latin America." *StSU* 1968 8(2): 1-184.

[2666] "The Soviet Union and 'The Great Proletarian Cultural Revolution.'" *Sur* 1967 (63): 3-194.

[2667] *The Soviet Union in Europe and the Near East: Her Capabilities and Intentions.* London: Royal United Services Institute for Defense Studies, 1970.

[2668] "The Soviet-West German Treaty." *NT* 1970 (33): 5.

[2669] "Soviet Writing on India." *Miz* 1968 10: 199-205.

[2670] *Sovremennoe mezhdunarodnoe pravo. Sbornik statei* [Contemporary international law. Collection of articles]. Moscow: Progress, 1969.

[2671] SPANDARIAN, V. "Soviet Trade With Iran." *NT* 1967 (13): 10-11.

[2672] SPAULDING, WALLACE. "Ceylon's Relations With the Communist Bloc, 1956-1965: The Role of Ideological Affinity in the Making of Foreign Policy." *DAI* 1970 30: 2596-A.

[2673] SPELLER, JON P. "Russia, America, and the Panama Canal." *EE* 1971 20(2): 28-30.

[2674] ———. "Soviet Aims in Greece." *EE* 1971 20(12): 33-34.

[2675] *Spetsializirovannye uchrezhdeniia OON v sovremennom mire* [The specialized institutions of the UN in the present world]. Moscow: Nauka, 1967.

[2676] SPINELLI, ALTIERO. "Soviet Security and the West." *ACQ* 1968 6: 43-60.

[2677] SPINRAD, BERNARD I. "Implications of SALT." *BAS* 1971 17(1): 22-25.

[2678] "SSSR i bor'ba protiv agressivnoi politiki imperializma" [The USSR and the struggle against the aggressive policy of imperialism]. *Komm* 1967 (5): 3-13.

[2679] *SSSR i zarubezhnye strany posle pobedy Velikoi Oktiabr'skoi Sot-sialisticheskoi Revoliutsii. Statisticheskii sbornik* [The USSR and foreign countries after the victory of the Great October Socialist Revolution. Statistical collection]. Moscow: Statistika, 1970.

[2680] SSSR, MINISTERSTVO INOSTRANNYKH DEL. *Dokumenty vneshnei politiki SSSR. vols. 12-16 covering 1929-1933.* [Documents of the foreign policy of the USSR]. Moscow: Politizdat, 1967-1970.

[2681] SSSR, MINISTERSTVO VNESHNEI TORGOVLI *Vneshniaia torgovlia SSSR. Statisticheskii obzor* [Foreign trade of the USSR. Statistical survey]. Moscow: I.M.O., published annually.

[2682] *SSSR v velikoi otechestvennoi voine 1941-1945. Kratkaia khronika* [The USSR in the Great Patriotic War, 1941-1945. A short chronicle]. Moscow: Voenizdat, 1970.

[2683] ST. JOHN, JACQUELINE D. "John F. Stevens: American Assistance to Russian and Siberian Railroads, 1917-1922." *DAI* 1970 30: 2953-A.

[2684] STAAR, RICHARD F. *The Communist Regimes in Eastern Europe.* Stanford, 1968.

[2685] ———. "What is Next in East European Intrabloc Relations." *EE* 1969 18(11-12): 19-28.

[2686] ———, ED. *Aspects of Modern Communism.* Columbia: University of South Carolina, 1968.

[2687] ———, ED. *Yearbook on International Communist Affairs: 1970.* Stanford: Hoover Institution, 1971.

[2688] ———, ED. *Yearbook on International Communist Affairs, 1971.* Stanford: Hoover Institution, 1971.

[2689] ———, AND MILORAD POPOV, EDS. *Yearbook on International Communist Affairs, 1969.* Stanford: Hoover Institution, 1970.

[2690] STALLER, GEORGE J. "Patterns of Stability in Foreign Trade: OECD and COMECON, 1950-1963." *AER* 1967 57: 879-888.

[2691] STANLEY, TIMOTHY, AND DARNELL M. WHITT. *Détente Diplomacy: United States and European Security in the 1970's.* Cambridge, Massachusetts: University Press of Cambridge, 1970.

[2692] ———. "Détente in the 1970's." *ACQ* 1970 8: 224-313.

[2693] ———. "A European Security Conference: Assessing the Soviet Involvement." *EE* 1971 20(2): 12-16.

[2694] STAPLETON, KEN. *See* 1054.

163

[2695] STAROBIN, JOSEPH R. "Origins of the Cold War: The Communist Dimension." *FA* 1969 47: 681-696.

[2696] _____.*See* 2777.

[2697] STARTSEV, V. "New Elements in European Economic Intercourse." *NT* 1970 (43): 26-27.

[2698] "Statement by the Delegations of the Socialist Countries on the Second Decade of Development and Social Progress." *IA(M)* 1970 (12): 67-70.

[2699] *Statisticheskii ezhegodnik stran Chlenov Soveta Ekonomicheskoi Vzaimopomoshchi* [Statistical yearbook of the member countries of the Council for Mutual Economic Assistance]. Moscow: Izdatel'stvo Sekretariata SEV, published annually.

[2700] STAVROU, NIKOLAOS A. "The Sino-Albanian Friendship." *WA* 1971 134: 234-242.

[2701] STEHLE, HANSJAKOB. "Vatican Policy Towards Eastern Europe." *Sur* 1968 (66): 108-116.

[2702] STEIBEL, GERALD L. *Détente: Dilemma or Disaster?* New York: National Strategy Information Center, 1969.

[2703] STEIN, ARTHUR. *India and the Soviet Union: The Nehru Era.* Chicago: University of Chicago Press, 1969.

[2704] _____. "India and the USSR: The Post-Nehru Period." *AsS* 1967 7: 165-175.

[2705] STEIN, BARRY N. "The Boundaries of Eastern Europe With Emphasis on the Oder-Neisse Boundary." *DAI* 1970 30: 3530-A-3531-A.

[2706] STEIN, MICHAEL K. "Finnish-Soviet Relations in the Khrushchev Decade 1955-1964." *MA* 1967 5(5): 23.

[2707] STEPANOV, G. "East-West Trade Relations." *IA(M)* 1969 (12): 29-33.

[2708] STEPANOV, V. "Edinstvo natsional'nykh i internatsional'nykh interesov rabochego klassa" [The unity of the national and international interests of the working class]. *Komm* 1970 (16): 89-101.

[2709] _____. "Mirovaia sistema sotsializma—vedushchaia revoliutsionnaia sila sovremennosti" [The world socialist system—the leading revolutionary force of the present]. *Komm* 1969 (10): 20-31.

[2710] STEPHEN, JOHN J. "Sakhalin Island. Soviet Outpost in Northeast Asia." *AsS* 1970 10: 1090-1100.

[2711] STERN, GEOFFREY. "The Crisis of Communism—The First World Political Creed." *IA(L)* 1970 (special issue): 72-87.

164

[2712] STETTINIUS, EDWARD R. *Roosevelt and the Russians: The Yalta Conference.* [Reprint of 1949 edition]. Westport, Connecticut: Greenwood Press, 1970.

[2713] STEVENS, CHRISTOPHER. "Africa and the Soviet Union." *IR* 1971 3: 1014-1025.

[2714] STOCKHOLM INTERNATIONAL PEACE RESEARCH INSTITUTE. *Yearbook of World Armaments and Disarmament.* Stockholm: Almqvist & Wicksell, published annually.

[2715] STOESSINGER, JOHN G. *Nations in Darkness: China, Russia, and America.* New York: Random House, 1971.

[2716] _____. *The United Nations and the Super-Powers: United States-Soviet Union Interaction at the United Nations.* 2d ed. New York: Random House, 1969.

[2717] STOKKE, BAARD RICHARD. *Soviet and East European Trade and Aid in Africa.* New York: Praeger, 1967.

[2718] STOLTE, STEFAN C. "The Boycotted Congress." *B,ISUSSR* 1969 16(5): 40-45.

[2719] _____. "COMECON at the Crossroads?" *B,ISUSSR* 1969 16(3): 26-34.

[2720] _____. "COMECON in the New Decade." *B,ISUSSR* 1971 18(3): 24-38.

[2721] _____. "Communist Polycentrism and the Conferences in Belgrade, Peking and Moscow." *B,ISUSSR* 1969 16(7): 3-19.

[2722] _____. "The Consequences of Polycentrism in the World Communist Movement." *B,ISUSSR.* 1968 15(1): 3-13.

[2723] _____. "East-West Trade in the Seventies." *B,ISUSSR* 1970 17: 16-30.

[2724] _____. "Features of Soviet-Bloc Economic Development." *B,ISUSSR* 1968 15(5): 3-13.

[2725] _____. "The Present State of the World Communist Movement as Illustrated by the Prospects for a World Communist Conference." *B,ISUSSR* 1968 15(12): 9-18.

[2726] _____. "Three Problems Facing the Soviet Bloc." *B,ISUSSR* 1967 14(7): 20-28.

[2727] _____. "The World Communist Conference and the New Direction of Soviet Foreign Policy." *B,ISUSSR* 1969 16(4): 18-24.

[2728] _____. "The World Economy in 1968: Communist Propaganda and Communist Empiricism." *B,ISUSSR* 1969 16(11): 19-26.

[2729] STONE, JEREMY J. *Containing the Arms Race.* Cambridge: Massachusetts Institute of Technology Press, 1967.

[2730] ———. "The First Nuclear War? Signals Point to the Possibility That the Soviet Union May Be Considering a Pre-Emptive Attack on China's Nuclear Facilities." *W/PR* 1969 9: 9-11.

[2731] ———. "When and How To Use SALT." *FA* 1970 48: 262-273.

[2732] STRANG, LORD WILLIAMS. "Prelude to Potsdam: Reflections on War and Foreign Policy." *IA(L)* 1970 44: 441-454.

[2733] ———. *The Moscow Negotiations 1939.* Leeds: Leeds University Press, 1968.

[2734] *Strany mira. Kratkii politiko-ekonomicheskii spravochnik* [The countries of the world. A short political-economic reference book]. Moscow: Politizdat, 1967.

[2735] "Strategic Arms Limitation: Do the Europeans Need S.A.L.T.?" *Ag* 1969 12: 42-43.

[2736] STRAUS, FRANZ JOSEF. *See* 291.

[2737] STREET, DAVID P. "The Break-Up of the Soviet Monolith in Eastern Europe: Domesticism, Polycentrism, and National Communism." *JICSt* 1971 4: 37-56.

[2738] STROVER, ANTHONY J. *See* 2011.

[2739] SUAREZ, ANDRES. *Cuba: Castroism and Communism, 1959-1966.* Cambridge: Massachusetts Institute of Technology Press, 1967.

[2740] SUKHAREVSKII, B. "Problem of Economic Incentives in CMEA Countries." *WMR* 1970 13(8): 53-56.

[2741] SUMBATIAN, Y. "Lenin on the Non-Capitalist Path of Development." *NT* 1969 (42): 14-16.

[2742] SUMMERS, HARRY G., JR. "Power: The Crucible of Conflict in the Sino-Soviet Dispute." *MR* 1971 51(3): 56-66.

[2743] "The Superpowers." In *Strategic Survey 1970,* pp. 3-17. London: Institute for Strategic Studies, 1971.

[2744] SUSLOV, M. "Leninism and Our Age." *WMR* 1969 12(5): 3-17.

[2745] ———. "Leninizm i revoliutsionnoe preobrazovanie mira" [Leninism and the revolutionary transformation of the world]. *Komm* 1969 (15): 13-37.

[2746] ———. "Pod znamenem internatsionalizma" [Under the banner of internationalism]. *Komm* 1969 (5): 3-10. Translated as: Under the Leninist Banner of Proletarian Internationalism. *NT* 1969 (14): 6-9.

166

[2747] SUTTON, ANTHONY. *Western Technology and Soviet Economic Development, 1917 to 1945.* 2 of 3 volumes. Stanford: Hoover Institution, 1968-1971.

[2748] SVERDLOV, A. "GDR, FRG i OON" [The GDR, the FRG and the UN]. *MEMO* 1970 (5): 79-81.

[2749] SVERDLOVA, M. N., AND L. R. KLETSKII. *Novyi etap natsional'no-osvoboditel'nogo dvizheniia* [New stage of the national liberation movement]. Leningrad: Un-Ta, 1967.

[2750] SWANSON, JOHN ROBERT. "Soviet and Local Communist Perception of Syrian and Lebanese Politics, 1944-1964." *DAI* 1970 31: 450-A.

[2751] SWEARINGEN, RODGER. *See* 2777.

[2752] SYLVESTER, ANTHONY. "The Soviet Bloc Presence in East Africa." *EE* 1968 17(7): 15-19.

[2753] SYLVESTER, HAROLD J. "American Public Reaction to Communist Expansion: From Yalta to NATO." *DAI* 1970 31: 2859-A.

[2754] SZAMUELY, TIBOR. *See* 918.

[2755] SZAWLOWSKI, RICHARD. "The International Economic Organizations of the Communist Countries." *CSIP* 1968 10: 254-278; 1969 11: 82-107.

[2756] SZENT-MIKLOSY, ISTVAN. "The Brezhnev Doctrine in International Relations." *CEF* 1969 17(June): 7-19.

[2757] SZITA, JANOS. "Some Aspects of East-West Economic Relations." *Co* 1968 5: 129-140.

[2758] SZNAJDER, EDWARD. "Polish Trade Today and Tomorrow." *NT* 1971 (44): 14-15.

[2759] TABORI, PAUL. "Another East-West Encounter." *EE* 1968 17(7): 12-14.

[2760] TABORSKY, EDWARD. "The Class Struggle, the Proletariat, and the Developing Nations." *RP* 1967 29: 370-386.

[2761] ———. "Communism and the Peasantry of the Third World." *CSISt* 1969 3: 663-676.

[2762] ———. "The Communist Parties of the 'Third World' in Soviet Strategy." *Orb* 1967 11: 128-148.

[2763] ———. "Where is Czechoslovakia Going?" *EE* 1967 16(2): 2-12.

[2764] TALTIN, E. "Vneshniaia politika SSSR nakanune i v gody velikoi otechestvennoi voiny" [The foreign policy of the USSR on the eve of and during the great patriotic war]. *Komm* 1970 (7): 112-122.

[2765] TANHORN, G. K. *Communist Revolutionary Warfare.* New York: Praeger, 1967.

[2766] TANSKY, LEO. *U.S. and USSR Aid to Developing Countries: A Comparative Study of India, Turkey, and the U.A.R.* New York: Praeger, 1967.

[2767] TARASOV, K. "Economic Expansion in the Guise of Trade." *IA(M)* 1969 (3): 43-47.

[2768] TARONOVSKII, O. *See* 837.

[2769] TARSCHYS, DANIEL. "Neutrality and the Common Market: The Soviet View." *CaC* 1971 6(2): 65-76.

[2770] TATU, MICHEL. "The East: Détente and Confrontation." *AP* 1970 (70): 17-41.

[2771] ———. "European Security Conference. It Might Actually Take Place." *ACQ* 1970 8: 309-312.

[2772] ———. "European Security Conference: What's in it For Whom?" *Int* 1970 3: 4-8.

[2773] ———. "The Future of Two Foreign Policies: I. The Soviet Union." *Int* 1968 2(4): 4-7.

[2774] ———. "Kremlinology: The Mini-Crisis of the 1970's." *Int* 1970 3: 13-19.

[2775] ———. "Something More Than an Interlude?" *ACQ* 1971 9: 50-55.

[2776] ———, WOLFGANG LEONHARD, MALCOLM MACKINTOSH, AND ADAM ULAM. "The Future of the Soviet Union: A Symposium." *Int* 1969 2(10): 4-9.

[2777] ———, HUGH SETON-WATSON, BERNARD S. MORRIS, RODGER SWEARINGEN, KLAUS MEHNERT, ALEC NOVE, DONALD W. TREADGOLD, MASAMICHI INOKI, REX MORTIMER, AND JOSEPH STAROBIN. " 'Commentaries' on Andrew Ezergailis, 'Monolithic' vs. 'Crumbling' Communism." *PoC* 1970 19(1): 8-27.

[2778] ———. *See* 333.

[2779] TAYLOR, JOHN W. R. "Soviet Airpower." *MR* 1967 47(12): 16-20.

[2780] TEKINER, SULEYMAN. "The Role of Central Asia in Soviet Foreign Policy." *StSU* 1968 7(4): 62-77.

[2781] ———. "Sinkiang and the Sino-Soviet Conflict." *B,ISUSSR* 1967 14(8): 9-16.

[2782] ———. "Soviet Policy Toward the Arab East." *B,ISUSSR* 1968 15(3): 29-37.

[2783] _____. "Soviet-Turkish Relations and Kosygin's Trip to Turkey." *B,ISUSSR* 1967 14(3): 3-13.

[2784] TELEFUS, A. *See* 589.

[2785] TEPLINSKII, L. B. *50 let Sovetsko-Afganskikh Otnoshenii (1919-1969).* [50 years of Soviet-Afghan relations (1919-1969)]. Moscow: Nauka, 1971.

[2786] TEREKHOV, V. "Technological Progress in the CMEA Countries." *NT* 1970 (18-19): 32-34.

[2787] _____. *See* 252.

[2788] TESSADORI, HENRY J. "Soviet Foreign Policy as Reflected in the Hungarian and Czechoslovak Crises." *NWCR* 1969 22(2): 59-90.

[2789] THAYER, GEORGE. "The Communists as Arms Traders." In *The War Business: The International Trade Armaments,* Chapter 8, pp. 324-358. New York, 1970.

[2790] THEOHARIS, ATHAN G. *The Yalta Myths.* Columbia: University of Missouri Press, 1970.

[2791] "Theses of the Central Committee, Communist Party of the Soviet Union, on the Centenary of the Birth of Vladimir Ilyich Lenin, Especially Part III: Leninism is the Banner of the Peoples' Struggle Against Imperialism, for the Revolutionary Renewal of the World." *IA(M)* 1970 (2-3): 3-26; also in NT 1970 (1): 41-63.

[2792] "Third World Socialisms: A Harder Soviet Look." *Miz* 1968 10: 151-155.

[2793] THOMAS, BRIAN. "What's Left of the Cold War?" *PQ* 1969 40: 173-186.

[2794] _____. *See* 2420.

[2795] THOMAS, DAVID. *See* 2026.

[2796] THOMAS, JOHN REED. "Sino-Soviet Relations." *CH* 1971 60: 210-214.

[2797] _____. "Soviet Foreign Policy and the Military." *Sur* 1971 17: 129-156.

[2798] _____. "Soviet Policy Toward Communist China and the 1958 Taiwan Straits Crisis." *DAI* 1970 31: 316-A.

[2799] _____. "Soviet Russia and Southeast Asia." *CH* 1968 55: 275-280, 302-303.

[2800] _____. "U.S.-East European Relations: Strategic Issues." *Orb* 1968 12: 754-773.

[2801] THOMAS, STEPHAN G. "Germany and NATO Policy Toward the East." *Orb* 1969 13: 256-260.

[2802] THOMPSON, JAMES M. "Soviet Goals and Strategy in the Middle East." *ArQ* 1969 98: 75-83.

[2803] THOMPSON, JOHN M. *Russia, Bolshevism, and the Versailles Peace.* Princeton, New Jersey: Princeton University Press, 1967.

[2804] THOMPSON, ROBERT. *Revolutionary War in World Strategy, 1945-1969.* New York: Taplinger, 1969.

[2805] THORNTON, RICHARD C. *The Comintern and the Chinese Communists, 1928-1931.* Seattle: University of Washington Press, 1969.

[2806] THORTON, THOMAS P. "South Asia and the Great Powers." *WAf* 1970 132: 345-358.

[2807] TIAGUNENKO, V. L. "Leninskii analiz kolonializma i nekotorye problemy sovremennosti" [The Leninist analysis of colonialism and some problems of the present]. *MEMO* 1969 (12): 3-13.

[2808] ———. "Oktiabr' i sovremennaia natsional'no-osvoboditel'naia revoliutsiia" [October and the present national liberation revolution]. *MEMO* 1967 (1): 3-18.

[2809] ———. *Problemy sovremennykh natsional'no-osvoboditel'nykh revoliutsii* [Problems of the contemporary national liberation revolution]. Moscow: Nauka, 1966.

[2810] ———, ED. *Klassy i klassovaia bor'ba v razvivaiushchikhsia stranakh* [Classes and class struggle in the developing countries]. 3 volumes. Moscow: Mysl', 1967.

[2811] TIGRID, PAVEL. *Why Dubcek Fell.* London: Macdonald, 1971.

[2812] TIKHEMENEV, V. "Leninizm i revoliutsionnyi protsess v Latinskoi Amerike" [Leninism and the revolutionary process in Latin America]. *Komm* 1971 (3): 114-119.

[2813] TIKHONOV, V. "The Soviet Merchant Fleet." *NT* 1971 (10): 20-21.

[2814] TIKHVINSKII, S. "UNESCO and Work for Peace and Progress." *IA(M)* 1970 (2-3): 102-105.

[2815] ———. "The Victory of 25 Years Ago." *NT* 1970 (36): 4-6.

[2816] TIKOS, LASZLO M. "Waiting for the World Revolution: Soviet Reactions to the Great Depression." *JCH* 1969 4(4): 87-99.

[2817] TIMAR, I. "Sovetsko-Vengerskoe soglashenie o vzaimnoi okhrane avtorskikh prav" [Soviet-Hungarian agreement on the mutual protection of authors rights]. *SGP* 1969 (8): 93-95.

[2818] TIMERBAEV, R. *Mirnyi atom na mezhdunarodnoi arene* [The peaceful atom in the international arena]. Moscow: I.M.O., 1969.

[2819] TIMOFEEV, T. T. "Rabochee dvizhenie i bor'ba za ukreplenie mirovogo antiimperialisticheskogo fronta" [The workers' movement and the struggle for the strengthening of the world anti-imperialist front]. *Komm* 1967 (18): 79-90.

[2820] ———. "Velikaia Oktiabr'skaia Sotsialisticheskaia Revoliutsiia i mirovoe rabochee dvizhenie" [The Great October Socialist Revolution and the world workers' movement]. *VI* 1967 (10): 15-36.

[2821] ———. *Velikii Oktiabr' i mezhdunarodnoe rabochee dvizhenie* [The great October and the world workers' movement]. Moscow: Mysl', 1967.

[2822] TING, CHUNG KIANG. "Russia in the Mediterranean." *AO* 1970 5(8): 14-17.

[2823] TIUNOV, O, I. *Neitralitet v mezhdunarodnom prave* [Neutrality in international law]. Perm': Permskii Universitet, 1968.

[2824] TIWARI, S. N. "The Sino-Soviet Rift: A Legacy of Imperialism." *UA* 1968 20: 152-162.

[2825] TOKAREVA, P. A. "Novye mezhdunarodnye organizatsii stran sotsializma" [New international organizations of the socialist countries]. *SGP* 1970 (7): 108-111.

[2826] TÖKES, RUDULF L. "Popular Front in the Balkans: Hungary." *JCH* 1970 5(3): 83-94.

[2827] TOLLEY, KEMP. "Our Russian War of 1918-1919." *USNI,P* 1969 145(792): 58-72.

[2828] TOLMACHEV, O. "Europe in the Modern World." *IA(M)* 1971 (6): 82-89.

[2829] TOLSTIKOV, V. "The World Revolutionary Movement and Contemporary International Relations." *IA(M)* 1967 (5): 79-85.

[2830] TOMA, PETER A. "Sociometric Measurements of the Sino-Soviet Conflict: Peaceful and Nonpeaceful Revolution." *JP* 1968 30: 732-748.

[2831] ———, ED. *The Changing Face of Communism in Eastern Europe.* Tucson: University of Arizona Press, 1970.

[2832] TOMASHEVSKII, D. G. *Leninskie idei i sovremennye mezhdunarodnye otnosheniia* [Leninist ideas and contemporary international relations]. Moscow: Politizdat, 1971.

[2833] ———. "Leninskii printsip mirnogo sosushchestvovaniia i klassovaia bor'ba" [The Leninist principle of peaceful coexistence and class struggle]. *Komm* 1970 (12): 101-113.

[2834] ———. "Some Questions of International Relations Research in the Light of Lenin's Teaching." *IA(M)* 1970 (6): 72-79.

[2835] ———.See 2254.

[2836] "Soviet Power and Policy: 1917-1939." *MR* 1968 48(1): 37-43.

[2837] TOMILIN, IU. "Keeping the Sea-Bed Out of the Arms Race." *IA(M)* 1970 (1): 41-45.

[2838] TOOLE, WYCLIFFE D., JR. "Soviet Interest in Arabia." *MR* 1968 48(5): 91-97.

[2839] TOSCANO, MARIO; GEORGE A. CARBONE, ED. AND TRANS. *Designs in Diplomacy.* Baltimore, Maryland: Johns Hopkins Press, 1970.

[2840] TOUSSAINT, MARCEL. "East European Trade: The Long Hard Road to Profits." *ACQ* 1971 8(4): 461-469.

[2841] "Towards an All-European Conference." *NT* 1969 (47): 1-3.

[2842] TOYNBEE, ARNOLD J. "Russian-American Relations: The Case for Second Thoughts." *JIA* 1968 22: 1-4.

[2843] "Trade and Economic Progress." *NT* 1968 (5): 10-13.

[2844] "Trade of the East European Countries and the Soviet Union." *EBE* 1970 21(1): 18-32.

[2845] TRAGER, FRANK N., ET AL., EDS. *The Military Unbalance: Is the U.S. Becoming a Second-Class Power?* New York: National Strategic Information Center, 1971.

[2846] TRAVIS, TOM ALLEN. "A Theoretical and Empirical Study of Communications Relations in the NATO and Warsaw Intrabloc and Interbloc Systems." *DAI* 1970 31: 3005-A.

[2847] TREADGOLD, DONALD W., ED. *Soviet and Chinese Communism: Similarities and Differences.* Seattle: University of Washington Press, 1967.

[2848] ———.See 2777.

[2849] *Treaties of the World: An International Survey Covering Treaties in Force and Communities of States.* New York: Charles Scribner's Sons; Bristol: Keesing's Publications; Bonn, Vienna, Zurich: Siegler, 1968.

[2850] *The Treaty Between the Federal Republic of Germany and the People's Republic of Poland.* Bonn: Press and Information Office, 1971.

[2851] "Treaty Between the Federal Republic of Germany and the Union of Soviet Socialist Republics of August 12, 1970." *NYUJIL* 1971 4(1).

[2852] "Treaty Between the USSR and the Federal Republic of Germany." *IA(M)* 1970 (10): 32-34.

[2853] TREPCZYNSKI, S. "The Bedrock of Poland's Foreign Policy." *NT* 1971 (29): 4-5.

[2854] TRETIAK, DANIEL. "Cuba and the Communist System: The Politics of a Communist Independent, 1967-1969." *Orb* 1970 14: 740-764.

[2855] ———. "Cuba and the Soviet Union: The Growing Accomodation." *Orb* 1967 11: 439-458.

[2856] ———. *Cuban Relations With the Communist System. The Politics of a Communist Independent, 1967-1970.* Waltham, Massachusetts: Westinghouse Corporation Advanced Studies Group, ASG Monograph no. 4, 1970.

[2857] TREVOR-ROPER, HUGH. "The Philby Affair: Espionage, Treason, and Secret Services." *Enc* 1968 3(4): 3-26.

[2858] TRISKA, JAN F., AND DAVID D. FINLEY. *Soviet Foreign Policy.* New York: Macmillan, 1968.

[2859] ———. *See* 3089.

[2860] ———, ED. *Communist Party States: Comparative and International Studies.* Indianapolis: Bobbs-Merrill, 1969.

[2861] TROFIMENKO, G. "Anti-Communism and Imperialism's Foreign Policy." *IA(M)* 1971 (1): 49-54.

[2862] TROFIMOVA, I. "Great Power Chauvinism: Basis of Peking Foreign Policy." *NT* 1971 (23): 22-23.

[2863] ———. "Moscow—Tokyo." *NT* 1970 (26): 21-23.

[2864] TROFIMOVA, L. I. *See* 3205.

[2865] TROTTER, RICHARD GORDON. "The Cuban Missile Crisis: An Analysis of Policy Formulation in Terms of Current Decision Making Theory." *DAI* 1971 32: 515-A.

[2866] TRUKHANOVSKII, A. A., ET AL. *Letopis' Sovetskoi Vneshnei Politiki: 1917-1967. Daty i fakty* [Chronicle of Soviet Foreign Policy, 1917-1967. Dates and facts]. Moscow: Politizdat, 1968.

[2867] TRUKHANOVSKII, V. G. "An Important Stage in the Struggle for Socialism." *IA(M)* 1967 (10): 12-20.

[2868] ———. *V. I. Lenin i Sovetskaia vneshniaia politika* [Lenin and Soviet foreign policy]. Moscow: I.M.O., 1969.

[2869] ———. "The Leninist Policy of Peace and Cooperation Among Nations." *IA(M)* 1971 (4): 3-9.

[2870] ———. "Lenin's Foreign Policy Activity (January-March 1921)." *IA(M)* 1969 (10): 36-39.

[2871] ———. "Lenin's Ideas and Contemporary International Relations." *IA(M)* 1970 (4): 13-18.

[2872] ———.*Leninskim vneshnepoliticheskim kursom. (Vneshniaia politika SSSR)* [On the Leninist course of foreign policy. (The foreign policy of the USSR)]. Moscow: Znanie, 1971.

[2873] ———. "Proletarian Internationalism and Peaceful Coexistence— Foundation of the Leninist Foreign Policy." *IA(M)* 1968 (11): 54-62.

[2874] ———. "Vazhnyi etap Leninskoi vneshnei politiki mira" [An important stage of the Leninist foreign policy of peace]. *VI* 1969 (7): 9-33.

[2875] ———. "Vneshniaia politika Sovetskogo gosudarstva" [The foreign policy of the Soviet state]. *PS* 1971 (2): 19-26.

[2876] ———. "Vsemirnoistoricheskoe znachenie pobedy Sovetstogo naroda v velikoi otechestvennoi voine" [The worldwide historical meaning of the victory of the Soviet people in the great patriotic war]. *Komm* 1970 (9): 90-100.

[2877] ———, ED. *Diplomaticheskaia deiatel'nost' V. I. Lenina* [The diplomatic activity of V. I. Lenin]. Moscow: I.M.O., 1970.

[2878] ———, ED. *Istoriia mezhdunarodnykh otnoshenii i vneshnei politiki SSSR 1917-1967 gg. tom I. 1917-1939 gg. tom II 1939-1945 gg. tom III 1945-1967 gg.* [The history of international relations and the foreign policy of the U.S.S.R., 1917-1967]. Moscow: I.M.O., 1967.

[2879] TRUSH, M. I. "Lenin's Foreign Policy Activities (September-December 1920)." *IA(M)* 1969 (9): 46-49.

[2880] ———. "Lenin's Foreign Policy Activity (April-July 1922)." *IA(M)* 1970 (1): 63-66.

[2881] ———. "Lenin's Foreign Policy Activity (August 1922-March 1923)." *IA(M)* 1970 (2-3): 34-37.

[2882] ———.*Soviet Foreign Policy-Early Years.* Moscow: Novosti, 1971.

[2883] ———.*Vneshnepoliticheskaia deiatel'nost' V. I. Lenina, 1921-1923. Den' za dnem* [The foreign policy activity of V. I. Lenin, 1921-1923. Day by day]. Moscow: I.M.O., 1967.

[2884] TSEDENBAL, IUMZHAGIIN. "Lenin's Ideas of Proletarian Internationalism are Communists' Battle Standard." *WMR* 1970 13(4): 73-77.

[2885] ———. "Torzhestvo Leninskikh idei proletarskogo internatsionalizma" [The triumph of the Leninist idea of proletarian internationalism]. *Komm* 1970 (6): 27-38.

[2886] ———. "Velikii Oktiabr' i narody Vostoka" [The Great October and the peoples of the East]. *Komm* 1967 (15): 104-115.

[2887] "Tsentral'nomu Komitetu Kommunisticheskoi Partii Chekhoslovakii" [To the Central Committee of the Communist Party of Czechoslovakia]. *Komm* 1968 (11): 4-9.

[2888] TSITSIASHVILI, ABON. *Leninskie printsipy vneshnei politiki Kommunisticheskoi Partii i Sovetskogo pravitel'stva* [The Leninist principles of foreign policy of the Communist Party and the Soviet government]. Tbilisi: Sabochota Sakartvelo, 1970.

[2889] TUCHKIN, G. M. *Ekonomicheskaia effektivnost' vneshnei torgovli (nekotorye teoreticheskie i metolodologicheskie problemy)* [The economic effectiveness of foreign trade (some theoretical and methodological problems)]. Moscow: I.M.O., 1969.

[2890] TUCKER, FRANK H. "The 'Cultural Revolution' and the Sino-Soviet Rift." *CA* 1967 5(6): 10-17.

[2891] ———. "The Sino-Soviet Rivalry in Africa, 1960-1965." *RMSSJ* 1967 4(1): 114-124.

[2892] TUCKER, ROBERT C. *The Marxian Revolutionary Idea.* New York: W. W. Norton, 1969.

[2893] ———. *Paths of Communist Revolution.* Research memograph no. 29. Princeton, New Jersey: Princeton University, Center of International Studies, 1968.

[2894] ———. "United States-Soviet Co-operation: Incentives and Obstacles." *A,AAPSS* 1967 (372): 1-15.

[2895] TUCKER, ROBERT W. "The Czech Intervention and Soviet-American Relations." *TSJIA* 1969 4(1): 16-24.

[2896] TUGANOVA, O. E. *Mezhdunarodnye otnosheniia na Blizhnem i Srednem Vostoke* [International relations in the Near and Middle East]. Moscow: I.M.O., 1967.

[2897] "Tukushchie problemy mirovoi politiki" [Current problems of world politics]. *MEMO.* A quarterly review of current events published each year in issues 1, 4, 7, and 10.

[2898] TUNG, WILLIAM L. *China and the Foreign Powers: The Impact of and Reaction to Unequal Treaties.* Dobbs Ferry, New York: Oceana, 1970.

[2899] TUNKIN, G. I. "Dva napravleniia v mirovoi politike i mirnoe sosushchestvovanie" [Two trends in world politics and peaceful coexistence]. *MEMO* 1971 (2): 3-13.

[2900] ———. *Ideologicheskaia bor'ba i mezhdunarodnoe pravo* [The ideological struggle and international law]. Moscow: I.M.O., 1967.

[2901] ———. "International Law and Ideological Struggle." *IA(M)* 1971 (11): 25-31.

[2902] ———. *Teoriia mezhdunarodnogo prava* [The theory of international law]. Moscow: I.M.O., 1970.

[2903] ———. "The U.N. and Human Rights." *NT* 1968 (9): 4-6.

[2904] TUVE, JEANNETTE ECKMAN. "The Role of Foreign Trade and Foreign Capital in the Development of the USSR to 1927." *DAI* 1970 30: 3895-A.

[2905] TUZMUKHAMEDOV, R. A. *See* 1371.

[2906] ———. *See* 1432.

[2907] "The 24th Congress of the CPSU and International Issues." *IA(M)* 1971 (8): 3-39.

[2908] "Twenty Years of COMECON: Á la Schweik." *Ag* 1969 14: 56-57.

[2909] "UAR and USSR: The Dialogue on Socialism." *Miz* 1968 10: 38-43.

[2910] "Uchenie V. I. Lenina ob imperializme i sovremennost'" [The teaching of V. I. Lenin on imperialism and the present]. *MEMO* 1967 (5): 3-22.

[2911] *Ukraina na mezhdunarodnoi arene* [The Ukraine in the international arena]. Kiev: Politizdat Ukrainy, 1968.

[2912] ULAM, ADAM B. "Communist Doctrine and Soviet Diplomacy." *Sur* 1970 76: 3-16.

[2913] ———. *Expansion and Coexistence: The History of Soviet Foreign Policy, 1917-1967.* New York: Praeger, 1968.

[2914] ———. *The Rivals: America and Russia Since World War II.* New York: Viking, 1971.

[2915] "The Twenty-fourth Soviet Party Congress." *CH* 1971 60: 222-226.

[2916] ———. *See* 2776.

[2917] UL'IANOVSKII, R. A. "Bor'ba Kominterna za Leninskuiu strategiiu i taktiku v natsional'no-osvoboditel'nom dvizhenii" [The struggle of the Comintern for Leninist strategy and tactics in the national liberation movement]. *NAA* 1969 (3): 3-16.

[2918] ———. "Lenin and the National Liberation Movement." *NT* 1970 (16): 8-11.

[2919] ———. "Leninism, Soviet Experience and the Newly-Free Countries." *NT* 1971 (1): 18-22; 1971 (2): 20-24.

[2920] ———. "Marxist and Non-Marxist Socialism." *WMR* 1971 14(9): 119-127.

[2921] ———. "Nauchnyi sotsializm i osvobodivshiesia strany" [Scientific socialism and the liberated countries]. *Komm* 1968 (4): 92-106.

[2922] ———. "O nekotorykh chertakh sovremennogo etapa natsional'no-osvoboditel'nogo dvizheniia" [On some traits of the present stage of the national liberation movement]. *NAA* 1967 (5): 21-36.

[2923] ULLMAN, RICHARD H. *Anglo-Soviet Relations, 1917-1921. vol. 2: Britian and the Russian Civil War: November 1918-February 1920.* Princeton, New Jersey: Princeton University Press, 1968.

[2924] ULSTEIN, EGIL. "Nordic Security." *AP* 1971 81: 1-32.

[2925] "The U.N. and International Security." *NT* 1970 (27): 1-3.

[2926] *Unbreakable Friendship: Soviet Party and Government Delegation in Prague. Soviet-Czechoslovak Treaty of Friendship, Cooperation and Mutual Assistance. 25th Anniversary Celebration of Czechoslovakia's Liberation by the Soviet Army From Nazi Occupation.* Prague: Rude Pravo; Moscow: Pravda, 1970.

[2927] UNDASYNOV, I. "Lenin—Vozhd' mezhdunarodnogo Kommunisticheskogo dvizheniia" [Lenin—the leader of the international Communist movement]. *PS* 1970 (3): 48-56.

[2928] "Union of Soviet Socialist Republics: Decree on the Procedure for Conducting Work on the Continental Shelf and the Protection of Natural Resources." *ILM* 1970 9: 975-977.

[2929] "Union of Soviet Socialist Republics: Draft Treaty Concerning the Moon." *ILM* 1971 10: 839-846.

[2930] "Union of Soviet Socialist Republics-United Arab Republic: Agreement on Friendship and Cooperation." *ILM* 1971 10: 836-838.

[2931] "Union of Soviet Socialist Republics-United States: Agreement on Cooperation in Exploration and Use of Outer Space." *ILM* 1971 10: 617-629.

[2932] "Union of Soviet Socialist Republics-United States: Agreements To Reduce Risk of Nuclear War." *ILM* 1971 10: 1172-1176.

[2933] "The United Nations and International Security." *IA(M)* 1969 (11): 5-9.

[2934] "The United States and the Soviet Union." In *The Military Balance 1971-1972*, pp. 1-7. London: International Institute for Strategic Studies, 1971.

[2935] "The U.S. and the USSR in the Middle East: Cooperation and Confrontation." In *Middle East Record, Vol. III (covering 1967)*. New York: Keter, 1971.

[2936] U.S. ARMY INSTITUTE FOR ADVANCED RUSSIAN AND EAST EUROPEAN STUDIES. *The Present Stage of Soviet Global Expansion: Sources, Goals and Prospects*. Garmisch, Germany: 5th Annual Soviet Affairs Symposium, April 20-22, 1971.

[2937] U.S. CONGRESS, JOINT ECONOMIC COMMITTEE. *Economic Performance and the Military Burden in the Soviet Union: A Compendium of Papers*. Washington, D.C.: United States Government Printing Office, 1970.

[2938] U.S. DEPARTMENT OF STATE. *The Sino-Soviet Economic Offensive in the Less Developed Countries*. Reprint of 1958 edition. New York: Greenwood Press, 1969.

[2939] U.S. DEPARTMENT OF STATE, BUREAU OF INTELLIGENCE AND RESEARCH. *Communist Governments and Developing Nations: Aid and Trade in 1967*. Research Memorandum, RSE-120, August 14, 1968.

[2940] _____.*Communist Governments and Developing Nations: Aid and Trade in 1968*. Research Memorandum RSE-65, September 5, 1969.

[2941] _____.*Communist States and Developing Countries: Aid and Trade in 1969*. Research Study, RECS-5, July 9, 1970.

[2942] _____.*Communist States and Developing Countries: Aid and Trade in 1970*. Research Study RECS-15, September 22, 1971.

[2943] _____. *Communist Governments and Developing Nations: Economic Aid and Trade [1966]*. Research Memorandum, RSB-80, July 21, 1967.

[2944] _____.*Educational and Cultural Exchanges Between Communist and Non-Communist Countries in 1965*. Research Memorandum, RSB-10, January 25, 1967.

[2945] _____.*Educational and Cultural Exchanges Between Communist and Non-Communist Countries in 1966*. Research Memorandum, RSB-40, May 12, 1967.

[2946] _____.*Educational and Cultural Exchanges Between Communist and Non-Communist Countries in 1967*. Research Memorandum, RSB-65, May 31, 1968.

[2947] _____.*Educational and Cultural Exchanges Between Communist and Non-Communist Countries in 1968*. Research Memorandum, RSE-25, May 7, 1969.

[2948] _____. *Educational and Cultural Exchanges Between Communist and Non-Communist Countries in 1969.* Research Study, RSES-35, August 12, 1970.

[2949] _____. *Soviet Diplomatic Relations and Representation.* Research Memorandum, RSB-75, June 11, 1968.

[2950] _____. *Soviet Diplomatic Relations and Representation.* Research Memorandum, RSE-70, September 9, 1969.

[2951] _____. *Soviet Diplomatic Relations and Representation.* Research Study, RSES-45, November 8, 1971.

[2952] U.S. DEPARTMENT OF THE ARMY. *Communist Eastern Europe: Analytical Survey of Literature.* Washington, D.C.: United States Government Printing Office, 1971.

[2953] U.S. HOUSE, SUBCOMMITTEE ON INTER-AMERICAN AFFAIRS, COMMITTEE ON FOREIGN AFFAIRS. *Soviet Naval Activities in Cuba. Hearings, September 30-November 24, 1970.* Washington, D.C., 1971.

[2954] U.S. JOINT ECONOMIC COMMITTEE, SUBCOMMITTEE ON FOREIGN ECONOMIC POLICY. *East-West Economic Relations, Part IV of a Foreign Economic Policies for the 1970's.* Washington, D.C.: United States Government Printing Office, 1971.

[2955] U.S. SENATE, COMMITTEE ON AERONAUTICAL AND SPACE SCIENCES. *Space Cooperation Between the United States and the Soviet Union. Hearing, March 17, 1971.* Washington, D.C.: United States Government Printing Office, 1971.

[2956] U.S. SENATE, COMMITTEE ON FINANCE. *The Role of the United States in East-West Trade, Report by Sen. Abraham Ribicoff, August 10, 1971.* Washington, D.C.: United States Government Printing Office, 1971.

[2957] U. S. SENATE, COMMITTEE ON GOVERNMENT OPERATIONS, SUBCOMMITTEE ON NATIONAL SECURITY AND INTERNATIONAL OPERATIONS. *The Soviet Approach to Negotiation: Selected Writings.* Washington, D.C.: United States Government Printing Office, 1969.

[2958] U.S. SENATE, SUBCOMMITTEE ON ARMS CONTROL, INTERNATIONAL LAW AND ORGANIZATION, SENATE FOREIGN RELATIONS COMMITTEE. *ABM, MIRV, SALT, and the Nuclear Arms Race.* Washington, D.C.: United States Government Printing Office, 1970.

[2959] U.S. SENATE, SUBCOMMITTEE ON NATIONAL SECURITY AND INTERNAL OPERATIONS; 91ST CONGRESS, 1ST SESSION. *Czechoslovakia and the Brezhnev Doctrine.* Washington, D.C.: United States Government Printing Office, 1969.

[2960] U.S. SENATE, SUBCOMMITTEE ON NATIONAL SECURITY AND INTERNATIONAL OPERATIONS, COMMITTEE ON GOVERNMENT OPERATIONS. *International Negotiations: The Great Power Triangle.* Washington, D.C.: United States Government Printing Office, 1971.

[2961] U.S. SENATE, SUBCOMMITTEE TO INVESTIGATE THE ADMINISTRATION OF THE INTERNAL SECURITY ACT AND OTHER INTERNAL SECURITY LAWS, SENATE JUDICIARY COMMITTEE. *Threat to U.S. Security Posed by Stepped-Up Sino-Soviet Hostilities.* Washington, D.C.: United States Government Printing Office, 1970.

[2962] "United States-Union of Soviet Socialist Republics: Draft Treaty on the Prohibition of the Emplacement of Nuclear Weapons and Other Weapons of Mass Destruction on the Seabed and Ocean Floor." *ILM* 1970 9: 392-395.

[2963] UNTERBERGER, BETTY MILLER. *America's Siberian Expedition, 1918-1920: A Study of National Policy.* New York: Greenwood Press, reprint, 1969.

[2964] _____, ED. *American Intervention in the Russian Civil War.* Boston: Heath, 1969.

[2965] URBAN, G. R. "Eastern Europe After Czechoslovakia." *StCC* 1969 2: 50-68.

[2966] UREN, PHILIP E. *See* 310.

[2967] "The Urgent Task of Consolidating Peace in Europe." *IA(M)* 1971 (3): 23-28.

[2968] USENKO, E. T. "Sotrudnichestvo stran-chlenov SEV i sotsialisticheskii internatsionalizm" [The cooperation of the member countries of CMEA and socialist internationalism]. *SGP* 1970 (4): 79-87.

[2969] USHAKOV, N. A. "Sovremennoe mezhdunarodnoe pravo—iuridicheskaia osnova otnoshenii mezhdu gosudarstvami" [Contemporary international law—the juridical basis of relations among states]. *SGP* 1970 (10): 69-77.

[2970] USIEVICH, M. "Problemy povysheniia effektivnosti proizvodstva v Evropeiskikh stranakh-chlenakh SEV" [Problems of raising the effectiveness of production in the European member countries of CMEA]. *VE* 1971 (2): 78-86.

[2971] USSR ACADEMY OF SCIENCES, AFRICA INSTITUTE. *Africa in Soviet Studies.* Moscow: Nauka, 1969.

[2972] "USSR and Developing Countries (Facts and Figures on Economic Relations)." *IA(M)* 1967 (10): 98-101.

[2973] "The USSR and the Middle East." In *Middle East Record, Vol. III (covering 1967)*. New York: Keter, 1971.

[2794] "The USSR and the Persian Gulf." *Miz* 1968 10: 51-59.

[2975] "The USSR and the Sudan." *Miz* 1968 10: 185-193.

[2976] USTINOV, I. N. *Vneshneekonomicheskaia ekspansiia gosudarstvennykh predpriiatii* [The foreign economic expansion of state enterprises]. Moscow: I.M.O., 1972.

[2977] USTINOV, N. "Mathematical Methods in the Analysis of International Relations." *IA(M)* 1968 (12): 74-82.

[2978] VAGABOV, M. V. *Internatsional'nye sviazi narodov Dagestana* [The international ties of the peoples of Dagestan]. Makhachkala: Dagknigoizdat, 1968.

[2979] VAGANOV, B. "The Leninist Foreign Trade Policy." *IA(M)* 1969 (5): 49-53.

[2980] VAGO, BELA. "Popular Front in the Balkans: Failure in Hungary and Rumania." *JCH* 1970 5(3): 95-118.

[2981] VAHDAT, FARIA. *See* 1210.

[2982] VAIDYANATH, R. "The Soviet View of the Tibetan Situation." *IS* 1969 10(4).

[2983] VAJDA, IMRE, AND MIHALY SIMAI, EDS. *Foreign Trade in a Planned Economy [Hungary]*. New York: Cambridge University Press, 1971.

[2984] VALEVKAIA, V. A. "Torgovlia Pol'skoi Narodnoi Respubliki s razvivaiushchimisia stranami" [The trade of the Polish People's Republic with the developing countries]. *NAA* 1968 (6): 115-121.

[2985] *Valiutnye otnosheniia vo vneshnei torgovle SSSR (pravovye voprosy)* [Financial relations in the foreign trade of the USSR (legal questions)]. Moscow: I.M.O., 1968.

[2986] VALKENIER, ELIZABETH K. "New Soviet Views on Economic Aid." *Sur* 1970 76: 17-29.

[2987] ———. "New Trends in Soviet Economic Relations With the Third World." *WP* 1970 22: 415-432.

[2988] ———. "Recent Trends in Soviet Research on the Developing Countries." *WP* 1968 20: 644-659.

[2989] ———. "Sino-Soviet Rivalry in the Third World." *CH* 1969 56: 201-206, 240.

[2990] VANIN, I. "Security Guarantees for Non-Nuclear Countries." *IA(M)* 1968 (10): 35-38.

[2991] Van Zanten, John W. "Communist Theory and the American Negro Question." *RP* 1967 29: 435-456.

[2992] _____. "The Soviet Evaluation of the American Negro Problem: 1954-1965: A Study of Ideology and Propaganda." *DAI* 1967 27: 3504-A.

[2993] Varis, Tapio. "The Control of Information by Jamming Radio Broadcasts." *CaC* 1970 5: 168-184.

[2994] Varner, Nellie M. "The Flexibility of the Soviet and American Governments in Foreign Policy: A Comparative Study." *DAI* 1969 29: 3202-A.

[2995] Varsanyi, Julius. "Ethnic Law and Central European Integration." *StNCE* 1971-72 3(1): 64-72.

[2996] Vasianin, I. "Vneshniaia torgovlia SSSR so sotsialisticheskimi stranami Evropy" [The foreign trade of the USSR with the socialist countries of Europe]. *VT* 1968 (4): 16-25.

[2997] Vasil'ev, A. *See* 44.

[2998] Vasil'ev, K. "From the History of Soviet-Finnish Relations. Juho Kusti Paasikivi (Birth Centenary)." *IA(M)* 1970 (12): 63-65.

[2999] Vasil'ev, P. "Scandinavia and Security." *IA(M)* 1969 (8): 44-48.

[3000] Vasil'eva, R. *See* 45.

[3001] Vasil'evskaia, E. G. "Osvoenie Luny: Nekotorye perspektivy pravovogo regulirovaniia" [Exploitation of the Moon: Some prospects of legal regulation]. *SGP* 1971 (4): 92-99.

[3002] _____. *Razvitie vzgliadov V. I. Lenina na imperializm (1893-1917 gg)* [The development of the views of V. I. Lenin on imperialism (1893-1917)]. Moscow: Izdatel'stvo Moskovskogo universiteta, 1969.

[3003] Vassilev, Vassil. *Policy in the Soviet Bloc on Aid to Developing Countries.* Paris: Organization for Economic Cooperation and Development, 1970.

[3004] Vayrynen, R. "A Case Study of Sanctions: Finland and the Soviet Union in 1958-1959." *CaC* 1969 4: 205-233.

[3005] Veber, A. "Leninskaia teoriia imperializma: Nekotorye sotsiologicheskie aspekty" [The Leninist theory of imperialism: Some sociological aspects]. *MEMO* 1970 (1): 13-22.

[3006] Vekshin, G. "CMEA and the Developing Countries." *NT* 1971 (40): 22-23.

[3007] Velebit, Vladimir. "The Future of East-West Trade." *JIA* 1968 22: 79-88.

[3008] *Velikaia Oktiabrskaia Sotsialisticheskaia Revoliutsiia i mirovaia sotsialisticheskaia sistema* [The Great October Socialist Revolution and the world socialist system]. Moscow: Nauka, 1969.

[3009] *Velikaia Oktiabrskaia Sotsialisticheskaia Revoliutsiia i natsional'noosvoboditel'noe dvizhenie narodov Azii, Afriki i Latinskoi Ameriki* [The Great October Socialist Revolution and the national liberation movement of the peoples of Asia, Africa, and Latin America]. Moscow: Nauka, 1969.

[3010] "Velikii Oktiabr' i internatsionalizm" [The Great October and internationalism]. *AAS* 1968 (11): 2-5.

[3011] "Velikii Oktiabr' i istoricheskie sud'by narodov Vostoka" [The Great October and the historical destiny of the East]. *NAA* 1967 (1): 5-18.

[3012] *Velikii Oktiabr' i mirovoi revoliutsionnyi protsess. (piat'desiat let bor'by rabochego klassa vo glave revoliutsionnykh sil sovremennoi eopkhi)* [The Great October and the world revolutionary process (fifty years of struggle of the working class at the head of the revolutionary forces of the present epoch)]. Moscow: Politizdat, 1967.

[3013] VEL'TOV, IU. *Uspekhi sotsializma v SSSR i ikh vliianie na SShA* [Successes of socialism in the USSR and their influence on the USA]. Moscow: I.M.O., 1971.

[3014] VEREIN, A. V. " 'Apostoly mira' na trekh kontinentakh" ["Apostles of peace" on three continents]. Moscow: I.M.O., 1971.

[3015] VERESHCHETIN, V. S. "Pravovaia priroda mezhdunarodnykh nauchno-tekhnicheskikh soglashenii po kosmosu" [The legal nature of international scientific-technical agreements concerning outer space]. *SGP* 1968 (5): 86-89.

[3016] VERNER, RICHARD L. "The Nuclear Test-Ban Treaty and American-Soviet Relations." *MA* 1968 6: 20.

[3017] VETROV, A. "Economic Ties Between Socialist and Capitalist States." *IA(M)* 1970 (9): 7-11.

[3018] ———. "Sovetsko-Frantsuzskoe torgovoekonomicheskoe sotrudnichestvo" [Soviet-French trade and economic cooperation]. *VT* 1969 (4): 14-17.

[3019] VIDIASOVA, L. "Moscow—Paris. December 1966." *IA(M)* 1967 (1): 79-85.

[3020] ———. "The USSR in the Struggle Against Aggression and War." *IA(M)* 1969 (3): 65-70.

[3021] "Vietnam and the Sino-Soviet Dispute." *StSU* 1967 6(2): 1-118.

[3022] VIGOR, P. M. "The Soviet Conception of Neutrality." *B,ISUSSR* 1968 15(11): 3-18.

[3023] VIKENT'EV, A. I., AND B. P. MIROSHNICHENKO. *Proizvodstvo i potreblenie v stranakh SEV. O sootnoshenii podrazdelenii sotsialisticheskogo obshchestvennogo proizvodstva* [Production and consumption in the countries of CMEA. On the correlation of the elements of socialist social production]. Moscow: I.M.O., 1969.

[3024] VIKTOROV, FELIX. "Economic Association of Countries of Socialism." *EEQ* 1967 1: 261-276.

[3025] VIL'K, MARIAN. "Ekonomicheskaia pomoshch' SSSR Pol'skomu narodu na zakliuchitel'nom etape voiny (1944-1945 gg)." [Economic aid of the USSR to the Polish people in the final stage of the war (1944-1945)]. *NNI* 1968 (2): 53-59.

[3026] VILLMOW, JACK R. "International Relations—German Democratic Republic." *CSISt,BS* 1968 2(2): 69-70.

[3027] VINOGRADOV, V. M., ET AL., EDS. *Sovetsko-Afganiskie otnosheniia 1919-1969 gg. Dokumenty i materialy* [Soviet-Afghan relations, 1919-1969. Documents and materials]. Moscow: Politizdat, 1971.

[3028] VIRE-TUOMINEN, M. "European Security—Imperative of Our Time." *WMR* 1971 14(5): 148-154.

[3029] VISER, TESTUS J., ED. *The USSR in Today's World.* Memphis, Tennessee: Memphis State University Press, 1969.

[3030] VISHNEVSKII, S. "The Ideological Struggle and Current International Relations." *IA(M)* 1970 (2-3): 38-45.

[3031] VISHNIAKOV-VISHNEVETSKII, K. A. *Internatsional'nye sviazi Rossiiskogo i Nemetskogo proletariata* [The international ties of the Russian and German proletariat]. Leningrad: Obshchestvo Znanie RSFSR, 1968.

[3032] VISHWANATHAN, SAVITRI. "Peace With Honour Through Soviet Mediation: An Abortive Attempt by Japan." *IS* 1970 12(1).

[3033] VISKOV, S. I. "Vystupleniia v SShA za sotrudnichestvo s SSSR (1945-1949 gg)" [Support in the U.S.A. for cooperation with the USSR (1945-1949)]. *NNI* 1969 (4): 68-77.

[3034] VITAL, DAVID. *The Survival of Small States: Studies in Small Power-Great Power Conflict [Sections on USSR-Israel and USSR-Finland].* London-New York: Oxford University Press, 1971.

[3035] VLADIMIROV, IU. V. "K voprosu o Sovetsko-Kitaiskikh ekonomicheskikh otnosheniiakh v 1950-1966 godakh" [The question of Soviet-Chinese economic relations in 1950-1966]. *VI* 1969 (6): 63-79.

[3036] ———. "Soviet-French Cooperation: Steady Progress." *IA(M)* 1971 (8): 69-71.

[3037] VLADIMIROV, M. "Sotrudnichestvo SSSR i KNDR" [The cooperation of the USSR and North Korea]. *VT* 1969 (12): 16-17.

[3038] VLADIMIROV, T. "USSR-France: Important Step in Development of Relations." *IA(M)* 1970 (12): 57-58.

[3039] VLADIMIROV, V. "Sotsialisticheskie strany i politicheskaia strategiia imperializma" [The socialist countries and the political strategy of imperialism]. *MEMO* 1968 (8): 3-15.

[3040] ———, AND I. ORLOV. "Socialist Foreign Policy Promoting Peace and Social Progress." *IA(M)* 1969 (2): 51-57.

[3041] *Vneshniaia politika Germanskoi Demokraticheskoi Respubliki* [The foreign policy of the German Democratic Republic]. Moscow: I.M.O., 1969.

[3042] *Vneshniaia politika Sovetskogo Soiuza i mezhdunarodnye otnosheniia. Sbornik dokumentov* [The foreign policy of the Soviet Union and international relations. Collection of documents]. Moscow: I.M.O., published annually.

[3043] VOITOV, V. "Po puti sotsialisticheskoi ekonomicheskoi integratsii" [On the path of socialist economic integration]. *VT* 1971 (2): 2-4.

[3044] VOITOVICH, S. D. *BSSR v bor'be za mir i sotrudnichestvo mezhdu narodami* [The Belorussian SSR in the struggle for peace and cooperation among peoples]. Minsk: Nauka i Tekhnika BSSR, 1968.

[3045] ———.*Sotrudnichestvo BSSR s sotsialisticheskimi stranami* [The cooperation of the Belorussian SSR with the socialist countries]. Minsk: Nauka i tekhnika, 1970.

[3046] VOLGY, THOMAS. *See* 1080.

[3047] VOLKOV, N. V. *Frantsiia i sotsialisticheskie strany Evropy. Ekonomicheskie i nauchno-tekhnicheskie sviazi* [France and the socialist countries of Europe. Economic and scientific-technical ties]. Moscow: I.M.O., 1971.

[3048] VOLKOV, V. "Sovetsko-Efiopskie torgovye otnosheniia" [Soviet-Ethiopian trade relations]. *VT* 1968 (12): 13-14.

[3049] VOLOSHIN, F. "Antikommunizm—vrag 'tret'ego mira' " [Anti-Communism—the enemy of the "third world"]. *AAS* 1971 (3):12-14.

[3050] VOLOVA, L. I. *Plebitsit v mezhdunarodnom prave* [The plebiscite in international law]. Moscow: I.M.O., 1972.

[3051] DE VOLPI, ALEXANDER. "Expectations From SALT." *BAS* 1970 26: 6-8, 30-34.

[3052] VOL'SKII, V. V. "Sovetskaia Latino-Amerikanistika: Nekotorye itogi i zadachi" [Soviet Latin American studies: Some developments and tasks]. *LA* 1971 (3): 6-17.

[3053] _____, ED. *SSSR i Latinskaia Amerika, 1917-1967 gg* [The USSR and Latin America, 1917-1967]. Moscow: I.M.O., 1967.

[3054] VORONIN, V. "The Beginnings of Friendship and Neighbourliness (50th Anniversary of the Moscow Treaties With Iran, Afghanistan and Turkey)." *IA(M)* 1971 (4): 48-54.

[3055] _____. "Sovetsko-Gvineiskoe sotrudnichestvo" [Soviet-Guinean co-operation]. *VT* 1968 (11): 21-24.

[3056] VORONOV, A. "Anti-Communism—The Machinery and the Doctrines." *NT* 1971 (34): 18-19.

[3057] _____. "Soviet Central Asia and the Developing Countries." *NT* 1971 (37): 10-11.

[3058] VORONOV, K. G., AND K. A. PAVLOV. *Organizatsiia i tekhnika vneshnei torgovli* [The organization and technique of foreign trade]. Moscow: I.M.O., 1970.

[3059] VOSHCHENKOV, K. P. *Mezhdunarodnoe polozhenie Sovetskogo Soiuza* [The international position of the Soviet Union]. Moscow: Znanie, 1971.

[3060] VOSLENSKII, M. S. *Tainyi soiuz protiv Oktiabria. O sekretnykh sviaziakh imperialistov SShA i Germanii v 1917-1919 gg* [The secret union against October. On the secret ties of the imperialists of the USA and Germany in 1917-1919]. Moscow: Nauka, 1967.

[3061] _____. *'Vostochnaia' politika FRG (1949-1966)* [The 'eastern' policy of the FRG (1949-1966)]. Moscow: Nauka, 1967.

[3062] VYSHINSKY, ANDREI Y. *The USSR and World Peace.* Freeport, New York: Books for Libraries Press, 1969.

[3063] VYSOTSKII, V. N. "Landmark in the Struggle for Détente (West Berlin Negotiations)." *IA(M)* 1971 (11): 12-16.

[3064] _____. "Potsdam: Results of the War and Programme for Postwar Structure." *IA(M)* 1970 (8): 20-25.

[3065] _____. *Zapadnyi Berlin i ego mesto v sisteme sovremmykh mezhdunarodnykh otnoshenii* [West Berlin and its place in the system of contemporary international relations]. Moscow: Mysl', 1971.

[3066] WACLAWEK, J. "The International and National in Communist Policy." *WMR* 1969 12(8): 55-63.

[3067] WAGNER, WOLFGANG. "Basic Requirements and Consequences of the Ostpolitik." *ACQ* 1971 9: 20-33.

[3068] WAINHOUSE, DAVID W., ET AL. *Arms Control Agreements.* Baltimore, Maryland: Johns Hopkins Press, 1968.

[3069] WALKER, DAREK J. "Chinese Perception of Soviet-American Relations, 1962-1970: A Pilot Study." *PSR* 1970 9: 258-269.

[3070] WALTERS, ROBERT S. *American and Soviet Aid: A Comparative Analysis.* Pittsburgh: University of Pittsburgh Press, 1970.

[3071] WALTON, RICHARD J. *America and the Cold War.* New York: Seabury Press, 1969.

[3072] WANDYCZ, PIOTR S. *Soviet-Polish Relations, 1917-1921.* Cambridge, Massachusetts: Harvard University Press, 1970.

[3073] WARNER, GEOFFREY. "The United States and the Origins of the Cold War." *IA(L)* 1970 44: 529-544.

[3074] WARREN, VERNON C., JR. "Russo-German Relations, 1933-1936: Years of Uncertainty." *DAI* 1970 30: 2955-A.

[3075] "The Warsaw Pact." *MR* 1967 47(10): 18-21.

[3076] WASOWSKI, STANISLAV, ED. *East-West Trade and the Technology Gap: A Political and Economic Appraisal.* New York: Praeger, 1970.

[3077] WATT, D. C. "America and Russia: The Rise of the Super-Powers." *IA(L)* 1970 (special issue, November): 19-33.

[3078] ———. "Russians Need Middle East Oil." *NME* December 1969 (3): 21-23.

[3079] ———. "The Soviet Presence in the Mediterranean: A Study in the Application of Political Influence." *NME* October 1968 (1): 14-19.

[3080] WEEKS, ALBERT L. *The Other Side of Coexistence: An Analysis of Russian Foreign Policy.* New York: Pitnam, 1970.

[3081] WEINER, ROBERT. "The USSR and UN Peacekeeping." *Orb* 1969 13: 115-130.

[3082] WEINSTEIN, MARTIN E. "Japan and the Continental Giants." *CH* 1971 60: 193-199.

[3083] WEISBAND, EDWARD. *See* 767.

[3084] ———. *See* 768.

[3085] WEISS, GERHARD. "The German Democratic Republic and Socialist Economic Integration." *IA(M)* 1971 (6): 24-28.

[3086] WEISSMAN, BENJAMIN M. "The American Relief Administration in Russia, 1921-1923: A Case Study in Interaction Between Opposing Political Systems." *DAI* 1969 30: 782-A.

[3087] WELCH, WILLIAM. *American Images of Soviet Foreign Policy.* New Haven and London: Yale University Press, 1970.

[3088] ———. "Soviet Expansionism and Its Assessment." *JCR* 1971 15: 317-328.

[3089] ———, AND JAN F. TRISKA. "Soviet Foreign Policy Studies and Foreign Policy Models." *WP* 1971 23(4): 704-734.

[3090] WERTH, ALEXANDER. *Russia: Hopes and Fears.* New York: Simon & Schuster, 1970.

[3091] WESSELL, N. H. "NATO and the Changing Russian Threat." *APS,P* 1968 29: 7-20.

[3092] WESSON, ROBERT G. *Soviet Foreign Policy in Perspective.* Homewood, Illinois: Doresey, 1969.

[3093] ———. "The Soviet Interest in the Middle East." *CH* 1970 59: 212-219.

[3094] ———. "Soviet Ideology: The Necessity of Marxism." *SSt* 1969 21: 64-70.

[3095] WETTERN, DESMOND. "NATO's Northern Flank." *USNI,P* 1969 95(798): 52-59.

[3096] WETTIG, GERHARD. "The SED-SPD Dialogue: Communist Political Strategy in Germany." *Orb* 1967 11: 570-581.

[3097] ———. "Soviet Policy on the Nonproliferation of Nuclear Weapons, 1966-1968." *Orb* 1969 12: 1058-1084.

[3098] WHALEY, BARTON. *Soviet Journalists in China.* Cambridge: Center for International Studies, Massachusetts Institute of Technology, 1970.

[3099] WHEELER, GEOFFREY. "Russia and China in Central Asia." *WT* 1967 23: 89-92.

[3100] ———. "Soviet Interests in Iran, Iraq, and Turkey." *WT* 1968 24: 197-202.

[3101] WHETTEN, LAWRENCE L. "Appraising the Ostpolitik." *Orb* 1971 15: 856-878.

[3102] ———. "Changing Soviet Attitudes Towards Arab Radical Movements: More Revisions To Come in 1970." *NME* March 1970 (18): 20-27.

[3103] ———. "Crisis in Prague and Moscow." *B,ISUSSR* 1969 16(5): 27-35.

[3104] ———. "Empire or Revolution: The Limits of Russian Policy." *NME* May 1969 (8): 11-15.

[3105] _____. *Germany's Ostpolitik: Relations Between the Federal Republic and the Warsaw Pact Countries.* New York: Oxford University Press, 1971.

[3106] _____. "The Mediterranean Threat." *Sur* 1970 (74-75): 270-281. Correction reprinted in *Sur* 1971 12: 252-259.

[3107] _____. "Military Aspects of the Soviet Occupation of Czechoslovakia." *WT* 1969 25: 60-67.

[3108] _____. "The Military Consequences of Mediterranean Super Power Parity." *NME* November 1971 (38): 14-25.

[3109] _____. "Moscow's Anti-China Pact." *WT* 1969 25: 385-393.

[3110] _____. "Moscow's Story of Success [In the Middle East]." *NME* August 1970 (23): 24-29.

[3111] _____. "The 1969 World Conference and the Future of the Communist Movement." *B,ISUSSR* 1969 16(7): 20-26.

[3112] _____. "Recent Changes in East European Approaches to European Security." *WT* 1970 26: 277-288.

[3113] _____. "The Role of East Germany in West German-Soviet Relations." *WT* 1969 25(12): 507-519.

[3114] _____. *The Soviet Presence in the Eastern Mediterranean.* New York: National Strategy Information Center, 1971.

[3115] WHITAKER, PAUL M. "Arms and the Nationalists: Who Helps?" *AfR* 1970 15: 12-14.

[3116] WHITE, JOHN A. *The Siberian Intervention.* Reprint of 1950 edition. New York: Greenwood, 1971.

[3117] WHITE, RALPH K. "Communicating With Soviet Communists." *AR* 1967 27: 458-476.

[3118] _____. *See* 634.

[3119] WHITESIDE, H. O. "Kennedy and the Kremlin: Soviet-American Relations, 1961-1963." *DAI* 1969 29: 3964-A.

[3120] WHITT, DARNELL M. *See* 2691.

[3121] _____. *See* 2692.

[3122] _____. *See* 2693.

[3123] WIESNER, JEROME S. "Arms Control: Current Prospects and Problems." *BAS* 1970 26: 6-8.

[3124] WILBER, CHARLES K. *The Soviet Model and Underdeveloped Countries.* Chapel Hill: University of North Carolina Press, 1969.

[3125] WILCOX, WAYNE. "The Protagonist Powers and the Third World." *A,AAPSS* 1969 336: 1-9.

[3126] WIECZYNSKI, JOSEF L. "Economic Consequences of Disarmament: The Soviet View." *RR* 1968 27: 275-285.

[3127] ――――. *The Economics and Politics of East-West Trade*. New York: Praeger, 1969.

[3128] WILES, PETER J. D. *Communist International Economics*. New York: Praeger, 1969.

[3129] ――――. "The Declining Self-Confidence of the Super-Powers." *IA(L)* 1971 47: 289-301.

[3130] ――――. "Trade and Peace." *StCC* 1968 1: 104-140.

[3131] WILRICH, MASIC. *See* 280.

[3132] WILSON, DESMOND P., JR. "Strategic Projections and Policy Options in the Soviet-Cuban Relationship." *Orb* 1968 12: 504-517.

[3133] WILSON, JOAN H. "American Business and the Recognition of the Soviet Union." *SSQ* 1971 52(2): 349-368.

[3134] ――――. "The Role of the Business Community in American Relations with Russia and Europe, 1920-1933." *DAI* 1967 27: 2491-A.

[3135] WINDSOR, PHILIP. *Germany and the Management of Détente*. New York: Praeger; London: Institute for Strategic Studies, 1971.

[3136] ――――. "NATO and European Détente." *WT* 1967 23: 361-368.

[3137] ――――, AND ADAM ROBERTS. *Czechoslovakia 1968: Reform, Repression and Resistance*. New York: Columbia University Press, 1969.

[3138] WINZER, OTTO. "Strengthen International Position of the GDR—A Goal in Battle for Peace and Socialism." *WMR* 1971 14(8): 99-106.

[3139] ――――. "Twenty Years of GDR Foreign Policy." *IA(M)* 1969 (10): 3-8.

[3140] ――――. *Vneshniaia politika Germanskoi Demokraticheskoi Respubliki (1949-1970)* [The foreign policy of the German Democratic Republic (1949-1970)]. Moscow: Progress, 1971.

[3141] WISE, DAVID, AND THOMAS B. ROSS. *The Espionage Establishment*. New York: Random House, 1967.

[3142] WODDIS, JACK. "Lenin and the International Communist Movement." *WMR* 1969 12(6): 12-21.

[3143] WOJNA, RYSZARD. "A Step Towards Normalcy in Europe." *NT* 1970 (47): 8-9.

[3144] WOLFE, BERTRAM D. *An Ideology in Power: Reflections on the Russian Revolution.* New York: Stein and Day, 1969.

[3145] WOLFE, JAMES H. "Bonn's Struggle for Détente." *CEJ* 1971 19: 355-357.

[3146] ———. "West Germany and Czechoslovakia: The Struggle for Reconciliation." *Orb* 1970 14: 154-179.

[3147] ———. "West Germany's Ostpolitik." *WA* 1971 134: 210-219.

[3148] WOLFE, THOMAS W. "Evolution of Soviet Military Policy." In *The Soviet Union Under Brezhnev and Kosygin,* edited by John W. Strong. New York: Van Nostrand Reinhold, 1971.

[3149] ———. "The Projection of Soviet Power." *Surv* 1968 10: 159-165.

[3150] ———. "Russia's Forces Go Mobile." *Int* 1968 1(8): 28, 33-37.

[3151] ———. "Soviet Approaches to SALT." *PoC* 1970 19: 1-10.

[3152] ———. "Soviet Military Policy at the Fifty Year Mark." *CH* 1967 52: 208-216, 244-246.

[3153] ———.*Soviet Military Policy Trends Under the Brezhnev-Kosygin Regime.* Santa Monica, California: RAND Corporation, 1967.

[3154] ———.*Soviet Power and Europe: 1945-1969.* Santa Monica, California: RAND Corporation, 1969.

[3155] ———.*Soviet Power and Europe, 1945-1970.* Baltimore, Maryland: Johns Hopkins Press, 1970.

[3156] ———. "The Soviet Union and SALT." *WT* 1971 27: 162-173.

[3157] ———. *The Soviet Union's Strategic and Military Stakes in the GDR. P-4549.* Santa Monica, California: RAND Corporation, 1971.

[3158] ———. "The Soviet Union's Strategic Stake in the G.D.R." *WT* 1971 27: 340-349.

[3159] WOLFSON, MURRAY. "A Mathematical Model of the Cold War." *P,PRS* 1968 9: 107-124.

[3160] WOODS, JOHN W. "Soviet Attitudes Toward China and the West Between 1959 and 1963: An Approach Through Content Analysis." *DAI* 1971 31: 4245-A.

[3161] "The World as Seen From Moscow." *RCIIS* 1971 1: 67-104.

[3162] WORSNOP, RICHARD L. *See* 834.

[3163] WU, AITCHEN K. *China and the Soviet Union.* Port Washington, New York: Kennikat Press, 1967.

[3164] WULLFERT, N. F. VON. "The Problem of Political Asylum as Illustrated by Communist Eastern Europe." *B,ISUSSR* 15(11): 34-41.

[3165] YELLON, R. A. "The Winds of Change." *Miz* 1967 9: 51-57, 155-173.

[3166] YINGER, JON A. "Cuba: American and Soviet Core Interests in Conflict." *DAI* 1967 28: 758-A.

[3167] YIU, MYUNG KUN. "Sino-Soviet Rivalry in North Korea Since 1954." *DAI* 1970 31: 1353-A.

[3168] YODFAT, ARYEH Y. "Arms and Influence in Egypt: The Record of Soviet Military Assistance Since June 1967." *NME* July 1969 (10): 27-33.

[3169] ———. "Communist Parties in the Arab World: A Chilling Account of Soviet Penetration." *NME* May 1971 (32): 29-33.

[3170] ———. "How Strong is the Soviet Hold on the Lebanon?" *NME* May 1970: 23-37.

[3171] ———. "Iraq—Russia's Other Middle East Pasture." *NME* November 1971 (38): 26-30.

[3172] ———. "Moscow Reconsiders Fatah." *NME* December 1969 (15): 15-19.

[3173] ———. "The Soviet Union and the Palestine Guerrillas." *Miz* 1969 11: 8-17.

[3174] ———. "Unpredictable Iraq Poses a Russian Problem." *NME* 1969 (13): 17-20.

[3175] ———. "The USSR and Jordan." *IP* 1971 10(1-2): 57-62.

[3176] ———. "The USSR and the Inter-Arab Relations." *IP* 1970 9(3-4): 25-28.

[3177] ———. "The USSR and the North African Countries." *ISp* 1971 25: 2126-2143.

[3178] ———. "The USSR, Jordan and Syria." *Miz* 1969 11: 73-93.

[3179] ———. "USSR Proposals to Regulate the Middle East Crisis." *IP* 1971 10(3-4): 20-28.

[3180] ———. "What Soviet Interest in Lebanon." *NME* May 1970 (20): 23-27.

[3181] YOUNG, ELIZABETH. "The Control of Proliferation: The 1968 Treaty in Hindsight and Forecast." *AP* 1969 56.

[3182] ———. "Ocean Policy and Arms Control." *WT* 1970 26: 401-407.

[3183] YOUNG, KATSU HIRAI. "The Japanese Army and the Soviet Union, 1936-1941." *DAI* 1968 29: 860-A.

[3184] YOUNG, ORAN R. "Intermediaries and Interventionists: Third Parties in the Middle East Crisis." *IJ* 1968 23: 52-73.

[3185] *Za edinstvo vsekh antiimperialisticheskikh sil* [For the unity of all anti-imperialist forces]. Moscow: Novosti, 1970.

[3186] "Za edinstvo vsekh revoliutsionnykh sil, protiv imperializma!" [For the unity of all revolutionary forces, against imperialism!]. *AAS* 1969 (8): 2-5.

[3187] ZABELIN, V. "Dogovory morskoi perevozki SEV" [Agreements on maritime transport of CMEA]. *VT* 1970 (3): 52-54.

[3188] ZADOIAN, MESROB. "Soviet-Rumanian Relations." *StNCE* 1968-69 2(3): 122-133.

[3189] ZADOROZHNYI, GEORGII. *Peaceful Coexistence. Contemporary International Law of Peaceful Coexistence.* Moscow: Progress, 1968.

[3190] ZAGLADIN, A. "Engels and Proletarian Internationalism." *NT* 1970 (48): 7-10.

[3191] ZAGLADIN, V. V. "CPSU in the Fight for Peace and Progress." *NT* 1971 (18): 6-9.

[3192] ———. "World Communism on the Threshold of the Seventies." *NT* 1970 (1): 17-20.

[3193] ———, ED. *Mezhdunarodnoe Kommunisticheskoe dvizhenie. Ocherk strategii i taktiki* [The international Communist movement. A sketch of strategy and tactics]. Moscow: Politizdat, 1970.

[3194] ZAGORIA, DONALD S. *Vietnam Triangle: Moscow/Peking/Hanoi.* New York: Pegasus, 1967.

[3195] ZAKHAROV, M. "Lenin i Sovetskaia voennaia nauka" [Lenin and Soviet military science]. *Komm* 1969 (7): 52-62.

[3196] ———. "Policy of Peace and International Cooperation." *IA(M)* 1971 (3): 86-89.

[3197] ———. "Vazhneishie etapy bor'by Sovetskogo naroda protiv fashistskikh zakhvatchikov" [The most important stages of the struggle of the Soviet people against fascist aggressors]. *Komm* 1970 (6): 105-116.

[3198] ZAKHEM, SAMIR H. "Lebanon Between East and West: Big Power Politics in the Middle East." *DAI* 1970 31: 3006-A-3007-A.

[3199] ZALYOTNY, A. "F.R.G. and the Developments in Czechoslovakia." *IA(M)* 1968 (11): 22-27.

[3200] ZANERIN, B. *See* 1781.

[3201] ZAPUTSKII, M. "SSSR—Afrika: Sodeistvie bez korysti" [The USSR—Africa: Collaboration without profit]. *AAS* 1968 (7): 5-7.

[3202] ZAREV, K. "Forms of Socialist Integration." *WMR* 1971 14(5): 71-76.

[3203] ZARNITSKII, S. V., AND A. SERGEEV. "The Birth of Soviet Diplomacy." *IA(M)* 1967 (6): 58-66.

[3204] _____, AND L. I. TROFIMOVA. *Sovetskoi strany diplomat* [Diplomat of the Soviet country]. Moscow: Politizdat, 1968.

[3205] ZARTMAN, I. WILLIAM, ED. *Czechoslovakia: Intervention and Impact.* New York: New York University Press, 1970.

[3206] ZATSARINSKII, A. P. *Ekonomicheskie otnosheniia SSSR s zarubezhnymi stranami. 1917-1967* [The economic relations of the USSR with foreign countries, 1917-1967]. Moscow: I.M.O., 1968.

[3207] ZAVIALOV, L. "European Security: The Time is Ripe." *NT* 1970 (7): 4-5.

[3208] ZELENTSOV, V. *See* 1784.

[3209] ZEMAN, ZBYNEK A. B. *Prague Spring.* New York: Hill and Wang, 1969.

[3210] ZEMELKA, STANLEY A. "The Problem of Specialization in COMECON." *EE* 1969 18(5): 9-14.

[3211] _____. "Twenty Years of COMECON: Economic Integration or Disintegration?" *CEF* 1968 16(12): 35-43.

[3212] ZEUTNER, PETER. *East-West Trade: A Practical Guide to Selling in Eastern Europe.* London: Parrish, 1967.

[3213] ZEVIN, L. Z. "Ekonomicheskoe sotrudnichestvo sotsialisticheskikh i razvivaiushchikhsia stran" [Economic cooperation of the socialist and the developing countries]. *VE* 1970 (9): 73-83.

[3214] _____. "Nekotorye tendentsii v razdelenii truda mezhdu sotsialisticheskimi i razvivaiushchimisia stranami" [Some tendencies in the division of labor among the socialist and the developing countries]. *VE* 1967 (8): 84-92.

[3215] ZEVIN, L. V. *Novye tendentsii v ekonomicheskom sotrudnichestve sotsialisticheskikh i razvivaiushchikhsia stran* [New tendencies in the economic cooperation of the socialist and the developing countries]. Moscow: Nauka, 1970.

[3216] ZHAMIN, V., V. ZHUKOV, AND IU. OL'SEVICH. "Voprosy ekonomicheskoi integratsii stran-chlenov SEV" [Questions of economic integration of the member countries of CMEA]. *VE* 1970 (9): 62-72.

[3217] ZHIVKOV, T. "Lenin Principle of Unity of National and International Tasks." *WMR* 1970 13(4): 14-22.

[3218] ZHUKOV, E. "The Destinies of Europe." *WMR* 1970 13(10): 16-20.

[3219] Zhukov, L. "Sotrudnichestvo s Alzhirom v vodnokhoziaistvennom stroitel'stve" [Cooperation with Algeria in the development of water resources]. *VT* 1971 (7): 20-23.

[3220] Zhukov, V. G. *Komu vygodna politika Mao* [For whom is Mao's policy an advantage]. Moscow: I.M.O., 1967.

[3221] ———.*See* 3217.

[3222] Zhukov, V. N., and Iu. Ia. Ol'sevich. "International'nye zatraty i sotrudnichestvo stran SEV" [International expenditures and cooperation of the CMEA countries]. *VE* 1967 (3): 70-80.

[3223] ———, and Iu. Ia. Ol'sevich. *Teoreticheskie i metodologicheskie problemy sovershenstvovaniia tsenoobrazovaniia na rynke SEV* [Theoretical and methodological problems of the perfection of price formation in the CMEA market]. Moscow: Nauka, 1969.

[3224] Zimmerman, William. "Elite Perspectives and the Explanation of Soviet Foreign Policy." *JIA* 1970 24: 84-98.

[3225] ———. "International Relations in the Soviet Union: The Emergence of a Discipline." *JP* 1969 31: 52-70.

[3226] ———.*Soviet Perspectives on International Relations 1956-1967.* Princeton, New Jersey: Princeton University Press, 1969.

[3227] ———. "The Soviet Union." In *Conflict in World Politics,* pp. 38-54, edited by Steven L. Spiegel and Kenneth N. Waltz. Cambridge, Massachusetts: Winthrop, 1971.

[3228] Zinchenko, G., et al. *50 let Velikogo Oktiabria i sovremennyi Antikommunizm* [50 years of the Great October and contemporary anti-Communism]. Moscow: Znanie, 1967.

[3229] *Zionism: Instrument of Imperialist Reaction: Soviet Opinion on Events in the Middle East and the Adventures of International Zionism (February-March, 1970).* Moscow: Novosti, 1970.

[3230] Zlomanov, L. P. *Razvitie vneshneekonomicheskikh sviazei SSSR* [The development of the foreign economic ties of the USSR]. Moscow: Ekonomika, 1971.

[3231] ———.*Vneshneekonomicheskie sviazi SSSR—vazhnyi faktor povysheniia effektivnosti obshchestvennogo proizvodstva* [The foreign economic ties of the USSR—important factor in increasing the effectiveness of social production]. Moscow: Znanie, 1971.

[3232] Zlomanov, L., and G. Mikheeva. "CMEA: Progress Report." *NT* 1971 (3): 5-6.

[3233] Zolotarev, V. I. *Mirovoi sotsialisticheskii rynok* [The world socialist market]. Moscow: I.M.O., 1970.

[3234] ZOPPO, CIRO. "Soviet Ships in the Mediterranean and the U.S.-Soviet Confrontation in the Middle East." *Orb* 1970 14: 109-128.

[3235] ZOTOVA, N. A. *Torgovlia mezhdu stranami SEV v usloviiakh khoziaistvennykh reform* [Trade among the countries of CMEA in the conditions of economic reform]. Moscow: Ekonomika, 1969.

[3236] ZUAN, LE. "Leninizm osveshchaet revoliutsionnye tseli sovremennoi epokhi" [Leninism illuminates the revolutionary goals of the present epoch]. *Komm* 1970 (7): 39-54.

[3237] ZUBKOV, A. I. *Mezhdunarodnoe razdleenie truda i razvitie metallurgii sotsialisticheskikh stran* [The international division of labor and the development of metallurgy of the socialist countries]. Moscow: Nauka, 1968.

INDEX

Cuba (*continued*)
　　1497, 2219, 2739, 2854, 2855, 2856,
　　2953, 3132, 3166
Cuban Missile Crisis of 1962, 21, 54, 516,
　　562, 1552, 1699, 2414, 2603, 2865
Cultural relations. *See* USSR, Soviet foreign
　　policy implementation
Cyprus and USSR, 1758
Czechoslovakia, 122, 339, 522, 1404, 1617,
　　1708, 1709, 1964, 2460, 2763
　Bulgaria, 2079
　Canada, 2137
　East Europe, 339, 2565. *See also* 1968
　　Crisis and Invasion
　Foreign trade of, 288, 695, 1774
　Germany, Democratic Republic of, 491
　Germany, Federal Republic of, 3146, 3199
　Hungary, 1105
　1968 Crisis and Invasion (and aftermath),
　　60, 66, 111, 125, 172, 214, 228, 282,
　　297, 305, 306, 325, 328, 347, 442,
　　446, 473, 499, 527, 545, 623, 654,
　　719, 827, 834, 850, 914, 935, 988,
　　992, 1039, 1152, 1159, 1168, 1190,
　　1192, 1209, 1241, 1323, 1357, 1438,
　　1461, 1521, 1605, 1625, 1627, 1640,
　　1650, 1657, 1757, 1837, 1914, 2004,
　　2033, 2049, 2056, 2092, 2099, 2113,
　　2242, 2264, 2268, 2298, 2411, 2460,
　　2527, 2554, 2759, 2788, 2811, 2887,
　　2895, 2959, 2965, 3103, 3107, 3137,
　　3199, 3205, 3209
　United States, 373, 442
　USSR, 143, 213, 339, 500, 515, 978, 1287,
　　1462, 1915, 1990, 2055, 2072, 2314,
　　2436, 2565, 2926, 3103. *See also*
　　Czechoslovakia, 1968 Crisis and
　　Invasion

Dagestan. *See* USSR, Republics, role of in
　　foreign policy
Decisionmaking. *See* USSR, "Determinants"
　　of Soviet foreign policy,
　　Decision-making process
Denmark and USSR, 521, 1662
Detente, 223, 313, 329, 331, 340, 366, 474,
　　565, 629, 656, 884, 885, 964, 985,
　　1086, 1187, 1231, 1430, 1573, 1790,
　　1875, 2101, 2310, 2535, 2594, 2630,
　　2631, 2691, 2692, 2702, 2770, 3063,
　　3135, 3136. *See also* East-West
　　Relations; Europe, Eastern, and the
　　West; United States, USSR
Developing countries, 903, 1273, 1363, 1660,
　　1798, 1898, 2647, 2810. *See also*
　　National Liberation (Movement);
　　Non-capitalist development;
　　Imperialism

Communism, 391, 706, 1265, 1302, 1307,
　　1327, 1963, 2246, 2760, 2761, 2886,
　　2921
East Europe, 581, 1254, 1816, 1886, 1974,
　　2394, 2434, 2435, 2472, 2491, 2938,
　　2939, 2940, 2941, 2942, 2943, 2944,
　　2945, 2946, 2947, 2948, 3003, 3006,
　　3213, 3214, 3215
　Germany, Democratic Republic of, 1208
　Poland, 2984
　USSR, 46, 77, 197, 224, 290, 303, 448,
　　479, 555, 612, 665, 779, 780, 808,
　　841, 947, 1015, 1045, 1184, 1211,
　　1216, 1268, 1284, 1335, 1483, 1547,
　　1577, 1623, 1739, 1740, 1845, 1847,
　　1853, 1854, 1855, 1873, 1886, 1919,
　　1955, 2022, 2090, 2191, 2329, 2431,
　　2435, 2449, 2451, 2452, 2466, 2469,
　　2491, 2762, 2919, 2766, 2767, 2768,
　　2769, 2770, 2988, 2989, 3006, 3057,
　　3124, 3125, 3165. *See also* each
　　individual country
　Economic relations, 488, 532, 581, 871,
　　872, 894, 901, 1044, 1063, 1064,
　　1170, 1335, 1451, 1452, 1816, 1974,
　　2018, 2302, 2394, 2453, 2472, 2578,
　　2579, 2618, 2659, 2766, 2938, 2939,
　　2940, 2941, 2942, 2943, 2972, 2986,
　　2987, 3003, 3070, 3214, 3215
Diplomacy. *See* USSR, Soviet foreign policy
　　implementation, Diplomacy
　　(diplomats)
Disarmament. *See* Arms control
Division of Labor. *See* Council for Mutual
　　Economic Assistance
Domestic factors and foreign policy. *See*
　　USSR, "Determinants" of Soviet
　　foreign policy, Domestic factors and
　　foreign policy

East-West relations, 159, 211, 217, 310, 328,
　　329, 331, 340, 449, 539, 629, 630,
　　631, 641, 653, 654, 673, 680, 720,
　　756, 795, 919, 985, 1000, 1198, 1441,
　　1682, 1986, 1998, 2096, 2101, 2132,
　　2149, 2236, 2243, 2244, 2286, 2310,
　　2350, 2517, 2593, 2697, 2759, 3017.
　　See also Detente; Europe, Eastern
　　and the West; Trade, international,
　　East-West; United States, USSR
Economic integration. *See* Council for
　　Mutual Economic Assistance
Economic warfare, 13, 211, 773, 774, 822
Economic Assistance. *See* USSR, Soviet
　　foreign policy implementation,
　　Economic relations
Egypt. *See* United Arab Republic
Environmental control and international
　　politics, 392, 694, 2928

Germany (*continued*)
USSR, 1081, 1141, 1562, 1927, 1943,
2529, 3157, 3158
West, the, 1199, 2599
Germany, Federal Republic of
Czechoslovakia, 3146, 3199
East Europe, 498, 528, 696, 980, 1197,
1199, 1410, 1648, 1769, 2444, 2494,
2801, 3061. *See also* Ostpolitik
Ostpolitik, 204, 221, 498, 501, 582, 596,
893, 934, 980, 1009, 1197, 1409,
1410, 1478, 1761, 1883, 1959, 2168,
2282, 2629, 3061, 3067, 3101, 3105,
3135, 3145, 3147
Poland, 309, 1090, 1621, 2850
USSR, 32, 151, 206, 291, 528, 584, 704,
915, 917, 1081, 1408, 1756, 1761,
2098, 2249, 2262, 2289, 2359, 2668,
2801, 2851, 2852, 3061, 3113, 3135.
See also Ostpolitik
Great Britain and USSR, 136, 193, 397, 485,
570, 703, 765, 864, 874, 1008, 1110,
1409, 1481, 1666, 1745, 1924, 2016,
2028, 2145, 2303, 2378, 2556, 2733,
2857, 2923
Greece
East Europe, 1101
USSR, 2674
Guinea and USSR, 3055

Hungarian Revolution of 1956, 11, 1172,
1323, 1397, 1545, 2232, 2788
Hungary, 212, 339, 1172, 1404, 2230, 2826,
2980
Czechoslovakia, 1105
East Europe, 92, 339, 374
Foreign trade of, 2157, 2983
United States, 2233
USSR, 45, 220, 339, 1272, 1888, 2233,
2341, 2655, 2817

Iceland and USSR, 1109
Ideological struggle, 97, 420, 563, 758, 1270,
1293, 1426, 1427, 1428, 1819, 1876,
1877, 1932, 1942, 1991, 2170, 2900,
2901, 3030
Ideology. *See* USSR, "Determinants" of
Soviet foreign policy, Ideology
Imperialism; anti-imperialism, 48, 97, 133,
241, 259, 398, 685, 944, 1018, 1130,
1144, 1169, 1270, 1292, 1364, 1419,
1601, 1688, 1730, 1879, 1949, 1957,
2012, 2197, 2229, 2254, 2272, 2564,
2649, 2678, 2767, 2791, 2819, 2881,
3039, 3185, 3186
Theory of, 294, 295, 398, 506, 507, 595,
875, 903, 1175, 1589, 1590, 1599,
1764, 1786, 1787, 2119, 2352, 2910,
3002, 3005, 3226, 3030

India and USSR, 283, 435, 437, 518, 616,
649, 676, 840, 911, 954, 968, 996,
1075, 1110, 1112, 1236, 1264, 1347,
1476, 1829, 1885, 1895, 1902, 1903,
2058, 2240, 2250, 2313, 2358, 2440,
2441, 2442, 2450, 2459, 2478, 2551,
2552, 2553, 2591, 2664, 2669, 2703,
2704, 2766. *See also* Kashmir
Indian Ocean and USSR, 1188, 1803, 2029,
2407
Indonesia and USSR, 176, 287, 1062, 1068,
1074, 2227, 2557, 2636
Industrialization and diplomacy, 100
Integration. *See* Council for Mutual
Economic Assistance
International Labour Organization, 2522
USSR, 586
International law
of the Citizen (human rights), 99, 404,
405, 413, 1664, 2008, 2903
Economic (trade) law, 141, 257, 341, 517,
1078, 1434, 2124
Labor law, 67
of Outer space, 912, 965, 1100, 1390,
1391, 1404, 1500, 1659, 2347, 2929,
2931, 3001, 3015
of the Sea, 42, 355, 356, 359, 360, 361,
1554, 2129, 2130, 2499, 2928
Soviet views/studies of, 231, 232, 233,
239, 354, 357, 358, 399, 411, 412,
477, 669, 722, 941, 942, 1006, 1104,
1108, 1286, 1288, 1454, 1455, 1456,
1457, 1553, 1606, 1607, 1664, 1687,
1691, 1765, 1810, 1811, 1828, 1859,
1878, 2002, 2014, 2170, 2215, 2241,
2323, 2366, 2541, 2651, 2670, 2823,
2900, 2901, 2902, 2969, 3050, 3189
International organization, 1374, 1470, 1859,
1860, 2002, 2003, 2060. *See also* by
individual name
International relations. *See also*
Internationalism, proletarian;
Communist Movement
Current affairs, 1294, 1767, 1770, 1782,
1870, 1944, 1945, 2628, 2739, 2829,
2832, 2871, 2897, 3030, 3161
Theory of (Including Leninist theory),
195, 202, 358, 666, 832, 1134, 1223,
1225, 1227, 1235, 1557, 1827, 2038,
2185, 2294, 2372, 2373, 2374, 2375,
2433, 2646, 2648, 2834, 2871, 2888,
2977
Internationalism and nationalism (the
international and the national), 30,
132, 134, 352, 458, 598, 804, 1239,
1334, 1344, 1465, 1578, 1995, 2427,
2607, 2708, 3066, 3217
Internationalism, proletarian (socialist), 215,
406, 495, 617, 639, 711, 735, 1119,
1310, 1343, 1402, 1439, 1460, 1556,
1634, 1734, 1716, 1780, 1897, 1977,

Internationalism (*continued*)
1984, 2050, 2056, 2125, 2126, 2133,
2135, 2142, 2196, 2253, 2371, 2377,
2428, 2429, 2520, 2584, 2744, 2746,
2873, 2884, 2885, 2968, 3010, 3190
Intervention, Allied (1918–1921), 289, 729,
822, 958, 2303, 2556, 2589, 2679,
2827, 2923, 2963, 2964, 3060, 3116
Iran
East Europe, 163
USSR, 95, 135, 163, 590, 839, 1128, 1149,
1156, 1237, 1249, 1442, 1560, 1842,
1857, 2671, 3054, 3100
Iraq and USSR, 1317, 1359, 3100, 3171,
3174
Israel
East Europe, 1464
USSR, 503, 526, 760, 861, 1464, 1612,
1848, 2039, 2546, 2609, 3034
Italy
Communist Party of, 225
USSR, 225, 1142
Yugoslavia, 371

Japan
East Europe, 910
USSR, 471, 640, 716, 863, 873, 966, 999,
1017, 1036, 1340, 1753, 2047, 2275,
2474, 2513, 2556, 2638, 2863, 3032,
3082, 3183
Jordan and USSR, 3175, 3178

Kashmir and USSR, 1905, 2560
Kazakhstan, *See* USSR, Republics, role of in
foreign policy
Kollontai, Alexandra, 1678
Korea, North, and USSR, 5, 423, 1313,
1314, 1316, 1365, 1505, 1562, 1940,
3037, 3167
Korea, South, and USSR, 5
Krasin, L. B., 1679, 1868

Labor unions. *See* World Federation of
Trade Unions
Latin America
Communism in, 2355
East Europe, 1033
Imperialism and, 2495
Soviet studies of, 56, 2010, 2988, 3052
USSR, 197, 203, 382, 452, 557, 611, 809,
880, 1033, 1123, 1158, 1327, 1704,
2011, 2117, 2531, 2532, 2574, 2575,
2576, 2665, 2812, 3053
League of Nations and USSR, 157, 2198
Lebanon and USSR, 2750, 3170, 3180, 3198
Lenin, V. I., foreign policy activities of, 25,
26, 1151, 1586, 1595, 1620, 2868,
2870, 2879, 2880, 2881, 2883 (Other
items are entered under the relevant
subject matter.)

Maiskii, I. V., 1681
Malaysia and USSR, 1071
Mali and USSR, 1005, 1856
Maoism, Soviet views of, 90, 254, 270, 710,
1407, 1477, 1703, 2581, 3220. *See
also* China
Mediterranean and USSR, 69, 88, 235, 383,
384, 424, 585, 813, 946, 947, 997,
1029, 1085, 1303, 1471, 1488, 1541,
1720, 1760, 1789, 1791, 1893, 2026,
2208, 2317, 2548, 2822, 3079, 3106,
3108, 3114, 3234
Mertens, L., 81
Middle East
East Europe, 952, 2448
Rumania, 2404
Soviet Studies of, 1533, 1534, 2257
USSR, 1, 8, 18, 60, 146, 171, 277, 319,
350, 377, 426, 482, 497, 566, 594,
658, 760, 772, 782, 889, 890, 917,
952, 1028, 1034, 1087, 1091, 1093,
1182, 1183, 1215, 1260, 1327, 1341,
1348, 1359, 1399, 1531, 1535, 1536,
1540, 1541, 1558, 1561, 1570, 1571,
1612, 1671, 1759, 1775, 1776, 1802,
1836, 1843, 1846, 1848, 1849, 1907,
1983, 2020, 2065, 2067, 2089, 2107,
2208, 2225, 2226, 2257, 2258, 2317,
2448, 2484, 2543, 2544, 2545, 2592,
2667, 2782, 2802, 2896, 2935, 2973,
3078, 3093, 3102, 3104, 3110, 3169,
3172, 3173, 3176, 3179, 3184
Militarism, 130
Military Assistance. *See* USSR, Soviet
foreign policy implementation,
Military
Military Balance. *See* United States, USSR
Military Doctrine. Strategy. *See* USSR,
Soviet foreign policy implementation,
Military
Mongolia
East Europe, 339
USSR, 64, 168, 284, 339, 677, 1140, 1230,
1975, 2284, 2304, 2602
Morocco
East Europe, 2306
USSR, 1490, 2306

National democracy. *See* Non-capitalist
development
National images. *See* Psychological factors in
international relations
National Liberation (Movement), 131, 142,
392, 518, 618, 707, 708, 926, 1119,
1229, 1240, 1250, 1282, 1305, 1306,
1307, 1506, 1624, 1711, 1880, 1898,
2031, 2274, 2426, 2464, 2749, 2807,
2809, 2922
Communist countries, 254, 323, 1094,
1308, 1310, 1394, 1615, 1711, 1712,
2343, 2561, 2562

SALT. *See* Arms control
Scandinavia, 876, 877, 878, 2999
  USSR, 218, 1052, 2027, 2924
Scientific ties. *See* USSR, Scientific ties
Security, international. *See* European security
    and peace, international
Siberia. *See* USSR, Republics, role of in
    foreign policy
Singapore and USSR, 1071
Sino-Soviet relations. *See* China
Socialism, non-communist, 1350, 1351, 2605,
    2792, 2909, 2920
Socialist community. *See* Council for Mutual
    Economic Assistance; Communist
    Movement; Europe, Eastern
Somalia and USSR, 1050
Sovereignty, Soviet (Brezhnev) Doctrine of,
    62, 154, 155, 524, 766, 767, 793,
    1163, 1416, 1510, 1751, 1801, 2056,
    2401, 2756, 2959. *See also*
    Internationalism and nationalism;
    Internationalism, proletarian
Space, outer, 35, 902, 912, 965, 993, 1100,
    1390, 1391, 1404, 1433, 1500, 1659,
    2077, 2111, 2347, 2405, 2412, 2488,
    2489, 2492, 2493, 2521, 2929, 2931,
    2955, 3001, 3015
Sudan and USSR, 1329, 1844, 2975
Suez Canal and USSR, 1817, 2549
Suez Crisis of 1956 and USSR, 2199
Sweden and USSR, 201, 833, 1633, 2193
Syria and USSR, 2066, 2425, 2750, 3178

Territorial question, 158
Thailand and USSR, 2515
Third World. *See* Developing countries;
    National Liberation; Non-capitalist
    development
Tibet and USSR, 2982
Tourism, 70, 1154
Trade, international, 534, 561, 748, 776, 869,
    891, 1364, 1436, 1626, 1916, 2037,
    2120, 2124, 2445, 2767
  of Communist countries, 317, 431, 581,
    632, 747, 866, 940, 1176, 1255, 1434,
    2184, 2189, 2525, 2844, 3128. *See
    also* Council for Mutual Economic
    Assistance; USSR; each individual
    East European state
  East-West, 211, 316, 430, 528, 539, 567,
    576, 630, 724, 797, 900, 1253, 1393,
    1481, 1725, 1922, 1966, 1967, 2096,
    2114, 2256, 2270, 2430, 2517, 2593,
    2697, 2707, 2723, 2757, 2840, 2954,
    2956, 3007, 3017, 3076, 3127
  Socialist principles of, 263, 1511, 2062,
    2147
Trieste Question, 1844
Turkey
  USSR, 82, 175, 496, 537, 855, 1237, 1238,

1717, 1937, 1939, 2766, 2783, 3054,
    3100
Yugoslavia, 1101

Ukraine. *See* USSR, Republics, role of in
    foreign policy
Union of Soviet Socialist Republics. For
    Soviet relations with developing
    countries, Eastern Europe, the West,
    NATO, and individual countries see
    appropriate heading.
Chronological periods
  1917–1921, 25, 26, 81, 107, 289, 459,
    460, 485, 496, 502, 529, 542, 714,
    729, 822, 838, 958, 1012, 1082, 1149,
    1151, 1237, 1238, 1281, 1512, 1555,
    1576, 1586, 1595, 1882, 1890, 2127,
    2292, 2303, 2683, 2556, 2589, 2679,
    2747, 2803, 2827, 2836, 2870, 2877,
    2879, 2882, 2883, 2904, 2923, 2963,
    2964, 3060, 3072, 3116, 3203. *See
    also* Intervention, Allied; Revolution,
    Communist
  1921–1928, 107, 227, 529, 540, 542,
    575, 619, 670, 864, 938, 1012, 1082,
    1122, 1149, 1237, 1238, 1281, 1284,
    1512, 1577, 1595, 1620, 1706, 1882,
    2683, 2747, 2836, 2880, 2881, 2882,
    2904, 3086, 3135
  1928–1935, 227, 619, 671, 948, 999,
    1082, 1121, 1122, 1124, 1405, 1512,
    1706, 1747, 1804, 1807, 2016, 2680,
    2747, 2816, 2839, 3074, 3132, 3133
  1935–1939, 85, 227, 264, 571, 628, 873,
    948, 1023, 1530, 1706, 1747, 2028,
    2030, 2069, 2072, 2733, 2747, 2764,
    2836, 3074, 3183
  1939–1945, 83, 164, 192, 210, 264, 315,
    381, 408, 469, 559, 570, 628, 867,
    874, 966, 987, 1023, 1041, 1084,
    1096, 1179, 1189, 1415, 1482, 1513,
    1515, 1635, 1681, 1704, 1707, 1717,
    1729, 1745, 1748, 1924, 2030, 2069,
    2085, 2158, 2285, 2422, 2438, 2550,
    2653, 2682, 2732, 2747, 2764, 2815,
    2867, 2876, 3025, 3032, 3183, 3197:
    Wartime conferences (Potsdam,
    Teheran, Yalta), 193, 389, 439, 755,
    987, 1513, 1745, 1924, 2378, 2712,
    2732, 2790, 3064,
  1945–1953, 135, 530, 592, 593, 614,
    977, 1174, 1277, 1442, 1464, 2042,
    2597, 2653, 2914, 3033, 3154, 3155.
    See also Cold War
  1953–1964, 118, 311, 346, 382, 445,
    544, 580, 586, 591, 634, 658, 725,
    726, 761, 963, 1050, 1137, 1277,
    1279, 1295, 1541, 2042, 2617, 2652,
    2706, 2914, 3119, 3154, 3155. *See
    also* USSR, General analyses

76379